Praise for *The Progre*

TO283316

By examining the ways in which intelligent, critical, and creative readings of the Bible have played a pivotal role in advancing some of the
most significant social reforms in US history, Claudia Setzer offers us a
powerful counter to interpretations of the Bible that have served what
she calls "the wrong side of history." *The Progressives' Bible* is an indis-
pensable resource for anyone seeking a fuller understanding of American history and a more complete sense of the Bible's place and role in
America. A book I have long needed for my university classroom, it
will no doubt be a revelation to all readers.

—Mary F. Foskett, Wake Forest Kahle Professor of
Religious Studies, Wake Forest University

For those who want to understand the varied and creative ways that
social reformers have used the Bible to advocate for a more just, inclu-
sive, and equitable America, there is no better guide than *The Progressives' Bible*. Claudia Setzer treats the reader to the arguments of a
remarkably wide-ranging and diverse array of activists from the early
1800s to the present, highlighting scriptural passages that have figured
prominently in their thinking and the interpretive strategies they have
used to understand them. If, as Setzer argues, hope is the prerequisite
for reform, then readers concerned with the issues of our own day will
find tremendous hope in her accounts of the progressive champions
who have gone before us.

—Mark A. Chancey, professor of religious
studies, Southern Methodist University

This is a must-read volume for all who are captivated by how the Bible
has been interpreted in the (North) American context. From abolitionism to women's rights to temperance, progressive thinkers grap-
pled with conflicts in light of the wider culture's investment in biblical
interpretation, which became a guide for biblical interpreters in the
Civil Rights era. Prof. Setzer navigates these conversations with skill
and expertise and allows readers to follow how our nineteenth-century

forebears both tackled exegetical quandaries and expressed moral sensibilities in their interpretive strategies. Setzer proves what she admirably writes: "The Bible on its own did not and cannot reform society. It was the people."

—Emerson Powery, professor of biblical studies and interim dean of the School of Arts, Culture, and Society, Messiah University

Based on a broad and sophisticated understanding of the Bible, Setzer offers an insightful survey of how different biblical texts were used in discussing abolition, women's rights, temperance, and civil rights. She artfully combines sources from well-known figures and those that should be better known. This book is an important resource for scholars of American religion and for contemporary progressives who might want to utilize the Bible.

—Marc Zvi Brettler, Bernice and Morton Lerner Distinguished Professor in Judaic Studies, Duke University

THE PROGRESSIVES' BIBLE

THE PROGRESSIVES' BIBLE

HOW SCRIPTURAL INTERPRETATION BUILT A MORE JUST AMERICA

CLAUDIA SETZER

FORTRESS PRESS
Minneapolis

Library of Congress Control Number: 2023047367 (print)

Cover designer: Kristin Miller
Cover image: Praying Ministers (1962), Jacob Lawrence, © 2023 The Jacob and Gwendolyn Knight Lawrence Foundation, Seattle / Artists Rights Society (ARS), New York

Print ISBN: 978-1-5064-9708-2
eBook ISBN: 978-1-5064-9709-9

CONTENTS

CONTENTS

PREFACE

As a teenager I watched the drama of the civil rights movement on the news from my safe perch in suburban Minneapolis. Like most of America, I was riveted by the speeches of Martin Luther King, Jr., and simply took in his references to the valleys being exalted, the mountaintop, and justice flowing down like water. It was not until I read David Chappell's book, *A Stone of Hope,* in 2004 (introduced by David Brooks in his *New York Times* column on March 23, 2004), that I began to think about the biblical, especially prophetic themes that lent strength and endurance to those who battled for equal rights for African Americans.

I began to look at other places in American culture that were frankly biblical, or at least that employed biblical supports for their positions, discovering debates where both sides often invoked the Bible—slavery/abolitionism, nineteenth-century women's rights, evolution/creationism, and more. These interests led me to create a course on the Bible and American culture, a sourcebook, and a book of essays on the topic.

I want to focus here on the underappreciated use of biblical and traditional texts by progressive thinkers in American history. Abolition of slavery, equal rights for women, and civil rights are accomplishments that most of us point to as proud moments in our history. Temperance might seem a somewhat idiosyncratic addition to the survey, since it led to the highly unpopular and ill-advised prohibition of alcohol. But at its height in the nineteenth century, temperance was a popular, broadbrush movement to improve society. Many of the people we meet in this book, like Elizabeth Cady Stanton or Frederick Douglass, believed in temperance.

It was a delight to learn more of the biographies of some of our key thinkers, especially the women of color I have foregrounded. Recent scholarly work on many thinkers, like Elizabeth Cady Stanton, Susan B. Anthony, the Grimké family, and Frances Willard, have rightly invited us to consider their moral shortcomings or their limited worldviews stemming from their white, middle-class upbringings. I have not shied away from mentioning racist or nativist sympathies when relevant. I have tried to avoid both hagiography and hatchet jobs. But if my admiration for certain activists like Fannie Lou Hamer or Maria Stewart seeps into my prose, I am not sorry for that.

Many historians have noted the activation of religious and biblical principles in the words of our reformers. David Blight, in his authoritative biography of Douglass, for example, speaks often of Douglass's prophetic thunder. My hope is that, as a biblical scholar, I am contributing something more fine-grained in showing *how* such reformers used biblical material and the variety of methods they used to infuse their words with biblical power. It may surprise readers, as it did me, to discover how many contemporary movements unabashedly draw strength from biblical sources and from their own religious traditions. What I originally expected to be a short postscript on contemporary movements became an exercise in trying to pare down all the possibilities to fit into one chapter.

No one owns the Bible or has sole custody of its meaning. This book will show how it came to life when fused with the struggles of these activists to reduce suffering and build a more just world.

ACKNOWLEDGMENTS

I am very fortunate to have had the support of so many people in the rather extended journey of producing this book. My thanks to Steve Wiggins, who suggested years ago that I write a monograph stemming from our sourcebook on primary documents on the Bible and American culture, edited with my colleague David Shefferman. My thanks to Steve Wiggins, Mark Chancey, and Michael Greenwald, who have read portions of the project and encouraged me. J. Christopher Edwards allowed me to see his own work and offered advice on publication. Carey Newman never flagged in his enthusiasm and in his belief in the importance of the book. His energy has propelled it to publication.

Colleagues at Manhattan College have enriched this work. Adam Arenson provided bibliographic suggestions, Jawanza Clark taught me about Albert Cleage, Jr., Courtney Bryant introduced me to the remarkable Septima Poinsette Clark, and Kevin Ahern pointed me to religious calls to corporate responsibility. My wonderful friends and fellow scholars in the Religious Studies department at Manhattan College have always been cheerleaders for me and for one another. Friends in the Columbia University New Testament seminar have offered supportive and constructive comments on my work. Research assistant Kyle Hahn navigated the presence of biblical material in popular culture, especially gaming, and on social media.

New Testament scholars Alexandra Brown, Celia Deutsch, and Michael Winger have offered me enduring friendship and scholarly camaraderie since graduate school. My special thanks to Judith Baumel, who always makes me feel smart, and who suggested the painting by Jacob Lawrence for the cover. As always, I am sustained by my family. Leora, Alex, Asher, and Mena never fail to be sources of pride, love, and happiness. No words can quite express what I owe Michael R. Greenwald, my partner in matters of the mind and heart, who is always at the center of my life.

INTRODUCTION

When the Supreme Court issued the *Dobbs* decision in 2022, overruling *Roe v. Wade* and returning the power to regulate abortion to the states, Gavin Newsom, the governor of California, ordered billboards put up in seven of the most restrictive states, inviting women in need to come to California where abortion remained legal; many of the signs also cited the biblical verse from Mark 12:31, where Jesus declares the command to love one's neighbor as one of the two greatest commandments of the Law.[1] Similarly, statements supporting abortion rights from United Church of Christ minister Jes Kast, from Presbyterian minister Rebecca Todd Peters, and from groups including the Religious Coalition for Reproductive Choice and Catholics for Choice, and the Reform and Conservative denominations of Judaism, invoked biblical ideas as foundational to their pro-choice positions.[2]

Why did pro-choice advocates invoke the Bible at all? Surely arguments based on human rights, women's health, and the good of society lay closer to hand and did not risk alienating the larger, mixed religious and nonreligious constituency of American society. The overturning of *Roe v. Wade* laid bare the fierce national divide over abortion, and it is no surprise that biblical verses were entered into the fray, but it may surprise some that biblically inflected arguments came from both sides of the debate. Nor were the reproductive rights advocates the first on the more liberal end of the political spectrum to harness themselves to biblical authority. This book shows that earlier progressive movements in American life also steeped their arguments in the biblical text.

The Bible is not one thing; it is a library of works assembled over time containing a multiplicity of voices. Nor does the Bible say only one thing; on many social issues its witness conflicts or is silent and meaning must always be extracted through interpretation. This book looks at progressive social reform movements in American life that drew strength from biblical texts—verses, narratives, characters, and laws, often seeing their own experiences in its pages: abolitionism, nineteenth-century feminism, temperance, and the mid-twentieth century civil rights movement. "Progressive" here is with a small "p," meaning people seeking to promote individual rights, create a more equitable society, and reduce suffering from social and legal injustice.[3] Its topics are not specifically about what historians called the Progressive era in US history, although there is some overlap with that era in both time period and values. This is not an attempt to "save" the Bible by emphasizing its use in movements that cohere with ideas that most contemporaries accept. It is a set of observations on the biblical resources available to reformers and the clever and myriad ways they interpreted the texts.[4]

These four movements are connected to one another: many people belonged to two or three of them and worked for more than one kind of social change. The movements share a relationship with the biblical text that is deep and organic, showing playfulness, desperation, irritation, and love. Abolitionism was the foremother of other reform movements in its use of the Bible. Habits of thought and a deft, critical approach learned in one movement transferred to others, as abolitionists became suffragists, or civil rights speakers employed verses and tropes first heard in antislavery rhetoric. Temperance, populated by many abolitionists and women's rights advocates, was in some ways the most creative in using the biblical materials while undermining a literal understanding of them. Many other movements such as the social gospel movement or the radical Jesus movement have invoked Jesus in a general way or spoke of bringing the kingdom, but few tied themselves as closely to the biblical text as the movements discussed here. This work will show not only the fact that reformers cited the Bible, but *how* they used it.

The significance of the movements is apparent in today's controversies. Acknowledging the reality of American enslavement of African peoples has been politicized to the degree that education at all levels—in choice of textbooks, in access to school library books, and in use of the term "critical race theory"—is under scrutiny. Women's rights, which centered on women's right to vote in the nineteenth century, has evolved in multiple directions, but the bedrock belief in women's equal rights undergirds arguments for reproductive rights. Expanding conceptions of sex and gender have paved the way for LGBTQ+ rights and especially for current discussion of the legal rights and protections of transgender people. The civil rights movement of the mid-twentieth century began but hardly completed the goal of creating a society where access to housing, education, equal protection under the law, and health care would be available to all people in equal measure. The alarming rise of white nationalist groups and incidents of anti-Black violence, antisemitic attacks, anti-Asian violence, and Islamophobia call out for Americans to examine our national values and assess the continuing deep undercurrents of racism. Temperance and especially its successor, Prohibition, seem quaint in comparison to the other three movements. Its reformist beginnings and multi-pronged attempts to improve the lot of the poor, women, and children have been overshadowed by its negative consequences—corruption in law enforcement, loss of tax revenue, organized crime, and a failure to stem alcohol abuse. Prohibition stands as a symbol of government overreach and the dangers of trying to legislate particular kinds of morality.

These four movements show us determining the limits of who we Americans say we are, proponents of individualism and personal freedoms who also cling to an ideal of a nation with its own moral grounding. Each movement invites questions of human rights. Should a citizen enjoy freedom if others are not free? Should biological differences between sexes determine legal rights? Can a conviction that alcohol threatens families be translated into public actions or legislation?

Why Use the Bible?

Using the Bible was crucial for these movements because the text represented an alternative reality to inhabit, a reality beyond the external social world that all could see. Fusing their own experiences with the unfolding of the biblical drama allowed reformers to hitch themselves to a grander, more dramatic narrative in which God sided with the forces of justice, and the righteous would triumph. It was an authority that few would question, as it had a bedrock familiarity and emotional hold in the culture. Through a myriad of methods, these reformers accessed the biblical text's authority and made it their own. Recent surveys show the Bible retains considerable authority in today's culture, despite decreasing rates of Americans actually reading it.[5]

Many people are familiar with ways in which biblical texts have been incorporated on the wrong side of history. Slavery, subjugation of women, violence toward outsiders, domination of nature—all have with justification been laid at the door of the Bible. Reductionism, the impulse to reduce the Bible to one voice, is always a temptation. Scholars, pundits, and everyday conversation partners will readily assert of the biblical text that "It oppresses women," "It promotes violence," or "It teaches unhealthy attitudes towards the environment." No one would argue such ideas are not there but so are competing ones. Less appreciated in our culture are the ways in which the Bible was a resource for the great social reforms of America like abolitionism in the nineteenth century or the civil rights movement of the mid-twentieth century.

These movements have their own personalities and aims, but they share an assumption of the biblical word's authority, often tethering themselves to the text's authority while also freeing themselves from it. Temperance was especially able at this; it had to be to explain the story of the blessing of wine by Jesus at the Last Supper and other positive associations with wine. A panoply of methods was brought to bear on biblical interpretation in the service of arguing for each broad reform, from the most niggling scrutiny of individual words, the discipline called philology, to emotional appeals to imagine oneself in the place of those suffering under society's grave injustices. Individual writers and speakers employed many devices—whatever worked in the moment.

Abolitionist intellectuals combed the biblical text, producing a mountain of inventive rhetoric, but focused particularly on the ways that the institution of slavery violated particular laws in the Hebrew

Bible and New Testament, especially the law against kidnapping.[6] A second law forbids the return of a runaway enslaved person and requires one to shelter and care for them.[7] One rhetor shows how several of the Ten Commandments call out slavery. The result is that the institution of slavery is a sin, a violation of God's commands. This leads the way for the searing indictments against a sinful people by God's spokesperson, the prophet.

Women's rights advocates had learned much about biblical interpretation from their time in the abolitionist movement, including how to read the Bible with a critical eye, ferreting out its commitment to justice. Some arguments closely resemble the methods of argument that had been used against slavery, appropriately transferred to the issue of women's equality. But women's rights activists were far from uniform in their attitudes and some dismissed the Bible as an age-old deterrent to women, part of the institutional wall of religion, church, and state that mitigated against women's full participation in society. At least one argued that the Bible was irrelevant and that their case rested on the more universal argument of human rights. The Bible serves as enemy, ally, and bystander for different nineteenth-century feminists.

The temperance crusade was deeply rooted in Protestant Christianity, so its campaigners turned naturally to the Bible, both as a physical prop in the Victorian era and as a source of arguments against alcohol. The problem was that the Bible has a variety of positive statements about wine and describes its use in religious ritual in both the Hebrew Bible and the New Testament. Not least in importance is the institution of the Eucharist by Jesus at the Last Supper. Nonetheless, temperance advocates mounted massive arguments against the use of alcohol, using the Bible as proof. To bring the Bible into the temperance fold required a rejection of literalism, and some writers openly critiqued literalism as an evil, attributing it to Pharisees and other groups they disliked. Ironically, this group of relatively conservative Christians practiced a form of interpretation that imitated the kind of historical-critical scholarship emerging in Europe and popular in more liberal forms of Christianity.

The civil rights movement played out in oral and written materials, showing a wide variety of styles, but much of its memorable rhetoric is associated with the inspired performance of public speeches and sermons. Often the struggle for voting rights and the dignity of equality took the form of a sense of struggle against forces of evil within society. They were not just seeking their own betterment, but also engaged in a battle against "principalities and powers," the apostle Paul's term for the combined negative forces of cosmic and governmental persecution. Only a thorough transformation and remaking of society would fix the ills of the present social situation. Martin Luther King left only the title of his proposed last sermon, never written or delivered because of his assassination, "Why America May Go to Hell."

It may surprise some to find that the Bible has not ceased to be a resource for current progressives. The final chapter considers a few contemporary social justice movements and their engagement with the Bible and their own religious traditions. We might have expected such fervent use of the Bible as evidenced in earlier struggles to have died out in our own time, and indeed many other current reform movements do not invoke religious or biblical themes. Methods may differ and such groups are profoundly aware that social justice movements belong not exclusively to Christians and Jews but embrace people of many faiths and those who are nonreligious. Nevertheless, a number of groups call on biblical values to sustain themselves, some doing rather close readings of the text, but all extracting their values. By drawing on a longer arc of experience and tapping into the legacies of earlier reformers, some of today's movements are buoyed up by the sense that crises have been faced before and seemingly overwhelming odds have been overcome.

These groups were never completely about the Bible, nor did they lean exclusively on biblical supports to make their cases. They regularly argued from human rights perspectives, from arguments about the health of society, and from historical precedent. Arguments from emotion were entered into frequently: abolitionists presenting the plight of enslaved people and asking hearers to imagine themselves in their place, temperance advocates describing destitute mothers and children, or civil rights speakers recounting their horrific treatment at the hands of police and jailers.

Certain methods recur. For example, each movement produced its own "canon within a canon," a set of frequently rehearsed material that gained power from its repetition and familiarity. Many see themselves as doing a prophet's work: standing in the tradition of the Hebrew prophets whose primary thrust was a critique of social injustice. The jeremiad, a particularly intense form of prophecy, figures prominently in the anti-racist rhetoric of abolitionism and the civil rights movement. Reformers wielded the biblical material in many ways, sometimes citing a single verse as a proof-text, identifying with biblical figures, building meaning from a text that goes beyond its plain sense, and creating a counter-narrative that sees their own struggle as part of the cosmic battle between God and evil that plays out in history.

For academics, this work coincides with a number of recent works examining the role of the Bible in American history and culture, from a website that demonstrates the ubiquity of biblical verses in everyday, secular newspapers in the nineteenth and early twentieth century to discussions of the aims and methods of the Washington, DC, Museum of the Bible.[8] Much of the discussion of Bible in America is the purview of historians rather than biblical scholars, so does not always attend to particular methods of interpretation but rather to the broad strokes of literary or historical use.

Religious professionals represent traditions that are grounded in the Bible. How can it speak to the challenges of our lives? Today's moral questions do not come with easily imported answers from the biblical text. They never did. How did earlier people who were struggling against institutions, enemies, and customs that seemed starkly evil but firmly entrenched find a powerful ally in the biblical text? How did they work with it in creative ways?

This work foregrounds women and people of color in the movements. Readers will discover Maria Stewart, a free Black woman who in her short but dramatic career employed the jeremiad, using it earlier than the better-known speakers Sojourner Truth and Frederick Douglass.

They will meet Septima Clark, whose long lifetime of teaching literacy and voting rights to African Americans preceded and accompanied the more flamboyant male preachers of the civil rights movement. They will be inspired by Fannie Lou Hamer, who lacked the educational advantages of many of the male preachers but was a riveting speaker who placed the struggle of their own time on the larger canvas of the cosmic battle between God and Satan that ran through the ages. The biblical grounding is also a hedge against despair. By drawing on a longer arc of experience and tapping into the legacies of earlier reformers, some of today's movements are buoyed up by the sense that severe crises have been faced before and seemingly overwhelming odds have been overcome.

These movements speak to the peculiar attachment that many in the United States have for the Bible: a mix of reverence, nostalgia, and considerable ignorance as to its contents. For some it is like an elderly relative who has always been around, a beloved font of stories, identity, and authority; for others it is a tiresome nag. Discovering earlier radical uses of the Bible is a bit like finding out one's grandmother was once a beautiful firebrand. Biblical material is not limited to religious organizations but is out in the public square, in secular and religious corners of the country. The recent interactive site that surveys newspapers in the nineteenth and early twentieth century shows little clear distinction between the secular and the religious. Some nondenominational news publications could nevertheless display large numbers of biblical verses.[9]

For every reader, this work will show that no one owns the Bible or holds the exclusive key to its interpretation. The Bible on its own did not and cannot reform society. It was the people who saw themselves in its pages, who mined it for their own purposes, and who fused their own experience with the people and struggles in the text, who fashioned it into a force for improving society. Unless otherwise noted, citations are from the King James Version of the Bible, used by the majority of activists discussed in this book.

CHAPTER 1

The Bible and Abolitionism

As HE ESCAPED to England, the enslaved freedom-seeker Henry Watson happily left behind the United States, calling it "the land of Bibles and whips."[1] Proslavery forces had corralled both testaments for their purposes with such success that it seemed to many that the Bible was the enslaver's best ally. Slavery's defenders cited the so-called curse of Ham in Gen 9, patriarchs who kept enslaved people, rules that assumed slavery, statements in Paul's letters and the gospels, and perhaps most difficult, Jesus's silence on the subject. Verses from the Hebrew Bible about protecting and freeing enslaved people were simply ignored. No wonder that Frederick Douglass dreaded enslavers who embraced religion as the cruelest of all.[2]

Abolitionists, however, did not cede the Bible to proslavery nor abandon biblical religion but looked to different narratives and verses and applied their own principles of interpretation. The four antislavery activists examined here were African American or white; one was a formerly enslaved person, one was a free-born Black, and two were whites born to privilege. Maria Stewart was an African American woman born free. Angelina Grimké Weld and Theodore Dwight Weld were a white couple, one the daughter of a Southern enslaver and the other a descendant of Puritan clergy. Frederick Douglass had been enslaved from birth up to his escape in 1838 around the age of twenty and final manumission eight years later in 1846. While their disparate social locations provided them different lenses through which to read the Bible and history, all treated the Bible as a touchstone of truth, the carrier of their own message, and intermingled its voice with their own.[3] Their significance lies in their stance against the common and near-automatic reliance on the biblical text by proslavery clergy and politicians. Combing the text, these abolitionists served up God, the Hebrew prophets, Jesus, and Paul as slavery's fiercest opponents.[4]

Maria W. Stewart
Taking on the Prophet's Task

The young widow arrived at the offices of *The Liberator*, manuscripts in hand, in the fall of 1831. A free-born African American of limited means and education, she had studied the Bible on her own and attended Sabbath schools while working to support herself. When William Lloyd Garrison, editor of the well-circulated abolitionist newspaper, called for Black women to submit their writings, Maria Stewart quickly obliged. Stewart's essay was published as a pamphlet, *Religion and the Pure Principles of Morality, the Sure Foundation on Which We Must Build*, and she began a very brief but provocative speaking career calling for a radical restructuring of American society: the abolition of slavery, women's rights, and Black empowerment. She preceded more famous speakers and writers Frederick Douglass, Sojourner Truth, and Frances Harper.

Maria W. Stewart was both extraordinary and typical. She was extraordinary as the first Black woman political writer/speaker and the first American woman "platform speaker" to speak to mixed (called "promiscuous") public audiences of men and women. She was typical as a Black woman campaigning against slavery, exemplifying Manisha Sinha's remark that "women were abolition's most effective foot soldiers."[5] Women evangelical preachers Jarena Lee, Zilpah Law, Nancy Towles, and many others paved the way by preaching in churches and religious venues as early as the 1740s.[6] Stewart, however, delivered her 1832–1833 calls for America to repent of the sin of slavery and for Blacks to pursue lives of achievement and personal virtue in lecture halls for all to hear. Her message of social reform relied on the Bible as her proof text, "I have borrowed much of my language from the Holy Bible . . . During the years of childhood and youth, it was the book that I mostly studied."[7]

Born Maria Miller, a free Black in Hartford, Connecticut in 1803, and orphaned at age five, she worked as a domestic in the household of a white clergyman and his family, educating herself as best she could. In 1826 she married James W. Stewart, the couple joining Boston's small Black middle class community. When James Stewart died three years later and Miller was cheated of his inheritance, she went back into service and struggled to make ends meet. She became a protégé of radical David Walker, whose *Appeal to the Coloured Citizens of the World* (1829) drew on biblical motifs to advocate armed insurrection against the slave system. Walker and Stewart stood at the beginning of the second wave of abolitionism, the interracial call for an immediate end to slavery.[8] Their immediatism forcefully rejected gradualism, the argument for a slow phasing out of slavery, and colonization, the plan to send freed enslaved people out of the country to Liberia or Haiti.

Not long after Walker's death, Stewart had a conversion experience which galvanized her to spread her own "good news." All her speeches and writings, including her signature *Religion and the Pure Principles of Morality* (1831), were published by William Lloyd Garrison in *The Liberator*. She gave four public speeches from 1832 to 1833 in Boston, evoking criticism from friend and foe alike for the audacity of her rhetoric and for the mixed gender and mixed racial venues. A windfall late in life allowed her to publish a second edition of her work, *Meditations from the Pen of Maria W. Stewart* (1879).

Stewart used methods that became commonplaces in Black intellectual rhetoric and carried into civil rights oratory.[9] When enslaved Africans and their descendants in the Americas were converted to Christianity over a period of nearly a century, they saw in its Scripture stories of a God who took the side of the oppressed, bringing liberation and redemption. By the mid-eighteenth century they developed a durable communal body of interpretation that is both oral and written.[10] In particular, Stewart dons the mantle of a prophet, speaks in the tradition of the jeremiad, a stance popular with later African American interpreters, employs apocalyptic imagery, and calls for agency and action. In these approaches she echoes the Hebrew prophets, Jesus, and Paul. She also holds out the Ethiopianist vision, based on Psalm 68:31, "princes shall come out of Egypt; Ethiopia shall soon stretch out her hands unto God," celebrating an early, high African culture within God's plan. Valerie Cooper shows the subtle way that Stewart's use of biblical motifs and language carry meaning for her Black hearers that are not obvious on a superficial reading, creating "semiotic webs in which biblical metaphors are embedded."[11]

The prophets of the Hebrew Bible were unpopular figures in their own times, forcing the self-satisfied in society to look at uncomfortable truths. Speaking on behalf of those without voice or power, they call out hypocrisy in those who claim to be doing God's will but who mistreat the powerless. Like the Hebrew prophets, Stewart sees herself as called by God for an arduous mission, to bring the nation, both Black and white, back to God and to raise up her people in the eyes of white society. She describes her commission as she begins her lecture at Franklin Hall, Boston on September 21, 1832, "Methinks I heard a spiritual interrogation—'Who shall go forward, and take off the reproach that is cast upon the people of color? Shall it be a woman?' And my heart made this reply—'If it is thy will, be it even so, Lord Jesus!'"[12] In this short declaration, Stewart calls to mind two prophets and the psalms to justify her role to raise the esteem of her people. She evokes the famous commission of Isaiah that depicts God on his heavenly throne, "Also I heard the voice of the Lord, saying, Whom shall I send, and who will go for us? Then said I, Here am I; send me" (Isa 6:8). While the word "reproach," King James Version's translation of the Hebrew cherpah, "taunt or scorn," echoes frequently throughout the Hebrew Bible, she uses it as Nehemiah does, to address a people disgraced in the eyes of their enemies or surrounding peoples.[13] The psalms too, say the people are "a taunt to their neighbors."[14]

Some four women prophets appear in the Hebrew Bible—Miriam, Deborah, Huldah, and Noadiah, while the New Testament presents the prophet Anna and women who prophesy.[15] In her farewell address, Stewart defends herself from criticism for speaking publicly as a woman and for speaking to mixed male/female audiences, considered scandalous by some clergy,[16] by identifying with women prophets and heroines in the Hebrew Bible and noting Jesus's affirmation of the women around him, "What if I am a woman; is not the God of ancient times the God of modern days? Did he not raise up Deborah to be a mother and a judge in Israel? Did not Queen Esther save the lives of the Jews? And Mary Magdalene first declare the resurrection of Christ from the dead?" She notes one of the first to preach Jesus is the Samaritan woman in John 4. Stewart allows herself an excursus on holy women, from those who minister to Jesus to medieval divines and scholars.[17] Such contemplation of "the divine feminine" will surface later in disparate works like *The Women's Bible Commentary* (1992) and contemporary feminist theology. She engages in some gender politics by taking up the cause of Black women in particular and urging them to activism in several speeches but also criticizing Black men for lack of ambition and courage in her 1833 speech at the African Masonic Hall.

The apostle Paul might seem a surprising model for an African American woman, given his reputation for tolerance of slavery and silencing of women.[18] But in her farewell address, Stewart defends her right to speak by making numerous nods to Paul and identifies with him as another preacher who undergoes a transformation and suffers mightily for his preaching. Furthermore, Paul's sufferings in fulfilling his mission and his sense of being caught up in a cosmic battle against evil make him an appealing patron for many African American thinkers. By incorporating him into her sense of mission, Stewart neutralizes any problem passages: "Did St. Paul but know of our wrongs and deprivations, I presume he would make no objections to our pleading in public for our rights." Like him, she suffers from the slings of the devil and the principalities and powers (Rom 8:38–9), and like him, her conversion brings her to "the fulness of the gospel of Christ."[19]

Prophets were not just "back then" but continue through history. Luke's gospel implies the prophetic mantle passed from Isaiah to Jesus as he began his ministry, creating a verse that will become a mainstay of Black preaching,

> The Spirit of the Lord is upon me, because he hath anointed
> me to preach the gospel to the poor; he hath sent me to heal
> the brokenhearted, to preach deliverance to the captives, and
> recovering of sight to the blind, to set at liberty them that
> are bruised, To preach the acceptable year of the Lord (Luke
> 4:18–19; Isa 61:1–2).

The calls to become prophets of comfort and reform continue
throughout history. Stewart relates that after her conversion God spoke
to her, filling her with "a holy zeal" to fulfill a mission for her people, "I
felt that I had a great work to perform and was in haste to make a profession of my faith in Christ, that I might be about my Father's business, a
nod to Jesus's own claim.[20] Soon after I made this profession 'The Spirit
of God came before me, and I spake before many.'" She concludes that
only the Holy Spirit operating within her gives her strength to speak.[21]

The jeremiad, named after the acerbic prophet Jeremiah, is a tech-
nique that distills prophecy into its purest form, intensifying its themes:
chosenness of a people, indictment for their sins, near-despair at their
fallenness, and vigorous call for change. Jeremiah's career spanned a
traumatic period in Israel's history, including the Judahite king Josiah's
last-ditch efforts to reform the nation, and Judah's fall to the Babylonian
empire and deportation of her captive population to Babylon in 587
BCE. Jeremiah is tailor-made to speak to the trauma of Africa's
descendants in nineteenth-century America as it probes the reason for
suffering.[22] An early oracle asks the rhetorical why: "Is Israel a servant?
is he a homeborn slave? why is he spoiled?" (Jer 2:14). "Servant" (*'ebed*)
may also be translated "slave," and "spoiled" carries the sense of being
ruined. The chapter follows a lawsuit pattern, enumerating Israel's sins
and failure to acknowledge her guilt as the reason for her suffering.[23]
So too will Black activists lay the sin of slavery and racism at the feet of
the United States as the reason for her coming demise; God expected
more of her as the new Israel.[24]

Stewart engages freely in the jeremiad, a dual indictment and
call to reform rooted in one's authority as God's prophet.[25] The bid

for belonging is evident in the admiration for the flourishing of white Americans, which only intensifies the severity of her critique. America is guilty. Like other prophets, she begins with a seemingly idyllic image, then brings down the hammer. Isaiah presents the beginning of God's love song to the lush vineyard of his beloved people—a vineyard to which he will lay waste. Amos sees a vision of the people symbolized by a basket of summer fruit, ripe and delicious—destined to rot because of their sins. Similarly, in *Religion and the Pure Principles of Morality* she applauds white America's accomplishments,

> I see them thriving in arts and sciences, and in polite liter-
> ature. Their highest aim is to excel in political, moral and
> religious improvement. They early consecrate their children
> to God . . . and their poorest ones, who have the least wish
> to excel they promote! . . . But how very few are there among
> them that bestow one thought upon the benighted sons and
> daughters of Africa, who have enriched the soils of America
> with their tears and blood; few to promote their cause, none
> to encourage their talents. White Americans have fulfilled the
> promises of America, but only for themselves.[26]

In her third speech at Masonic Hall, she is more pointed and severe in addressing slavery as a betrayal of America, the reason "a thick mist of moral gloom hangs over millions of our race . . . While our minds are vacant and starving for want of knowledge, theirs are filled to over-flowing. Most of our color have been taught to stand in fear of the white man, from their earliest infancy, to work as soon as they could walk, and call 'master' before they scarce could lisp the name of 'mother.'"[27] She argues that given equal opportunities in education and work, her race too would produce scientists, statesmen, and philosophers. But white America has flourished because it defrauded her race of its rights, while living off the fruits of its labor. In her first essay she invokes images from Genesis to Revelation, drawing on the whole Christian Bible, "Oh America, America, foul and indelible is thy stain! Dark and dismal is the cloud that hangs over thee, for thy cruel wrongs and injuries to the fallen sons of Africa. The blood of the murdered ones cries to heaven for vengeance against thee (Gen 4:10). Thou art almost become drunken with the blood of her slain (Rev 17:6); thou hast enriched thyself through her trials and labor; and now thou refuseth to make even a small return."[28] All who share this convention of the Black jeremiad expect to prick the conscience of white America. Despite their severity, these works share an optimism that white America will actually *care* and can do better. Like the prophets, even the gloomiest of them, Stewart retains hope for change.

Stewart does not spare the African American community her critique. Despite her unblinking indictment of the sins of white America against her race and recognition of slavery and servitude as the reason they cannot use their talents and fulfill their potential, Stewart nevertheless critiques her own people for lassitude. She goes after parents, mothers in particular, to be more assertive in disciplining and teaching their children, as well as "the many highly intelligent men of color" who have not put in enough effort on behalf of their race, who are full of "talk without effort" and whose "gross neglect," she says, makes her blood boil.[29] In one of her favorite expressions she warns that the Black community will become "a hissing and reproach" in the eyes of the world, an instantly recognizable reference to Jeremiah 29:18 in the King James Bible, where God plans to rain down destruction on those in the land who ignored his words spoken through the prophets sent to them. If the Black community is a chosen people within a chosen people, it too is called to repent.

An apocalypse is a genre of literature that springs from a sense that the world is so thoroughly corrupted that only a clean sweep by divine power can make it right. From the period of the Second Jerusalem Temple, these works involve visions and symbols revealed and interpreted by angels that show the workings of another world under God's control. They predict imminent, often violent judgment against evildoers and confidence in the restoration of the suffering righteous. Typical biblical examples of apocalypses are the book of

Daniel and Revelation. A broader worldview that we call apocalyptic permeates first-century literature, including the New Testament. The dualistic view of opposing forces of good and evil battling it out on a cosmic plane moving toward God's victory for the righteous and punishment for the powerful had enormous appeal for people who felt powerless and fed a theology of resistance because it forcefully rejected the status quo.

Unsurprisingly, Stewart hews toward apocalyptic works, picking up strands from Daniel, Paul's letters, and Revelation. Her conversion experience includes receiving messages of comfort and commission, so she is not far from Paul and others who see a transcendent reality behind this world. Starkly apocalyptic in language, she puts the country on notice. She indicts the nation for the sin of slavery, comparing it to the enemies of God's people, Babylon, a cipher for the Roman empire in the book of Revelation, and to Egypt, the great enslaver. In her fiery conclusion to *Pure Principles*, she predicts a violent fate for white America and a blessed existence for her people, invoking Revelation and Daniel, "O ye great and mighty men of America, ye rich and powerful ones, many of you will call for the rocks and mountains to fall upon you, and to hide you from the wrath of the Lamb, and from him that sitteth upon the throne; whilst many of the sable-skinned Africans you now despise will shine in the kingdom of heaven as the stars forever and ever." Here she weaves together the image of Jesus as king over all, judging the nations, by citing Revelation 6:16, while leaving it to her hearers to complete the following verse 17, "for the great day of his wrath has come, and who shall be able to stand?" For those who have suffered, she predicts the eternal life given to the righteous, as visualized in Daniel, "And they that be wise shall shine as the brightness of the firmament; and they that turn many to righteousness as the stars for ever and ever (12:3)." She further prophesies the arrival of God's vengeance against the hypocrisy of Americans who admire those who rise up for freedom in countries like France or Ireland while crushing the same proud spirit in the Africans around them, suggesting God will "pour out upon you the ten plagues of Egypt."[30]

Lisa Bowens shows that Stewart understands the meaning of opposition as Paul did, coming from local and immediate circumstances, but reflecting a larger struggle of good and evil. Sin, for both thinkers, is a force that acts in the world to bring down humanity. Suffering and opposition affirm for Stewart that she is on the right side of the two-tier struggle, fighting slavery in America, but also locked in cosmic battle with the devil.[31] Like Paul, Stewart is a warrior. Bowens also notes that she absorbs Paul's apostolic identity, citing the experience of her conversion and the "heart-cheering promise" that "neither death nor life, nor principalities, nor powers, nor things present, nor things to come, should be able to separate me from the love of Christ Jesus, our Lord."[32] Bowens remarks, "As her life merges with Paul in the experience of opposition, so too does it merge in the experience of teaching the gospel of grace."[33]

Like her prophetic forerunners Jeremiah, Paul, and David Walker, Stewart issues a broadside against society's sins for one purpose—to call for reform. White society had but a short amount of time to destroy slavery and repent against its other sins against her race. But she also critiqued free Blacks for giving in to discouragement and goaded them to act. In *Pure Principles*, "it is no use to murmur nor to repine; but let us promote ourselves and improve our talents. And I am rejoiced to reflect that there are many able and talented ones among us, whose names might be recorded on the bright annals of fame. But 'I can't' is a great barrier."[34]

Stewart aims considerable moralizing at Black Americans for their lack of unity and neglect of their own people. She urges parents to discipline and educate their children, and the race as a whole to engage in "headwork" to lift themselves out of drudgery. A strong proponent of education in any form, she is not the first to sustain a cautious hope that prejudice from whites would disappear in the face of Black superior morality and education, "I am of a strong opinion that the day on which we unite, heart and soul, knowledge and improvement, that day the *hissing and reproach* among the nations of the earth against us will cease. And even those who now point at us with the finger of scorn, will aid and befriend us. It is of no use for us to sit with our hands folded, *hanging our heads like bulrushes*, lamenting our wretched condition; but let us make a mighty effort and arise; and if no one will promote or respect us, let us promote and respect ourselves."[35]

Her second address, at Franklin Hall on September 21, 1832, similarly suggests that the free Black community should mount an effort not only to fight slavery, but to free itself from the corrosive effects of domestic service and drudgery, states nearly as bad as slavery. Prejudice, ignorance, and poverty keep them in submission. Identifying with the founding narratives of the country, she urges Blacks to emulate the courage of the pilgrims and American revolutionaries, "my brethren, have you made a powerful effort? Have you prayed the legislature for mercy's sake to grant you all the rights and privileges of free citizens?"[36] In the same speech she argues that "if American free people of color turned to moral worth and intellectual improvement, prejudice would gradually diminish and the whites would be compelled to say, 'unloose those fetters!'" Here again, Stewart shows an unsubstantiated faith that becoming a model group would lead to a natural ebb of prejudice.

Stewart absorbed some nineteenth-century ideologies about women's roles, what scholar Barbara Welter called "the cult of true womanhood," where women reigned as moral exemplars in the home and influenced children and husbands, "chaste keepers at home." She also uses the presumption of female inferiority to needle men for their own lethargy, "I am sensible that there are many highly intelligent gentlemen of color in these United States, in the force of whose arguments, doubtless, I would discover my own inferiority." They have failed to work for their enslaved brothers, nor cultivated their own talents nor distinguished themselves, all things that might help remove the "reproach" that burdens their people. It makes her blood boil, she says, a sign that she does not really believe in feminine submissiveness. In her eyes, only one man showed the requisite courage and ambition but he is dead, no doubt a reference to Walker.[37]

More often, she preaches women's empowerment, urging "the daughters of Africa" to teach, to raise funds for schools, to build stores.

She urged them to imitate the confidence of white Americans and the strength of men, "Do you ask the disposition I would have you possess? Possess the spirit of independence. The Americans do, and why should not you? Possess the spirit of men, bold and enterprising, fearless and undaunted. Sue for your rights and privileges. Know the reason that you cannot attain them. Weary them with your importunities. You can but die if you make the attempt; and we shall certainly die if you do not."[38] Bowens shows that in Stewart's stridency, she weaves in considerable amounts of language from the apostle Paul in her calls to agency in the face of a pitched, seemingly mismatched, battle against sin's power, and in her taking on the persona of a warrior.[39] In so doing, she "conscripts Paul into the service of women," and "enlists him in the liberation war."[40]

Like her mentor David Walker, Stewart was an Ethiopianist. A hopeful ideology arose among nineteenth-century Black thinkers based on a verse in the psalms, 68:31, "Princes shall come out of Egypt; Ethiopia shall soon stretch out her hands unto God." While the Hebrew text of the verse harbors some complexities, it seems to refer to the kingdom of Judah's future elevation and respect shown by more powerful nations like Egypt and Ethiopia. In African American interpretation, it assumes the imminent elevation of the Black community after their period of enslavement.

The verse is a cornerstone of Stewart's rhetoric, cited in all of her speeches and in her written treatise *Pure Principles*, an antidote to the often cited "reproach." While Ethiopianist ideology in general was problematic because it seemed to legitimize slavery as necessary to Christianize the enslaved, it ultimately focused on God's coming deliverance. As Powery and Sadler say, "It was a complex and internally conflicted ideology. It celebrated the sovereignty of God as the one who allowed the enslavement of Africans in order for them to be civilized and Christianized by the Europeans who oppressed them."[41] Yet it showed God as the champion who would shortly deliver Africans and place them in their rightful place of respect. In Stewart's hands it functioned as shorthand for hope and the replacement of reproach with honor. Celebrating a high, ancient African culture, Ethiopianism proved they possessed pedigree and did not need "civilizing." This cultural pedigree became a basis for prodding African Americans, especially men, for failing to attain the same heights as white Americans, even as Stewart acknowledged the barriers of racism and poverty that had stood in their way. In the following, from her third speech at the African Masonic Hall, she combines her themes: the two-tiered battle against the cosmic forces of sin and the earthly forces of prejudice, the high pedigree and agency of Black Americans, and the hopeful promise of restoration to dignity:

> History informs us that we sprung from one of the most learned nations of the whole earth—from the seat, if not the parent of science; yes, poor, despised Africa was once the resort of sages and legislators of other nations, was esteemed the school for learning, and the most illustrious men in Greece flocked hither for instruction. But it was our gross sins and abominations that provoked the Almighty to frown thus heavily upon us and give our glory unto others. Sin and prodigality have caused the downfall of nations, kings, and emperors; and were it not that God in wrath remembers mercy, we might indeed despair; but a promise is left us; "Ethiopia shall again stretch forth her hands unto God."[42]

Angelina Grimké Weld and Theodore Dwight Weld
Condemning the Sin of Enslavement

A slim young woman mounted the platform as an angry mob swarmed and shouted outside. Angelina Grimké, a bride of two days, began to address the evening session of the first day of the Anti-Slavery Convention of American Women, querying the crowd with Jesus's words about John the Baptist in Matthew's gospel, "What came you out to see? A reed shaken by the wind?" A loud shout from outside penetrated. Weaving reasoned argument and biblical verses together, she warned and encouraged for an hour, as stones showered the building and a brick crashed through a window. Pennsylvania Hall was torched and destroyed the next day by anti-abolitionists. The year was 1838 and Grimké retired from public speaking soon after.[43]

Angelina and her sister Sarah Grimké became the first women agents of an abolitionist society in the country in 1836, lecturing to mixed-sex groups amidst threats of violence. That both were Southerners who had seen the grotesques of slavery in their own Charleston family added power to their words. When Angelina married Theodore Dwight Weld, a powerhouse in the antislavery movement, their wedding, with its multiracial guest list and clergy plus egalitarian vows, united two fervent reformers into "two bodies animated by one soul."[44] The two Welds, along with Sarah, gathered thousands of stories of life under slavery from Southern newspapers, judicial proceedings, letters, and eyewitnesses, in *American Slavery As It Is. Testimony of A Thousand Witnesses*, published in 1839, which became one of abolitionism's most influential writings. The Weld-Grimké household, which held three abolitionists, and at least two women's rights advocates, two Quakers and a Presbyterian, was doubtless the site of many discussions about the Bible and social change.

Angelina Grimké spent the summer of 1836 reading theology, the Bible, and abolitionist publications, and in September published her signal work, *Appeal to the Christian Women of the South*. Prepared with the precision of a legal brief and exquisitely argued, it was not the first attempt to argue against (or for) slavery using the Bible. But it was remarkable in its thoroughness and because it came from the pen of a daughter of Southern enslavers and was addressed to other Southern women.[45] Appealing to her Southern sisters as someone also forced to witness and participate in the system of slavery as a child, she regards the Bible as the "ultimate appeal in all matters of faith and practice" and labels "our fathers" as mistaken in using it as a defense.[46] Four main strategies allow her to dismantle earlier biblical arguments in defense of slavery.

In the major portion of the work, Grimké systematically snips the cords between biblical servitude and Southern slavery. Careful to always

call it "servitude" and not "slavery" in biblical instances, she argued
that the institution practiced by the patriarchs, or regulated by laws
in the Torah, was entirely different from the slavery practiced in the
southern United States. Many antislavery interpreters had made much
of the fact that the most common words for "slave" in Hebrew and
Greek can also mean "servant," but that was only her starting point.
The patriarchs, she shows, did not behave like enslavers: Abraham and
Sarah served the three angels themselves, unthinkable in a Southern
home, the servant Eliezer was expected to inherit Abraham's riches if
a son did not arrive, and servants were circumcised as members of the
household.[47] For Christians, baptism replaced circumcision as the rite
of belonging. Grimké pointedly asks if they were baptizing their slaves,
knowing many enslavers did.[48]

The Bible relates six ways to become a servant, including repayment
of a debt or restitution for theft. None characterize Southern slavery.
She maneuvers around some apparent parallels, like being born into
slavery, by saying children would be those of indentured servants or
sold by fathers to be wives, hardly positive outcomes, but still signs of
difference. In another barb, she notes that if Southern enslavers sell their
Black daughters conceived with their female enslaved people, they never
acknowledge them as such. The two biblical examples seemingly similar
to practices in Southern slavery, captives of war and those bought from
gentiles, are not the same as what is practiced in the South because the
servitude does not pass on to the next generation.[49]

The Bible puts safeguards in place against excessive cruelty to
enslaved people, principles ignored by Southern enslavers. For example,
enslaved people go free in the seventh year and a man's family goes
with him. Enslaved people rest on the Sabbath and festivals. If an
enslaver damages the servant's eye or knocks out a tooth (presumably
under punishment), he must free him. If a servant dies immediately as
a result of overzealous punishment, the enslaver is punished, she says
by death, under the principle of "a life for a life." Here she undermines
a favorite phrase of enslavers, that if an enslaved person survives a few
days after punishment and then dies, the enslaver goes free because "he

is his money," recognizing ownership's privilege. This verse, she says is singular, outweighed by the many laws protecting servants' rights. Female Jewish enslaved people, she argues, are usually given as wives, and if she does not please the husband, he cannot sell her; if he takes another wife, he may not reduce her support.[50]

Every biblical servant was guaranteed to be freed: Hebrews after six years or at the enslaver's death, and non-Jews at the Jubilee. More importantly, no one was allowed to return an escaped slave and was required to give the person shelter, effectively giving every servant the right to leave without fear of forced return. Thus, she argues, there is no similarity between Southern slavery and the biblical practices of servitude which protected the servants' rights, "the attributes of justice and mercy are shadowed out in the Hebrew code; those of injustice and cruelty, in the Code Noir of America."[51]

Regarding the claim that Jesus said nothing to undermine slavery, Grimké argues that he spoke only to Jews, so all her arguments undermining any support for slavery from the Hebrew Bible apply. She asks the rhetorical question, "Can you imagine Jesus as a slave-holder?" Paul is also innocent, despite his return of the runaway Onesimus to his enslaver Philemon, because Paul instructed Philemon to take him back as a brother. Paul's opposition to slavery is evident in the letters attributed to him where he pressed enslavers to treat enslaved people fairly and in First Timothy, where he called dealers in enslaved people "men-stealers."[52] Furthermore, recognition of the common humanity of all peoples is clear from Peter's words in Acts, "God is no respecter of persons," from the Golden Rule, and from the command to "love your neighbor as yourself."[53]

Grimké carefully scrutinizes individual words, combined with logic, to dismiss ambient ideas about racial inferiority or slavery as ordained by God. Copious examples appear to reject the translation of "slave" in favor of "servant." The creation of humans in God's image and giving them "dominion" over animals gave no such dominion over other human beings.[54] She calls this "that first charter of human rights that was given by God."[55] The well-worn "curse of Ham" from Gen

9:25–27, which those in the nineteenth century who were proslavery interpreted as ordering permanent servitude of African peoples to other nations, she let stand but argued for a distinction between "will" and "ought." The verse predicted what *would* happen, not what *should have* happened. All predictions do not indicate God's approval, since he predicted Israel's bondage in Egypt and Peter predicted "the Jews' " role in the crucifixion.[56]

A third argument revolves around biblical laws. Abolitionists underscored the law against "man-stealing" or kidnapping, a law whose transgression is a capital offense. Since enslaved people all came as the result of kidnapping them from their homes, their presence is evidence of a capital offense against God. She has already undermined the idea of slavery as inherited, so enslaving the children of enslaved people is doubly illegitimate. The law that one may not return a runaway slave and must shelter and care for him she interprets to mean that any servant under biblical law was free to leave. Angelina Grimké reports of a slave blinded during a flogging, who did not go free, as biblical law commands.[57] The later Fugitive Slave Law of 1850 clearly will contradict the command to feed, shelter, and shield a runaway slave.[58] Because all of these laws represent commands from God, violators are sinners and the institution of slavery reveals itself as founded on sin.

Grimké incorporates Jesus and Paul into the antislavery cause, despite Jesus's silence on slavery and Paul's actions in the case of Philemon and ambiguous remarks about whether to seek manumission.[59] She calls on her Southern sisters to take courage from biblical figures who violated unjust laws—Daniel, Peter, and John—to call out the sinfulness of slavery, to free their enslaved people, and to teach them to read. A long roll of biblical women who stood up for right includes many who will be cited by her sister Sarah in support of women's rights—Miriam, Deborah, Huldah, Esther, Elizabeth, Anna, Mary Magdalene and the women present at Jesus crucifixion, the women at Pentecost, and Paul's fellow preachers.[60] She calls out plaintively, "are there no Miriams among you who would rejoice to lead out the captive daughters taking courage from the biblical figures who violated unjust laws—Daniel, Peter, and John of the southern states to liberty and life?" "Is there no Esther among you who would plead for the poor devoted slave?" She calls on the Exodus for encouragement, "do you think God cannot deliver them?"[61]

The speech at Philadelphia Hall in 1838 is less of a legal argument and more of an appeal to feelings, peppered with biblical verses. Grimké again directed herself particularly to the women in the audience, who, lacking power in the courts or at the ballot box, might feel helpless to effect change by noting that God works through people of little status or power: "he hath chosen the foolish things of this world to confound the wise, and the weak to overcome the mighty."[62] She destroys the myth of "the happy slave," recalling her childhood on the family plantation when every Southern breeze carried the sound of wailing slaves and cursing taskmasters. She saw among the enslaved only the false mirth of the hopeless, who think "let us eat and drink for tomorrow we die." Hearing the noise of the mob outside, she asks if the mob broke in and attacked them, would their suffering be anything compared to the daily violence suffered by the enslaved? No one can be neutral on slavery. God was not neutral when he took sides against Egypt to free his people in the Exodus, or punished Judea for enslaving others. Some are deluded because they have visited the South and seen the outer trappings of gentility at enslavers' tables, or they have simply become desensitized to cruelty. To battle such indifference, Grimké brings forth a series of biblical examples of raising one's voice to call others to account: the trumpet at Sinai, David's lament over Saul, John the Baptist's call to the people to repent, and the prophets come to deliver the oppressed.[63] Finally, for those who claim they do not know what to do, she adjures them to read abolitionist writings, to arm themselves with knowledge, and using an image from Isaiah 6 and Proverbs 25, to "scatter 'the living coals of truth' upon the naked heart of the nation." If speeches and writings had no power, she assures her sisters and brothers, the South would not censor them.[64]

Toward the end of her published tract appealing to Southern women, Grimké calls out the economic interests, racism, and classism both of North and South that keep slavery in place. Northern merchants' livelihoods depend on slave labor, "making *their* fortunes out of the *produce of slave labor*; the grocer is selling your rice and sugar." Their second motive is their deep fear of amalgamation, the term for mixing of races in marriage and offspring. Technically, the North does not approve of slavery, but views amalgamation as repugnant. So many Northerners want emancipation with expatriation. Despite knowing that slavery is sinful, they cannot support full and immediate emancipation, showing that "prejudice against color is the most powerful enemy we have to fight with at the North." She identifies classism in the Northerners' refusal to extend to Blacks the same access to education and employment that they enjoy, "determined to keep them as low as they can." Against these crimes she easily employs the biblical injunction to "Love your neighbor" and the Golden Rule, and the reminder from Heb 13:3 that "they are in bonds as bound with them."[65] While some critics paint Grimké as a sentimental Victorian, her sharp rebuke of classism, racism, and economic self-interest strike a courageous note.[66] Furthermore, her co-editing of *American Slavery As It Is*, with its horrific true stories of life under slavery, precludes the idea of her being hampered by feminine modesty in pointing to rape and sexual abuse of enslaved women by enslavers and overseers. In *Appeal* she points to the reality that white enslavers have fathered daughters but do not acknowledge them. She does not acknowledge, however, that her own brother Henry continued to hold enslaved people and fathered three children with one of them, Nancy Weston.[67]

Angelina's husband, Theodore Dwight Weld, the son and grandson of Congregationalist ministers, came under the influence of revivalist preacher and abolitionist Charles G. Finney. The climate of revivalism made public talks and sermons a respectable way to engage the public and preachers like Weld easily brought into relief the absurdity of trying to combine Christianity and slaveholding. A leader at Presbyterian Lane Seminary in Cincinnati, he was an organizer of a student-led, nine-day set of debates over slavery, immediatism, gradualism, and colonization.

These debates and the students' work with the free Blacks of Cincinnati stirred controversy that led the president, Lyman Beecher, under pressure from the board of trustees, to shut down the student abolitionist society and threaten Weld. Weld, along with fifty others, left the school in 1834, earning the name "the Lane rebels."

Weld devoted his time to lecturing and organizing for the Anti-Slavery Society. In training new recruits, he met the first women agents, the Grimké sisters. By 1836 his health and voice were diminished and he was forced to take up his pen to plead the cause in *The Bible Against Slavery*, summarizing the arguments he had made in public debates.[68] He unravels the arguments of proslavery preachers, drawing on an arsenal of quotations of biblical material, targumim (early Aramaic translations and interpretations of the Hebrew Bible), philology, and ideas of the mutability of language over time. An effective rhetor, he uses sarcasm, humor, and an overwhelming accumulation of examples. He heaps scorn on those who try to justify slavery from the Bible, "the Bible defences thrown around slavery by professed ministers of the Gospel do so torture common sense, Scripture, and historical facts, it were hard to tell whether absurdity, fatuity, ignorance or blasphemy predominates in the compound."[69]

Like Stewart and Grimké, Weld repeats the charge that slavery violates the prohibition against man-stealing in Exodus 21:26, but also argues that slavery is a sin that violates two of the Ten Commandments, the commandment against stealing and the commandment against coveting. By making someone a slave, the owner takes away the most fundamental right of a person, the right to his own person, "The eighth commandment presupposes the right of every man to his powers, and their product. Slavery robs of both. A man's right to himself is his only absolute right—his right to anything else is *relative* to this, is derived from it, and held only by virtue of it. **SELF-RIGHT** is the *foundation-right*—the *post in the middle*, to which all other rights are fastened."[70]

Like his wife, Weld says slavery perverts the plan of creation by turning a human being into a thing, taking away personhood:

> We repeat it, **the reduction of persons to things!** Not robbing a man of privileges, but of *himself*; not loading him with burdens, but making him a *beast of burden*; not restraining liberty, but subverting it; not curtailing rights, but abolishing them; not inflicting personal cruelty, but annihilating *personality*; not exacting involuntary labor, but sinking man into an *implement* of labor; not abridging human comforts, but abrogating human *nature*; not depriving an animal of immunities, but despoiling a rational being of attributes—uncreating a **man** to make room for a *thing!*

> This is American slavery. The eternal distinction between a person and a thing, blotted out—the crowning distinction of all others.[71]

Making humans into merchandise is part of the sin of man-stealing, which explains why its punishment is death. In response to proslavery arguments that the Bible sanctions slavery, he asks why the punishment for stealing a person is so much more severe than for stealing any other form of "property?" His rejoinder goes back to his first principle, the violation of God's natural order:

> The sin in stealing a man is not the transfer from its owner to another of that which is property, but the turning of *personality* into *property*. It is the first law of reason to regard things and beings as they are; and the sum of religion, to feel and act toward them according to their value. Knowingly to treat them otherwise is sin; and the degree of violence done to their nature, relations, and value, measures its guilt.[72]

By extension, slaveholders also break the commandment against coveting, as Weld asks, "who ever made human beings slaves without *coveting* them?" Enslaved people are deprived of all human rights to satisfy desires of owners for a host of evils, including "[financial] gain, lust of dominion, of sensual gratification, of pride and ostentation."[73] He joins other abolitionist exegetes as he cites the law in Deuteronomy that forbids the return of a runaway slave. It is as though God had said that sending him back would recognize the right of the slaveholder to keep him.[74]

Weld ridicules the proslavery uses of Gen 9:25, the so-called curse of Ham, with angry humor, calling it a favorite trinket of enslavers, who "never venture abroad without it, a pocket-piece for sudden occasion, a keepsake to dote over, a charm to spell-bind opposition." His arguments echo his wife's, who was writing at the same time. He questions whether the text means servitude or slavery, which he has established is not service, but theft of personhood. He asks why it is interpreted as extending to a whole race or nation, rather than one individual. Finally, he says proslavery proponents have mistaken a prediction for a prophecy. If merely predicting a crime justifies it, then God's prophecy of Israel's subjection in Egypt absolves the pharaohs of guilt, not to mention those who crucified Jesus. They, he suggests, would be saints![75] These arguments become standard in antislavery rhetoric.

Frederick Douglass
Prophetic Indictment of Hypocrisy

The young enslaved Frederick was startled by his mistress reading from the book of Job in her pleasing voice. He followed her instruction as she taught him the alphabet and a few short words. Her husband, however, became enraged at the idea of teaching an enslaved boy to read, saying, "it would forever unfit him to be a slave" and halted the lessons. Frederick saw it as a revelation—now he understood that reading and gaining knowledge was "the pathway from slavery to freedom." Determined, he learned to read from the white children in the street, exchanging bread from the house for lessons.[76]

Frederick Douglass, the only one of our four writers to have suffered enslavement, looms large in American letters as a prolific writer, editor, and orator of the abolitionist movement. We know about his life in copious detail, thanks to his three autobiographies, where he both narrates his life and reflects on slavery's stain on the nation, damaging both the enslaved and the enslaver. Born in Maryland in 1818 to Harriet Bailey, an enslaved woman, and to an unknown white father (presumed by most to be the enslaver Aaron Anthony), Douglass was moved to different households before finally escaping slavery in 1838. Traveling through Delaware, Philadelphia, and New York, he settled in New Bedford, Massachusetts. Despite the danger of being identified and returned to slavery, he became an agent of the Massachusetts Anti-Slavery Society, touring New England and New York State, Ohio, and Indiana in 1841–1843, testifying to the realities of life under slavery. In 1845 he traveled to England, Scotland, and Ireland, speaking to antislavery audiences. He was legally freed while in England in 1846, when friends and supporters raised money to pay for his freedom. He continued writing, traveling, and speaking to the final day of his life, when he attended a women's rights meeting, all while supporting a large extended family.

Douglass speaks in the tradition of the prophets and the Black jeremiad, and does not engage in the biblical proof-texting and argument of the Welds and others. He appeals to emotion and conscience, having in his arsenal what none of our other writers possess: years of personal experience caught in slavery's vise. Douglass's use of the Bible shows the paradox voiced by Richard Newton, "America is a strange new world in which some are *bound in* (i.e. the enchained, the castigated, the conquered) just as it can be the promised land where others *are bound for* (i.e. the invigorated, the cheered, the conquerors)."[77] Douglass narrates his early experiences showing religious enslavers bound their cruelty to Bible-based arguments, but he saw himself as bound for liberation and a better society.

Douglass' best-known speech, popularly known as "What to the Slave is the Fourth of July?"[78] sounds the classic prophetic themes of censoring national hypocrisy and warning of disaster, with a minor chord of hope. Delivered on July 5, 1852, it came at a moment when slavery was still ascendant, the Civil War far off, and the multiple revolutions in Europe of 1848 in tatters. David Blight calls it "a symphony in three movements," and it is the second movement whose frightening intensity displays the Black jeremiadic style.

The books of the Hebrew prophets typically begin with an announcement, sometimes biographical, declaring their right to speak, followed by condemnation of the people for sins against the covenant between God and Israel, calls for change, and promises of hope. The levels of reassurance vary according to the prophet. The covenant between God and Israel is the basis for the various "lawsuits" or enumeration of crimes leveled at the people. Douglass extrapolates his right to speak by combining two covenants—the one between God and humanity to do justice and the one outlined by the nation's founding documents, the Declaration of Independence and the Constitution. The latter has been misused: properly interpreted, it is a "glorious liberty document." In the first part of the speech, Douglass lays the groundwork by lauding the principles of the nation's founding, comparing July 4 to the Passover and Exodus, the United States to the "emancipated people of God," and the British government to all tyrants from Pharaoh onward. The fathers of the nation, believing in peace and freedom, preferred revolution to submission, and thus "lay deep the corner-stone of the national superstructure, which has risen and still rises in grandeur around you." For the moment, Douglass ignores the problematic history of founders like Jefferson and Washington as enslavers.

But now, he says, Americans rely on the merit of their forefathers, while betraying their principles. They are like those who "boast we have 'Abraham as our father' when they had long lost Abraham's faith and spirit." Knowledgeable hearers will recognize the reference to the acrimonious debate between Jesus and some Jews who had believed in him in chapter 8 of the Gospel of John. Jesus disputes their reliance on Jewish pedigree, both descent from Abraham and being children of God, because they attack him. They are rather the offspring of the devil and perform his works, "ye are of your father the devil, and the lusts of your father ye will do."[79] These hateful words are understood by most New Testament scholars today as not coming from the historical Jesus, but as a projection of the gospel author's own struggles with some people in his community over faith in Jesus.[80] Douglass, of course, was not a critical text scholar, but a rhetor.

Similarly, he invokes the bitter invective of chapter 23 of the Gospel of Matthew, equating America with the Pharisees indicted for hypocrisy, outward piety and inner corruption, the killing of the prophets, and spilling the blood of the righteous and innocent. Douglass uses these references to turn the tables on his hearers: after lulling them into pride at their heritage, he, like the voice of Jesus in these two examples, tells them they have betrayed their founders' principles by not extending them to Douglass and his people, "Are the great principles of political freedom and of natural justice, embodied in that Declaration of Independence, extended to us? . . . I am not included within the pale of this glorious anniversary." The tone of the speech changes as he brings the classic indictment of the prophet against those who consider themselves righteous but mistreat the poor and downtrodden, "the sunlight that brought life and healing to you, has brought stripes and death to me . . . Do you mean, citizens, to mock me by asking me to speak today?" He moves to the famous lament of Psalm 137, of the pain of exiles in a strange land, "by the rivers of Babylon, we sat down," reminding them of their kidnapping of Africans from their land.

Douglass spends little time undoing the biblical arguments for slavery, "must I argue that a system thus marked with blood, and stained with pollution, is wrong? . . . The time for such argument is passed." He draws searing images of slavery: the procession of enchained enslaved people, including the young mother with her baby, weeping as she moves along, faltering under the sun and the whip, the waiting slave ships he saw off the coast of Baltimore, the processions of enchained feet shuffling by his door.

The most pungent charge of prophets then and now is that of hypocrisy. Douglass bears down on public displays of religiosity, on church and on clergy, saying, "the hypocrisy of the nation must be exposed." He borrows directly from Isaiah and Amos, where God shows disgust at the prayers and sacrifices of the publicly pious who rest on their religious rituals while mistreating the powerless.[81] God rejects the public spectacle. Like the basket of summer fruit that will soon rot in Amos 8, such people only appear righteous and beautiful, but are corrupt and

will soon be destroyed. Douglass borrows these ideas and words, but
the real judge is the enslaved person himself,

> to him, your celebration is a sham: your boasted liberty, an
> unholy license; your national greatness, swelling vanity; your
> sounds of rejoicing are empty and heartless; your denuncia-
> tions of tyrants, brass fronted impudence; your shouts of liberty
> and equality, hollow mockery; your prayers and hymns, your
> sermons and thanksgivings, with all your religious parade,
> and solemnity, are, to him, mere bombast, fraud, deception,
> impiety, and hypocrisy—a thin veil to cover up crimes which
> would disgrace a nation of savages.

Douglass's critique of the churches and clergy could not be more
severe as they not only promote slavery but stand as the biggest obsta-
cles to abolition. He cites the abolitionist minister Albert Barnes, who
says, "there is no power out of the church that could sustain slavery an
hour, if it were not sustained in it." Douglass holds the church guilty
not just for propping up slavery, but "superlatively guilty" in failing to
use its power to abolish it. Reversing Peter and the apostles' brave stance
against authority in Acts 5:29, he says today's churches teach "that we
ought to obey man's law before the law of God." In the face of such
perversion of religion, he welcomes infidelity and atheism as superior.

Douglass can indulge in such invective because he has the full
force of both testaments behind him. As often, he defines two kinds
of Christianity, a false one that oppresses and a true one that liberates.
In one sentence he alludes to multiple biblical passages, "But a religion
which favors the rich against the poor; which exalts the proud above the
humble; which divides mankind into two classes, tyrants and enslaved
people, which says to the man in chains, *stay there*; and to the oppressor,
oppress on; it is a religion which may be professed and enjoyed by all the
robbers and enslavers of mankind; it makes God a respecter of persons;
denies his fatherhood of the race, and tramples in the dust the great
truth of the brotherhood of man." Here he has woven in themes of

God as father and human responsibility to one another visible in the
Creation story, commands to love one's neighbor, and Cain's question
"Am I my brother's keeper?"[82] Two verses from Acts that will flourish in
abolitionist and civil rights rhetoric also appear, "And [God] hath made
of one blood all nations of men for to dwell on all the face of the earth,"
confirming the equality of all people, and Peter's statement that God "is
no respecter of persons," or shows no partiality.[83] The image of "trampling" echoes the prophet Amos, who castigates those who trample on
the poor.[84] Douglass brings Isaiah explicitly to deliver God's reaction
to religious piety that tries to gloss over these deeds,

> In the language of Isaiah the American church might be well
> addressed, "Bring no more vain oblations; incense is an abom-
> ination unto me; the new moons and Sabbaths, the calling of
> assemblies, I cannot away with; it is iniquity even the solemn
> meeting. Your new moons and your appointed feasts my soul
> hateth. They are a trouble to me; I am weary to bear them;
> and when ye spread forth your hands I will hide mine eyes
> from you. Yea! When you make many prayers, I will not hear.
> YOUR HANDS ARE FULL OF BLOOD; cease to do evil,
> learn to do well; seek judgment; relieve the oppressed; judge
> for the fatherless; plead for the widow."[85]

After the verdict, however, comes hope for reform and restoration.
Prophets like Isaiah and Jeremiah (less so Amos) hold out the possibility
that the nation will return to the right path and repair their relationship with God. Douglass says, "I do not despair of this country." Both
the principles of liberty embedded in the founding of the country and
God's power to restore are at work in the land. "'The arm of the Lord
is not shortened,'[86] and the doom of slavery is certain." God's light that
arose in creation continues to shine, and the future strength of Africa,
the Ethiopianists hope, will grow.

In *My Bondage and My Freedom*, the second, more expansive
of Douglass's autobiographies, published in 1855, he mentions the

liberating and subversive quality of learning to read in general, and
reading the Bible in particular. Describing white landowners breaking
up his modest Sabbath schools, where he taught fellow enslaved people
to read by reading the Bible under the shade of an oak tree, he reflects
on the irony of enslavers indifferent to enslaved people drinking or
fighting, but who regarded enslaved people reading Scripture "a most
dangerous nuisance." He notes the attendant irony and hypocrisy that
in a Christian country, his students read the Bible in secret and under
threat of flogging by people who profess religion.[87]

Hypocrisy continues to be a major theme throughout this work,
as Douglass observes that the outward piety of an enslaver seemed to
correlate with his cruelty, "I have found them [religious slaveholders],
almost invariably, the vilest, meanest, and basest of their class."[88] He
cites Master Thomas Auld, who entertained visiting preachers lavishly,
stuffing his guests while starving his enslaved people in the kitchen.[89]
The infamous slave-breaker Covey, whom Douglass beats in a fight, was
known for his religiosity.[90] Implied in these tableaux, of course, is the
prophetic claim that their religion was a sham, its outward showiness
hiding corruption within. Douglass dubs it "slaveholding priestcraft."[91]

A second companion theme of the prophetic jeremiad appears in
this work: that God controlled history and would rain down judgment.
In violating the rights of humanity and the principles of the republic,
the proponents of slavery would trigger their own ultimate destruction. The enslaver is "every hour the violator of the just and inalienable
rights of man; and he is, therefore, every hour silently whetting the
knife of vengeance for his own throat."[92] Slave defenders were of their
father the devil, another reference to Jesus's opponents in John 8 and of
the "synagogue of Satan," a reference to enemies of Christ followers in
Revelation 2. He reports that some saw the cholera epidemic as God's
punishment against enslavers.

His narrative also contains the characteristic hope that springs from
the conviction of a just God in control. Douglass discovered the abolition
movement, experienced his own conversion, and found a religious mentor
in an older man named Lawson, all around the same time, bringing a

turn to hopefulness and the possibility of change. Young Douglass was taken with the idea that God had great work for him to do, unaware that he would become one of the greatest orators in US history. He reports a mystical experience, "the air seemed filled with bright, descending messengers from the sky,"[93] which he opined might be the coming of the Son of Man, a scene that combines Jacob's vision at Bethel that affirmed God's covenant and protection and the vision of the end of days described in Daniel, a new age of God's kingship and the destruction of persecuting empires.[94] He takes this as further comfort and direction, "in my state of mind I was prepared to hail Him as my friend and deliverer."[95]

Douglass's "Lessons of the Hour" speech, given numerous times in his final years, contains only a sprinkling of biblical verses but turns on the same great theme of prophetic irony that animated all his oratory, the hypocrisy of a professedly Christian nation denying the humanity of a large number of its inhabitants, "we claim to be a Christian country and a highly civilized nation, yet, I fearlessly affirm that there is nothing in the history of savages to surpass the blood chilling horrors and fiendish excesses perpetrated against the colored people by the so-called enlightened and Christian people of the south." His eloquent blast against lynching, colonization, and economic exploitation carried with it the prophet's inevitable warning: God is shaping history and will render final judgment, "it should be remembered that in the order of Divine Providence the man who puts one end of a chain around the ankle of his fellow man will find the other end around his own neck."[96]

Quite a different tone, one of joy, infuses Douglass's short speech on April 4, 1865, when the public came to celebrate the fall of the Confederate capital Richmond to Union troops.[97] He notes with pride that Black soldiers were some of the first to enter the city and that colored troops participated. The event included a band, a glee club, and the presence of the Black Fifth Massachusetts Cavalry regiment. He makes the case that he and his race were always citizens and had been gradually "read out of our citizenship." Biblical material caps the speech, as he refers to the Rich Man and Lazarus story, saying that "the negro is coming up—he is rising—rising. Why, only a little while ago we were the Lazaruses of the South; the Dives of the South was the slaveholder." Like Maria Stewart, he quotes the King James Version that the rich man, "fared sumptuously every day, and was arrayed in purple and fine linen."[98] Unlike Stewart, he describes the rich man looking up from hell "in torments," seeing Lazarus in Abraham's bosom and begging to have Lazarus come to help, or at least to warn his brothers still living. But one cannot pass over the great gulf between heaven and hell, or life and death.

Abraham himself refuses to intervene, "if they hear not Moses and the prophets, neither will they be persuaded, though one rose from the dead."[99] Here Douglass substitutes the names of the Union generals, "But Father Abraham says, 'If they hear not Grant nor Sherman, neither will they be persuaded though I send Lazarus to them.'" Douglass insists on the sense of ultimate justice and God's vengeance on enslavers. His prophetic voice always claims that Providence worked in history. The text notes this part is met with thunderous applause. He says that like Lazarus, "we are way up yonder now, no mistake," an ambiguous reference to both heaven and being beyond the reach of slavery. In this brief and exultant speech, with one allusion to a famous parable, Douglass harnesses themes of justice, vengeance against evil, and raising up of God's suffering people.

The Bible as an Antislavery Document
Overturning the Proslavery Argument

These four thinkers have demonstrated the many biblical arguments that arose in abolitionist rhetoric. Abolitionists had a few of their own literalist arguments in citing the biblical laws against kidnapping, theft, and returning a runaway slave. But frequently disarming their proslavery opponents meant going beyond the "plain sense" of certain verses, contextualizing the ancient institution of slavery, and arguing for overriding principles of love and reciprocity. Literalism would not really work on either side of the slavery debate, but the abolitionists in particular had to dismantle the literal sense of material that assumed slavery. Doubts about the literal truth of the Bible came from many quarters, most as legacies of the Enlightenment. German critical scholarship made its way to the United States and to the abolitionist movement via intellectuals like Theodore Parker, who preached and published in newspapers and general publications.[100] In quite a different way, the revivalism of the Second Great Awakening honored personal experience of the Spirit outside of institutionalized religion. J. Albert Harrill cites the wave of evangelicalism and the influence of Scottish common-sense realism, a philosophical movement that stressed humanity's inherent morality, noting, "with evangelical religion and moral philosophy combined, the 'plain sense' of the Bible became what one's personal experience intuited it to be."[101] Some groups—Quakers, Deists, and Unitarians—had never been literalists.

For Black Americans, scriptural antislavery was standard, as it was for most white Christians outside the United States.[102] "In fact, so securely did the Bible become the book for black Americans that in the years before the Civil War there seems to have been a diminishing need to rehearse arguments from the Bible against slavery. As was true for much of white Protestant Christendom outside the U.S., scriptural anti-slavery had simply become instinctive."[103]

Victims and opponents of slavery in North America had their own common-sense arguments that slavery and Christianity were incompatible. Threaded through so many of the slave narratives and arguments is the shared sense of outrage at the human toll of suffering exacted by slavery and its contradiction of laws of love and care for the less powerful, and the example of Jesus. Many noted with bitter sarcasm that being religious seemed to amplify the cruelty of enslavers, overseers, and dealers. Like Douglass, Henry Bibb considers religious enslavers the worst. Sold to a cotton planter named Whitfield, who was a deacon in the Baptist church and distinguished by his cruelty to his enslaved people, "he looked like a saint—talked like the best of slave holding Christians, and acted at home like the devil."[104] Describing the woeful scene at the auction block, where families are torn from one another, Bibb invites his reader to "exercise their own judgment whether a man can be a Bible Christian, and yet hold his Christian brethren as property, so that they may be sold at any time in market, as sheep or oxen, to pay his debts."[105]

Enslaved women in particular felt the hypocrisy of slavery. Sojourner Truth directly communed with God, praying in a secluded arbor about her experiences; she says, "Do you think that's right, God?"[106] Planning her escape from slavery, she took advice directly from God, considering each thought of when and where to go as divine guidance.[107] She loved the Bible, but rejected its literalism, saying God was a spirit who did not need to rest, nor wait for the cool of the evening to walk in the garden.[108] Harriet Jacobs, suffering the advances of her capricious enslaver Dr. Flint, also reports the demolition of a small church built by the enslaved people and the forbidding of their worship. Allowed to attend the white church, they are forced to sit in the balcony and invited down to receive communion after the rest of the congregation. She reports with irony, "They obeyed the summons, and partook of the bread and wine, in commemoration of the meek and lowly Jesus, who said 'God is your Father, and all ye are brethren.'"[109]

That biblical religion and slavery were incompatible was proven by enslavers' attempts to limit access to it. While a bit of religion might contribute to docility,[110] giving the Bible directly to captive people was dangerous, as they absorbed its liberationist and prophetic messages. It was not only Douglass who had biblical reading snatched away from him. Plantation owners carefully controlled who preached to those they kept enslaved. Attempts to learn on their own were punished. Henry Bibb reports that in his neighborhood in Kentucky in 1833 a poor white girl set up a Sabbath school to teach him and other enslaved people to read. Local authorities broke it up, Bibb noting that "for enslaved people this was called an incendiary movement."[111]

The Sin of Slavery

A foundational argument of abolitionists, as these writers have declared, was that slavery was a sin, the large number of Christians who were slaveholders providing no proof to the contrary. "A sin is still a sin, even if a Christian commits it, charged Parker."[112] Some point to particular commands willfully transgressed, while others claim the institution creates a life that is wholly sinful and contrary to God's plan of creation. "Sin" carries a variety of terms and meanings in the Hebrew Bible, ranging from unintentional mistakes to willful errors to moral guilt, but always carries the meaning of transgressing God's will and commands. Humans are inherently flawed and prone to sin, a truth God seems to accept when, after the Flood, he promises to never again curse the ground because of humanity's sins, "for the inclination of the human heart is evil from youth."[113] The New Testament maintains these meanings, but also includes the idea of being a "sinner" as a way of life. Paul introduces the idea of sin as an elemental power that works in the world through the flesh.[114]

Specifically, slaveholding was the biblical sin of "man-stealing," as Weld and others point out.[115] Because they were kidnapped from Africa, every enslaved person is stolen and his holder is a thief.[116] Clergyman George Bourne first proposed the idea in 1815, making the biblical argument against slavery in his work, *The Book and Slavery Irreconcilable*.[117] Bourne and Weld reflect that *all* Ten Commandments are transgressed by the system.

Abolitionists across the spectrum embraced the idea of the sin of slavery as an all-encompassing way of life that went against God's will and plan for creation, tainting the enslavers, the enslaved, and Northerners who did not participate directly. Grimké, whose Southern family continued as enslavers even as she campaigned for abolition, grieved at not only the suffering they caused but also the effect of its sin on the souls and hearts of her mother and siblings.[118] Henry Highland Garnet, a formerly enslaved Presbyterian minister serving in Troy, NY, indicts both slave owner and enslaved as guilty of sin for participating in the institution. At a convention of Blacks in Buffalo in 1843, he gave a speech that called for uprisings.

In every man's mind the good seeds of liberty are planted, and he who brings his fellow down so low, as to make him contented with a condition of slavery, commits the highest crime against God and man. Brethren, your oppressors aim to do this. They endeavor to make you as much like brutes as possible. When they have blinded the eyes of your mind— when they have embittered the sweet waters of life—when they have shut out the light which shines from the word of God—then, and not until then, has American slavery done its perfect work.

 TO SUCH DEGRADATION IT IS SINFUL IN THE EXTREME FOR YOU TO MAKE VOLUNTARY SUBMISSION. The divine commandments you are duty bound to reverence and obey. If you do not obey them, you will surely meet with the displeasure of the Almighty. He requires you to love Him supremely, and your neighbor as yourself— to keep the Sabbath day holy—to search the Scriptures— and bring up your children with respect for His laws, and to worship no other God but Him. But slavery sets all these at nought, and hurls defiance in the face of Jehovah. The forlorn condition in which you are placed does not destroy your obligation to God.[119]

Young Frederick Douglass disagreed with this strategy, and Garnet's measure calling for rebellion was defeated by one vote.

Northerners too were guilty of winking at slavery and benefiting from it. Parker implicates Northerners in his "A Sermon on Slavery," delivered in 1841 and 1843, rejecting claims that it was a problem for Southerners to solve alone, as long as Northerners bought food and clothing from the South, "Slavery! We have something to do with it. The sugar and rice we eat, the cotton we wear, are the work of the slave. His wrongs are imported to us in these things. We eat his flesh and drink his blood."[120] In early versions of today's Fair Trade movement, Quakers and African American women in Philadelphia founded Free Produce societies to sell goods produced by free farmers and artisans, leading to the establishment of the American Free Produce Association.[121]

No wonder that slavery was commonly depicted as a brothel. If speakers could not appeal to hearers on the basis of human rights, perhaps stories of sexual immorality might shock them. Douglass in an 1847 speech, notes the strangeness of people in the North who "talk coolly" about relatives who are enslavers and anticipate their visits, "if the Gospel were truly preached here, you would as soon talk of having an uncle or brother a brothel keeper as a slaveholder; for I hold that every slaveholder, no matter how pure he may be, is a keeper of a house of ill-fame. Every kitchen is a brothel, from that of Dr. Fuller's to that of [President] James K. Polk's . . . think of a million of females absolutely delivered up in to the hands of tyrants, to do what they will with them—to dispose of their persons in any way they see fit."[122] Harriet Jacobs relates the particular danger to a women under enslavement, subject to the sexual whims of her enslaver and to the jealousy of her mistress, making physical beauty a curse which "hastens the degradation of the female slave."[123] Jacobs suffers the leering and advances of her enslaver Dr. Flint as well as the anger and jealousy of his wife. Sarah Parker Remond, part of a distinguished African American abolitionist family in Massachusetts, lectured in England, speaking of "the sufferings perpetrated on her sisters . . . and the fearful amount of licentiousness which everywhere pervaded the Southern States," calling women the "worst victims" of slavery and pointing to the thousands of mixed-race people in the United States as proof of the widespread rape of enslaved women.[124]

The idea that slaveholding is sin is implied by enslaved people who see cruel enslavers and overseers struck down by illness and suffering shortly after inflicting pain on others. Formerly enslaved John Brown, in a speech in Plymouth, England in 1851, tells of an enslaved man in Virginia calling out to God for deliverance, whose enslaver taunted him, saying, "'now I will tie you to that tree and whip you, and you pray to the Almighty, and if he don't help you, we shall see who is the best man, then, shan't we?'" He beat him as the slave prayed, but nothing happened. "'Now,' said he, 'you see you have only one master, and that's me.' Shortly afterwards this cruel planter was ill, and he implored the enslaved people to wash his hands, and thought there was blood on his whip, and died cursing himself for all his wicked deeds."[125]

Exodus

The Exodus story provided a ready and frequent proof that God hated slavery and was on the side of the enslaved. References to Moses, the Red Sea, Pharaoh, and the plagues are ubiquitous in antislavery rhetoric. Herbert Marbury shows its model for African American thinkers as typified by two forms—pillars of fire, emphasizing God's vengeance on the oppressors, and pillars of cloud, showing God's care for the downtrodden.[126] David Walker, in his *Appeal to the Coloured Citizens* of 1829, skews toward the first model, as he identifies America as the new Egypt, guilty of the sin of slavery. In the tradition of the Black jeremiad and of apocalyptic, he predicts the downfall of the United States as punishment for slavery. He reminds readers of the destruction of thousands of Egyptians whom God drowned in the sea as a consequence "for afflicting *his people* in their land,"[127] yet Israelites were comparatively better off than enslaved people in America. In condemning all kinds of sin, most preachers do not mention the sin of slavery, "which is ten thousand times more injurious to this country than all the others put together . . . I tell you Americans! That unless you speedily alter your course, *you and your country are gone!!!!!*"[128]

Douglass cites the Exodus at many junctures, employing it as a shorthand for the double themes of liberation and vengeance and fusing it with the earlier story of Joseph, the beloved son sold to foreigners. He affirms its meaning for the enslaved, whose religion was all about freedom, "the preacher who wanted to raise a real hearty shout at the black camp meeting had but to describe the departure of the Hebrews out of Egypt and paint the destruction of Pharaoh and his hosts."[129] In a very different way, he laments the failures of Reconstruction because freed people had no possessions or land to begin new lives. Even Israel on its way out of Egypt provided the jewels of Egypt for their sustenance.[130] Finally, it is a metaphor for every personal and national struggle, "the Red Sea lies ever before the pilgrim and the promised land."[131]

The utility of the Exodus narrative is complicated somewhat by the importance of Egypt in the trope of Ethiopianism. As a rich and ancient African culture, Egypt, along with Ethiopia, figures in Psalm 68:31, where "princes shall come forth from Egypt." The high pedigree of Africans and their culture stemming from their belonging to these two advanced civilizations means that "Egypt" cannot function as a completely negative symbol in Black abolitionist rhetoric.

Refutation of "the Curse of Ham"

In the arguments of proslavery forces, the final verses of a relatively obscure tale in Genesis 9:20–28 become the justification for permanent subjection of the African race. In the story, Noah becomes drunk, falls asleep, and "lay uncovered," presumably exposing his genitals. His son Ham sees him, but the other sons, Shem and Japheth, cover Noah with a garment, walking backward so as to avoid seeing their father's nakedness. When he awakes, Noah knows what has happened and curses Canaan, the son of Ham, condemning him to be a slave to his brothers. In the so-called "Table of Nations," which follows in chapter 10 and traces the descendants of Noah, Ham's descendants are in Africa, including Egypt and Ethiopia, thus allowing the elision of slavery and race.[132]

Historical critical scholarship assigns the story to an early stratum of the biblical text, J or Yahwist for those who support the Documentary Hypothesis.[133] Among other things, these tales seek to make sense of the existence of other nations, including Canaan, and Israel's relationship to them. Chapter 10, the genealogy of Noah's descendants, is from the later, Priestly stratum, written in response to Babylonian exile hundreds of years later. The priestly editors tried to create a cohesive, unfolding grand story from the various disparate narratives, in part by adding genealogies.[134]

Obscure as it is, this passage assumed an outsize importance in nineteenth-century America because it allowed race to be folded into arguments about slavery. An anonymous proslavery pamphlet, *African Servitude* [1860], shows how proslavery advocates amplify the story's significance, throwing in the mark of Cain[135] for extra effect, ignoring the absence of any description of the mark as well as its role as a sign of God's protection:

> That there might not in after-ages be any mistake or doubt upon whom the curse was laid, it would seem that the Almighty put upon the descendants of Ham, not only the black mark of disobedience and condemnation to service, but also prepared and adapted both mind and body for the service required of them.
>
> The fall or defection of Ham, considered in all its results, is one of the most, if not the most, important event to the human race that has transpired since the flood; save, always, the advent and death of the Saviour, the great event of the universe.
>
> Before this important event (the fall of Ham) it might be truly said that "all men were born free and equal" in rights and privileges, but after the curse, who shall say, in opposition to God's Word, that there is an equality in conditions, rights, and privileges of all the inhabitants of the earth?[136]

This myth was ubiquitous in nineteenth-century America, accepted even by some African Americans as an origin story. Powery and Sadler note its dominance in American cultural assumptions of the day, so that even Black preachers and authors who attempted a historical approach were forced to respond to it.[137]

The curse of Ham allowed a conflation of race and slavery.[138] Those who undermined the story tried to cut the implied connection to racial origins. Weld used ridicule, calling this a favored accessory of enslavers that in truth implied no connection to whole peoples but was about individuals. Many others note that references to slavery in the Bible almost never specify race, although some distinguish a Hebrew slave from a non-Hebrew slave. During a debate in Kentucky in 1849 regarding a new constitution, Baptist preacher James M. Pendleton and author John G. Fee made the case that biblical statements about slavery did not specify race and surely many enslaved by Rome in her northern provinces were white.[139] Douglass similarly needles those who argue a permanent enslavement of Africans from scripture, saying that there are so many of mixed race due to white enslavers fathering children with slave women that a new class of enslaved people are not entirely descendants of Ham, so "it is certain that slavery at the south must soon become unscriptural."[140]

These arguments failed to dispel the general conflation of race and slavery, as racism and economic interests kept slavery in place in both North and South.[141] Ironically, people who promoted the "curse of Ham" idea were implicitly rejecting polygeny, an ancillary racist theory that Africans and Caucasians do not share a common ancestor, an idea that undergirded some theories of African inferiority. Yet since Ham is one of Noah's sons, along with Shem and Japheth, they have common ancestry and their descendants in chapter 10 represent the shared ancestry of different nations. Racist ideas were so illogical they sometimes worked against each other.

Refutation of Patriarchs as Enslavers and Laws That Assume Slavery

The biblical text refers to the patriarchs as having servants or enslaved people, but the English translations use terms that are more connotative than the Hebrew word עבד, *ebed*, which can be rendered by either word. For example, Genesis 24:2 refers to Abraham's "servant," a person who seemed to enjoy seniority and "had charge of all that he [Abraham] had." When Abraham answers God's call to go to Canaan in Gen 12:2-5, he takes not only his wife and nephew, but their possessions and "the souls that they had gotten in Haran." The word "gotten" is not the word "bought," but literally "made," suggesting at least to the ancient rabbis that they were converts to the one God.[142] Abram laments his lack of offspring saying he will have to adopt Eliezer of Damascus, "And Abram said, 'you have given me no offspring, and so a slave born in my house is to be my heir'" (Gen 15.3 NRSV). In the Hebrew text, no word for "slave" appears, merely *ben biti*, "son of my household." The NRSV renders it "slave born in my house," while the KJV is closer to the Hebrew with "one born in my house." These ambiguities in terminology opened the door for some antislavery exegetes like Albert Barnes. Barnes, a white biblical scholar and pastor in New Jersey and Philadelphia, was one of the "New School" Presbyterians, who stressed moral responsibility and activism against Calvinist fatalism.[143] Many New School adherents were abolitionists, including Lewis and Arthur Tappan, Gerrit Smith, and Arthur Jay. Barnes undertakes a detailed attack on slavery based on biblical material in his *An Inquiry into the Scriptural Views of Slavery*, arguing from general principles and from individual words and verses.[144]

To the claim that the patriarchs held enslaved people, he applies philological analysis, developing what opponents called "the Barnes hypothesis." He shows that the Hebrew word for slave,עבד *ebed*, encompasses a wide range of meanings in the Bible, including a servant of a king, an ambassador, a soldier, a worshipper of God or idols, a worker who is hired, or a slave who is bought or inherited.[145] He notes that the word is often employed to denote a servant, whether hired, bought, or inherited, "the Hebrews did not make distinctions between the various kinds of service with the accuracy of the Greeks."[146] Context determines meaning so "the use of the *term* nowhere in the Scriptures of necessity implies *slavery*."[147] He notes that nowhere does any patriarch sell a slave or consider one merchandise.[148] The only case where a servant is clearly bought refers to the command to Abraham to circumcise all in his house, including "the one bought with your money from any foreigner who is not of your offspring."[149] The example of Joseph sold as a slave is so negative that it can hardly help slaveholders' arguments. Yet even the word "buy" is open to interpretation, he argues, as God "bought" his people, or ransomed them for himself.[150] Like Grimké, Barnes assiduously severs the cords between biblical servitude and American slavery. He suggests that the example of Abraham bespeaks something gentler than Southern slavery, "servitude in the days of Abraham must have existed in a very mild form." When nearby marauders kidnapped Lot and his family in Gen 14, Abraham confidently armed his servants, and did not fear them rising against him. This is in marked contrast to the US situation where enslaved people are not allowed weapons and require a pass to travel away from their enslavers' homes.[151] A decade later, in *The Church and Slavery* (1857), Barnes rejects those who label slavery "patriarchal," rejecting any equation of ancient slavery and its practice in the United States. Such exhaustive arguments on philological grounds probably convinced no one on their own but went into the great arsenal of antislavery arguments.

Ethiopianism

Stewart and Douglass invoke a verse cited frequently among African American abolitionists from Psalm 68:31 in the KJV (68:32 in MT), "Princes shall come out of Egypt; Ethiopia shall soon stretch out her hands unto God." Powery and Sadler mention the dominance of the KJV (Authorized Version) in African American thought, writing, and preaching. With this verse, the KJV helped inspire an Ethiopianist ideology that explained slavery as a temporary period, not unlike Israel's time in Egypt, that God allowed to happen in order to prepare Africans for leadership. As Powery and Sadler point out, this interpretation has its own internal contradictions, as it both decried and apparently legitimized slavery.[152]

In its context, the verse is part of a psalm of praise that visualizes the triumph of the God of Israel and the tributes of other nations streaming to Jerusalem. The verse is "famous and infamous" for its textual variants and is part of a composite of verses that surround the core of the psalm, verses 12–28.[153] However, as an isolated verse it inspired African

Americans to expect a change in their lives brought by God. It looks to a restoration of the glorious past of Africa and explains enslavement as a temporary period ordained by God for the purpose of Christianization and instruction. For the enslaved, of course, it was a very severe lesson.

Sojourner Truth's narrative reports a man impressed by her preaching who sends her to Hartford bearing a letter, "I send you this living messenger, as I believe her to be one that God loves. Ethiopia is stretching forth her hands unto God. You can see by this sister, that God does by his Spirit alone teach his own children things to come."[154] Henry Highland Garnet, touring the UK, gave a speech at a music hall in Birmingham, drawing an optimistic picture of the eventual success of abolition, "he was satisfied that God's set time had come, in which he intended to favor Africa, and when the cheering prophecy was to be fulfilled, 'Ethiopia shall quickly stretch forth her hands unto God.' He knew he would be pardoned in saying England owes a great debt to Africa."[155]

Jesus and Paul

The New Testament texts present more problems for abolitionist exegetes. Paul, in genuine and pseudonymous letters, assumes the social fact of the slavery and returns the slave Onesimus to his enslaver Philemon, although the ambiguity of his words leaves room for the possibility he expected manumission.[156] Barnes emphasizes Paul did not force or even persuade Onesimus to return.[157] Formerly enslaved people remember Paul's words being used to keep them in subjection. Harriet Jacobs relates the preaching of Rev. Mr. Pike, brought in to preach to the enslaved people at a time after Nat Turner's insurrection, when "the slaveholders came to the conclusion that it would be well to give the enslaved people enough of religious instruction to keep them from murdering their masters."[158] He preaches from the text in Ephesians, "Servants, be obedient to them that are your masters according to the flesh, with fear and trembling, in singleness of heart, as unto Christ" (Eph 6:5). Although scholarship has determined that the letters to the Ephesians and the Colossians were probably not by Paul himself, this was not appreciated by most nineteenth-century readers who were not scholars or liberal clergy, and the letters are part of the canon. Theologian Howard Thurman tells the story of his grandmother, a former slave in Florida. Thurman often read to her from the Bible, but she never allowed him to read from Paul's writings, except the section on love in 1 Corinthians 13, because during her enslavement a white preacher regularly preached from Paul's works to admonish her and others to be obedient as it was God's will. She promised God and herself that if she became free, she would never read that part of the Bible again.[159] Paul, says Allen Callahan, became for both enslaved people and enslavers "the patron saint of the master class in the ante-bellum United States."[160]

James Gillespie Birney, a politician and former enslaver turned abolitionist, defends Paul as someone who saw slavery, but never held enslaved people himself. Birney constructs a fictional scene of Paul's church including Cassius, a Roman officer with thousands of enslaved people; Apicius, with forty to fifty enslaved people; and Megrinus, with one enslaved person. Would Paul refuse to admit their enslaved people to his church, or require them to sit in separate pews, or have separate churches, or withhold Scripture from them? Clearly not. Moreover, the poverty and identification with the poor that characterized both Jesus and Paul would not resonate with enslavers or slavery.[161] Slavery is "the work of the devil, which Christ came to destroy" and the Roman empire fell because of slavery. Bourne goes further—Paul is a champion of anti-slavery. Paul advises enslaved people to be free if they can accomplish it, hinting at it as best as is safe under watchful Roman eyes.[162] Nor could any man-stealer have belonged to the church at Corinth, says Bourne, where traders in enslaved people are one of the categories of people condemned by the Law."[163]

Turning the New Testament into an abolitionist ally calls for more ingenuity than doing so for the Hebrew Bible. Jesus never addresses slavery directly in his sayings or preaching and interpreters must take refuge in generalizations about the man and his teachings. Proslavery

proponents like Thornton Stringfellow argued that since the Old
Testament allowed slavery, Jesus's silence on the subject means he
agreed with their stance. Barnes countered with a general claim, "the
spirit of the New Testament is against slavery, and the principles of the
New Testament, if fairly applied, would abolish it."[164] Birney similarly
argued "the spirit of Christianity, to say the least of it, is *equalizing*."
One popular principle invoked by Birney uses a metaphor from the
parable in Mark 4:26–29 to say that Jesus's teaching was "a seed growing
secretly" that would spread and lead to the eventual demise of slavery.[165]
Jesus, he argues, did not encounter slavery among fellow Jews since there
was no proof it existed among Jews in his time. If it had, he would have
rebuked it. His refusal to go to the centurion's house, he suggests, was
a rejection of slavery as practiced in the Roman army.[166]

   Despite the forced quality of these arguments, many had staying
power against the more literalist hermeneutic of proslavery writers and
rhetors. The combination of antislavery argument and the beginnings
of critical scholarship undermined literalism. Moreover, arguments like
"the seed growing secretly" that started with biblical exegesis by clergymen made their way into public rhetoric via newspapers and speeches.
Much of it may have been for internal consumption, cementing attitudes
and producing cohesion within abolitionist groups.

   Bowens shows that understandings of Paul as the enslaver's ally
have been one-sided. In contrast to white interpretation of Paul, many
African Americans identified with Paul as early as the eighteenth
century and also understood Jesus's message through Pauline terms and
theology. They related to Paul typologically, as another person called by
God to witness to Christ and to endure suffering with strength.[167] Maria
Stewart, for example, adopts Paul's warrior language to make sense
of the intense opposition she faced. Considering her life a "complete
disappointment," she, like Paul, expected reward in the next world.[168]
Douglass shows an affinity with Paul on a visit to the Areopagus in
Greece, where he recalls Paul's speaking to the philosophers with the
truth of "one blood" doctrine. Similarly, Douglass identifies with the
apostle as another with "stripes on his back" who spoke the word of

God.[169] The conversion narratives of enslaved writers show Paul as a spiritual forebear, who suffered in body, but was transformed by God as his "chosen vessel." Like Paul, these thinkers trusted in God's overwhelming power, rejecting the apparent and temporary power structure in favor of a larger, supernatural reality of cosmic battle of forces and "divine interruptions of the demonic."[170]

The Golden Rule

While the arguments above rely on verses from the Hebrew Scriptures, Jesus's citation of the Golden Rule in Matthew 7:12 is also an obvious rejoinder to proslavery arguments. Many antislavery speakers simply invite people to consider whether they would change places with the enslaved or see their own families sold into slavery. Douglass incorporates the idea into his July 5 speech by simply saying, "there is not a man beneath the canopy of heaven that does not know that slavery is wrong for him."[171] Bourne cites the golden rule specifically, asking every slave-merchant to consider his emotions if he became a slave, or saw his wife and children sold into slavery, "would not the indignation and the anguish of the Merchant himself be almost inexpressible?"[172]

Birney's purpose is transparent in the title of his 1846 book, *The Sinfulness of Slaveholding in All Circumstances Tested by Reason and Scripture*. Addressed "To the Preachers of the Gospel in the United States," he says "I cannot withhold my surprise that any of you should still use the Book of God's *love* to countenance the practice of Man's *hate*."[173] In the comprehensive work he invokes the Golden Rule, the example of Paul, and argues that Jesus did not condemn slavery because Jews did not practice it in his time. He reasons that the guilt of slavery stems from its initial subjugation of people by force, beginning with the example of an African prince who captures a village, sells them to a Christian slave-trader, from whom a planter buys them. The plantation owner who buys the enslaved people "steps into the shoes of the slave-trader, as the slave-trader has before stepped into the shoes of the African prince."[174] All are guilty, but the planter is most guilty because he is the most educated and knows the Golden rule.[175] Birney should know. Born into a family of enslavers, he held enslaved people himself until his rejection of slavery and championing of gradualism, then immediatism, as a lawyer and politician. Like Bourne, he argues that guilt is not diluted by the oceans crossed in the Middle Passage.

Oddly enough, the Golden Rule had also been invoked by defenders of slavery like Virginia clergyman Thornton Stringfellow, who assumed a sort of patriarchal care and authority over the enslaved people instead of a reciprocity of equals.[176] Formerly enslaved Henry Watson relates a sermon by a white preacher to his slave group, applying the Golden Rule by asking the enslaved people to imagine if they were masters and mistresses. "Would you not desire that your servants should do their business faithfully and honestly, as well when your back was turned as while you were looking over them?"[177] Such contrived arguments show that, at least for the verse containing the Golden Rule, the plain meaning of the text favored the abolitionist side.

Acts One Blood doctrine

Not only was the KJV influential for African Americans, it was the regnant version for Protestants in eighteenth- and nineteenth-century America, with near-official status in the culture. In the case of the Acts 17:26, where Paul addresses the philosophers of Athens as fellow worshippers of the one God, the words of the KJV had lasting effect, "And he hath made of one blood all nations of men for to dwell on all the face of the earth." The Greek of today's authoritative Nestle-Aland text does not contain a word for "blood," but points to a single human ancestor, "and he made from one every nation of men to live on all the face of the earth, having determined allotted periods and the boundaries of their habitation." Codex Alexandrinus, one of the four most important manuscripts of the Greek Bible, contains the words "blood" and "all nations," words that make their way into the KJV.

Although the idea of common descent is common to both versions, the metaphor of "one blood" stuck and the verse became axiomatic in antislavery rhetoric. The verse is often paired with Acts 10:34 that shows God's impartiality, "Then Peter opened his mouth, and said, 'of a truth, I perceive that God is no respecter of persons.'"

Already in the eighteenth century, some Christians argued for the equality of the races on the basis of common descent from Adam, the family of man, God's showing no partiality, and the idea that all peoples were of "one blood." Benjamin Banneker, a distinguished mathematician and astronomer born free in Maryland, included the verse in a public letter to Jefferson, then secretary of state, in 1791. He challenged the person who wrote eloquently of the right to liberty in the Declaration of Independence to address its denial to those under slavery.[178] Less than fifty years later, the same verse appears in Garrison's address of July 4, 1838, delivered at the request of the Massachusetts Anti-Slavery Society and published in *The Liberator* on July 13, its impassioned rhetoric arguing for an immediate end to slavery. Showing his lack of faith in the Declaration of Independence and some lines later, the Constitution, as vehicles for liberation, he presents a mélange of biblical referents, "in the name of the God, who has made us of one blood, and in whose image we are created; in the name of the Messiah, who came to bind up the broken-hearted, to proclaim liberty to the captives, and the opening of the prison to them that are bound; in the name of the Holy Ghost, whom to despise is to perish; I demand the immediate emancipation of all who are pining in slavery."[179]

Antislavery writers bring the one blood metaphor to show the hypocrisy of those who allow slavery and profess Christianity, often with unfortunate similes about the Pharisees in the gospels and "the Jews" in the gospel of John.[180] Charges of hypocrisy and negative divine judgment easily transferred to the critique of slavery, with Acts 17:26 and Acts 10:34 as the true message of God.[181] Frederick Douglass attacks proslavery clergy as "ecclesiastical sneaks," who prostitute the Bible, calling them "children of the devil," a charge Jesus lays against "the Jews" in the gospel of John 8:44.[182]

Not only can the one blood verse promote the idea of equality, it
provides a rebuttal to theories of polygenism that had gained respectability in some scientific circles in the nineteenth century.[183] Explaining
racial differences had become a preoccupation of nineteenth-century
ethnologists. Polygenism asserted that the races had different origins,
so implicitly went against the idea that all humans descended from
Adam. Associated with naturalists George Gliddon, Josiah Nott, Louis
Agassiz, and others, it assumed a fixed and purposive idea of the natural
order that included the races. Some argued that racial traits were fixed
and traceable back through time. For proslavery rhetors it was a short
hop from the idea of unchanging racial difference to theories of racial
inferiority and the superiority of whiteness,[184] aided by the patina of
scientific respectability.

The idea of "one blood" is a direct assault on such ideas. It also
worked against the curse of Ham and claim of eternal servitude of
the African race. As Powery and Sadler note, Gen 9 and Acts 17
are not technically incompatible, since Genesis 9 indicates Shem,
Ham (and therefore Canaan), and Japheth are all sons of Noah, so
the nations delineated in Genesis 10, "the table of nations," are of
one blood. Yet Acts 17 was universally understood by antislavery
thinkers as implying equality between races as a consequence of
common descent.[185] Like the appeal to the glorious past and sophisticated cultures of Egypt and Ethiopia, this verse rebuked claims
of racial inferiority and helped dispose of the slaveholders' favorite
story, the curse of Ham.

This "one blood" verse was commonplace in the narratives of
enslaved people. Powery and Sadler show most were less interested
in ancient ethnography than in understanding it as a buttress to the
equality of all humans and a map forward to a future of possibility.[186]
The preface to William and Ellen Craft's narrative of their flight from
slavery, *Running a Thousand Miles for Freedom*, notes both this verse
and the founding document of the United States, "Having heard while
in Slavery that 'God has made of one blood all nations of men,' and
also that the American Declaration of Independence says, 'We hold

these truths to be self-evident, that all men are created equal; that they are endowed with their Creator with certain inalienable rights; that among these, are life, liberty, and the pursuit of happiness;' we could not understand by what right we were held as 'chattels.'"[187]

The Bible and the Constitution

A few abolitionists questioned whether the Bible was really antislavery and were willing to repudiate it if necessary. In 1850, the Anti-Slavery Society in Boston passed a resolution that declared the Bible a falsehood *if* it sanctions slavery.[188] Many more had problems with the Constitution. After some proslavery victories at the federal level, the passing of the Fugitive Slave Act (1850) and the Dred Scott decision (1857), it became increasingly difficult to see the Constitution or Declaration of Independence as pristine commitments to human liberty. In her 1861 speech, "No Union with Slaveholders," Susan B. Anthony castigates Joshua R. Giddings, an antislavery member of the House from Ohio, for his steadfast loyalty to a document that after 1850 supports the capture and return of fugitive enslaved people, "What does Mr. Giddings mean when he, with his hand on the Bible, solemnly swears to support the United States Constitution?"[189] In the same speech she even attacks Charles Sumner, who had years before been beaten unconscious on the Senate floor for his antislavery speech, as she pleaded for all who claim to hate slavery to stop swearing allegiance to the Constitution—a tall order for members of the House and Senate.

Garrison, Wendell Phillips, H. Ford Douglas, Robert Purvis, and others rejected the Constitution as a proslavery document, and loyalty to it was part of the source of a feud between Garrison and Frederick Douglass. Some defended it by comparing it to the Bible, which had its contradictions, but was deemed on the side of the slave. Frederick Douglass changed his views over time. In 1847 he decried the trampling of human rights using religion and the Bible but called it a *mis-use*. The Constitution, however, was flawed by design,

the Constitution I hold to be radically and essentially slaveholding, in that it gives the physical and numerical power of
the nation to keep the slave in his chains, by promising that
that power shall in any emergency be brought to bear upon the
slave to crush him in obedience to his master. The language of
the Constitution is you shall be a slave or die ... For my part I
had rather that my right hand should wither by my side than
cast a ballot under the Constitution of the United States.[190]

By 1851 Douglass, who had been Garrison's protégé, espoused a
different view. In "What to the Slave Is the Fourth of July?" he says
the Constitution, correctly understood, in no way supports slavery:
"I hold there is neither warrant, license, nor sanction of the hateful
thing: but interpreted as it ought to be interpreted, the Constitution is
a GLORIOUS LIBERTY DOCUMENT."[191]

Bitter experience made enslaved people less confident about the
ideals or the implementation of the founding secular or religious documents. William Wells Brown, who escaped slavery in 1834 to become
a major abolitionist orator, expressed the idea that Church and State
were in synchrony to bolster a slaveholding system. As he struggled with
fatigue during his journey to freedom, he reminded himself what lay
behind him, "when I thought of slavery with its Democratic whips—
its Republican chains—its evangelical bloodhounds, and its religious
slave-holders—when I thought of all this paraphernalia of American
Democracy and Religion behind me, and the prospect of liberty before
me, I was encouraged to press forward, my heart was strengthened, and
I forgot that I was tired or hungry."[192] Brown said it was a mistake, not
design of the Founding Fathers to incorporate the slave trade into the
Constitution.[193] As for Northerners' persistent discrimination in the
so-called Cradle of Liberty, "you have the cradle, but you have rocked
the child to death."[194] A few simply grew frustrated with the wordy
exchanges and Bible-quoting arguments that seemed to change nothing.
According to the New York Tribune, Henry Ward Beecher suggested

supplying the antislavery side in Kansas with Sharps rifles, earning them the name "Beecher's Bibles."[195]

Development of newer, scientific arguments did not render the religious or biblical arguments moot, however. Looking at the number of publications in this period suggests a parallel religious argument augmented human rights or political expediency arguments. The abolitionist writers who took on the Bible brought it over to their side and seriously undermined the proslavery advocates who had argued on the basis of the curse of Ham, literalist reading of the laws of slavery, or the need to Christianize Africans.[196]

CHAPTER 2

The Bible and Women's Rights in the Nineteenth Century

WHEN RUTH BADER Ginsburg argued the gender discrimination case *Frontiero v. Richardson* before the Supreme Court in 1973, she quoted a portion from the work of Sarah Moore Grimké, the first American woman to use biblical texts to argue for women's rights, "But I ask no favors for my sex. I surrender not our claim to equality. All I ask of our brethren is, that they will take their feet from our necks, and permit us to stand upright on that ground which God designed us to occupy."[1]

The Bible's conspicuous presence in nineteenth-century society meant that activists for women's rights could not ignore it, but the movement for suffrage and equality hosted a wide spectrum of views about the Bible's actual usefulness for their cause. While many activists like Grimké saw the Bible as a document founded on gender equality and their ally, others saw it as their enemy, which, aligned with churches and clergy, formed a stubborn obstacle to women's equal rights. A few others saw the Bible as largely irrelevant, since the movement sprang from universal human rights. But while the women's rights advocates may have debated its meaning and contents, they agreed that as a bulwark of institutional Christianity the Bible was usually a problem. Lucy Stone, part of the triumvirate of early suffrage leaders that included Susan B. Anthony and Elizabeth Cady Stanton, chided her friend Antoinette Brown, a Congregationalist minister, for her embrace of "that *wall* of Bible, brimstone, church and corruption which has hitherto hemmed *women* into *nothingness*."[2] God was manifest in nature, and pure spirit was accessible if only one could cut through the corrupting influence of culture on scripture. Stanton, Matilda Joslyn Gage, and most of the contributors to *The Woman's Bible*, a two-volume commentary centered on women's inclusion and exclusion from the text, also understood the Bible as a part of the institutional wall that blocked women's possibilities.

The movement for women's rights in the nineteenth century overlapped, not always comfortably, with the two other prominent reform movements of abolitionism and temperance; many key figures embraced all three reforms. A decade before the Seneca Falls convention, Grimké's letters to the head of the Boston Female Anti-Slavery Society in 1837 laid out an extensive argument for women's equality using biblical texts, and Sarah and her sister Angelina braved controversy as women speaking to mixed gender audiences as antislavery agents. Maria Stewart, a freeborn Black, had a brief, but passionate career in the 1830s as an abolitionist writer and platform speaker who also argued for women's equality. Women preachers had exercised their speaking abilities within churches since the early nineteenth century. Seneca Falls was a coalescing of elements already at work.

While the movement for women's rights shared members, strategies, and attitudes with abolitionism, the movements came to compete with one another and a bitter rift developed between some women's rights advocates and abolitionists over the Fifteenth Amendment (1870), which extended citizenship and the vote to all male citizens, regardless of race or former servitude but not regardless of sex. Frederick Douglass and others feared that insisting on women's enfranchisement would sink the whole enterprise. Wendell Phillips, a supporter of women's rights, voiced the winning sentiment at the 1865 meeting of the American Anti-Slavery Society, "So I say one question at a time. This hour belongs to the Negro."[3] Matters reached a crisis point when the American Equal Rights Association (AERA) meeting in 1869 became the scene of "the Great Schism" in the suffrage movement, between those willing to support the Fifteenth Amendment to give Black men the vote and those who insisted on the addition of women's suffrage. Elizabeth Cady Stanton and Susan B. Anthony had originally formed the AERA in 1866 to promote universal suffrage for both women and African

Americans. The women's movement split into two groups, a divide that would remain for twenty years.[4] Stanton and Anthony stooped to racist stereotypes in opposing a Fifteenth Amendment,[5] while those on the other side increased their ever-ready appeals to gender differences, as when Frederick Douglass said, "We . . . claim our rights as men among men."[6] Women had the right to vote since the eighteenth century in certain states and western territories but began to lose that right as states began revoking women's suffrage as the language of male citizenship codified women's exclusion.[7] The Black man's gain was women's loss.

The women's rights movement also overlapped with the temperance movement. Frances Harper held office in the Women's Christian Temperance Union headed by Frances Willard. Susan B. Anthony began her career as a public speaker in New York temperance circles and, along with Elizabeth Cady Stanton, founded the New York State Temperance Society in 1852. In a speech the following year to the society in Rochester, Stanton said, "We have been obliged to preach women's rights, because many, instead of listening to what we had to say on temperance, have questioned the right of a woman to speak on any subject. . . . Let it be clearly understood, then, that we are a woman's rights society."[8] Temperance lent a moral weight to the movement and provided a platform for women's public speaking. At the same time, it contributed to the idea of woman as the moral custodian of the family, a feature of the "separate spheres" idea that argued women reigned at home while men operated in the world, even as temperance's public actions plainly contradicted the idea. Stanton quickly became disillusioned with the temperance movement, however, telling Anthony in a letter of June 20, 1853, "Now Susan, I do beg of you to let the past be past, and to waste no powder on the Women's State Temperance Society. We have other and bigger fish to fry."[9] These "bigger fish" included reform of divorce law and the Married Woman Property Act, which Anthony promoted single-handedly all over New York state in 1855, and a restructuring of women's status in society. First, however, they had to battle the institutions keeping women in their place, including the big book that graced many a Victorian home.

The Bible as an Ally of Women's Rights
Sarah Grimké, Frances Willard, and Frances Harper

The Creation Story

Both opponents and advocates of women's equality relied heavily on the stories of creation and the first humans in the first three chapters of Genesis. When the first convention of the National Woman Suffrage Association (the Stanton–Anthony group formed after the schism) met in Washington in 1869, the invited chaplain of the House of Representatives referred to woman as "an afterthought of the Creator" in his prayer. Lucretia Mott, a pious Quaker, quickly raised her hand, took her Bible, and read aloud from Genesis 1:27–28, "So God created man in his own image, in the image of God created he him; male and female created he them. And God blessed them, and God said unto them, Be fruitful, and multiply, and replenish the earth, and subdue it; and have dominion over the fish of the sea, and over the fowl of the air, and over every living thing upon the earth." Both sexes were created in God's image and they exercised joint authority over nature.[10]

Biblical scholars had already noted that the Creation story in Genesis 1–3 is really two narratives from different time periods placed side by side, but the most frequently cited elements by opponents of women's equality are the creation from Adam's rib, indicating subordination, and the so-called "curse of Eve," where pain in childbirth and eternal subordination become the punishment for eating the forbidden fruit.[11] Feminist exegetes undercut the implications drawn by later interpreters, and drew on themes of equality evident in Gen 1:26–28 and/or even the suggestion that the word "help-meet" indicates some shared identity, since only she is "fit" or appropriate for him.[12]

"Eve's sin" in eating the forbidden fruit had done massive service to block women's possibilities. Typical is Dr. H. K. Root, who, when addressing the Woman's Rights Convention in New York in 1853, reminded his hearers of "an original command from God that man should rule." After a review of the Christian understanding of the Fall in Genesis, he said, to cheers and applause (not from the women), "you see that the original cause of sin was because man, being placed in the garden, gave way to woman, and the curse fell upon him; the original cause of sin was because man gave up his judgment to woman; and it may be, if we now give up our rights to woman, some great calamity may fall upon us. Had women only sinned, perhaps we might still have been in Eden."[13] Such remarks meant women's rights exegetes had much of their material selected for them and, like the abolitionists, worked with a relatively small "canon within a canon."

Sarah Moore Grimké joined her sister Angelina as they became two of the first women antislavery agents to speak publicly to mixed audiences. Living with Angelina and her husband, Theodore Dwight Weld, after their marriage in 1838, Sarah helped constitute a household of ardent abolitionists who understood the message of God in the biblical text as a forceful rejection of slavery. Although all three also supported women's equality, only Sarah carried over the lessons of abolitionist exegesis into the argument for women's rights. Grimké undercut the power of the so-called curse through philology and an early form of cultural criticism. In her *Letters on the Equality of the Sexes*, a series of analyses written to Mary Parker in 1837, the president of the Boston Female Anti-Slavery Society, and later published in a newspaper and as a book, Grimké presented the first extended analysis for women's rights that incorporates biblical texts. Just as her abolitionist brother-in-law Theodore Dwight Weld had brought Genesis 1:26–28 to argue against slavery,[14] she used it to argue for women's equality. Just as Lucretia Mott had parried the chaplain's claim of women's inferiority with this same verse, Grimké insisted in her first letter, "'so God created man in his image, in the image of God created he him, male and female he created them.' In all this sublime description of the creation of man, (which is a generic term including man and woman), there is not one particle of difference intimated as existing between them. They were both made in the image of God; dominion was given to both over every other creature, but not over each other. Created in perfect equality, they were expected to exercise the viceregence intrusted to them by their Maker, in harmony and love."[15]

Returning to the creation story several times, at one point Grimké calls women's subordination "unscriptural."[16] She turns the second creation story to egalitarian uses, too, saying the creation from Adam's rib indicates Eve's identity and sameness in moral power. Eve's role as "help-meet" is a role that can only be filled by an equal. Eve was "to give him a companion *in all respects his equal*; one who was like himself *a free agent*, gifted with intellect and endowed with immortality." They are partners, and "all good work on earth was meant to be the joint effort of men and women, a fulfillment of Job 38:7, 'the morning stars sang together, and all the sons of God shouted for joy.'"[17]

Grimké disposes of "the curse of Eve" by underscoring that both parties were guilty of eating the forbidden fruit. The so-called punishment of eternal subordination is simply a mistranslation that has become an excuse for men to lord it over women. She notes that the English language, unlike the French, distinguishes "shall" and "will," namely, a command as to what should happen versus a prediction of what will happen. Translators, operating under the influence of a culture that subordinated women, made a command out of what God meant merely as a regrettable prophecy, "the truth is that the curse, as it is termed, which was pronounced by Jehovah upon woman is a simple prophecy. The Hebrew, like the French language, uses the same word to express *shall* and *will*. Our translators having been accustomed to exercise lordship over their wives, and seeing only through the medium of a perverted judgment, very naturally, though I think not very learnedly or very kindly, translated it *shall* instead of *will*, and thus converted a prediction to Eve into a command to Adam."[18] Abolitionists had reasoned similarly, that if mere prediction indicated divine approval, the enslavement in Egypt must have been a positive! Prediction does not equal approval.

Lucy Stone repeated this reasoning in her speeches on the Moral and Religious Disabilities of Women, calling it "a fearful prophecy."[19] This verse had shocked her when she read it as a young girl, so that she went running to her mother to see if it were true. When her mother tried to calm her by saying Eve's sin was the reason for women's hard lot and "the Fall," Lucy resolved to go to college to learn biblical languages so as to discover what the Bible *really* said.[20] Like Grimké, whom she had read, she was certain that God preached gender equality. Eventually she did attend Oberlin College, learning biblical languages to make her own judgment. On the same verses, Sojourner Truth sensibly suggested, "Well, if woman upset the world, do give her a chance to set it right side up again."[21]

Frances Willard, the influential president of the Woman's Christian Temperance Union and the author of *Woman in the Pulpit*, an extended argument for women's ordination in the Methodist church, echoes Grimké and others by stressing the first creation story, underlining the first reference to male and female creation in God's image and with joint dominion.[22] She also needles clergy for the overuse of the verses around Eve's eating the fruit, while routinely avoiding others, such as New Testament prohibitions on ostentatious attire. Selective quotation never seems to favor women, "In life's prime and pride men like to quote 'Adam was first formed, then Eve,' but at the grave they are ready to declare that 'man, born of woman, is of few days and full of trouble.'"[23] Similarly, if clergy insist on taking the half verse of Genesis 3:16, "he shall rule over you" literally and permanently, they need to do so for others, such as the command to Adam to actually "eat his bread in the sweat of his face." "The argument is a two-edged sword, and cuts both ways."[24] In any case, Christ has nullified all curses, including any resulting from primeval sin, and restored what humanity's sin had lost.[25]

For Willard, the very act of biblical interpretation proved the need for men and women to work together. Some interpreters were woodenly literal, while others "played fast and loose with God's word." Women commentators would provide balance, "we need the stereoscopic view of truth in general, which can only be had when woman's eye and man's together shall discern the perspective of the Bible's full-orbed revelation."[26] Invoking the New Testament much more often than the Hebrew Bible in her argument, she appears to subscribe to a theory of "progressive revelation," a popular nineteenth-century view which sees civilization as achieving higher levels of morality as it moves on. One minister she cites expresses the belief, "as we approach a Christian civilization, subjection based on sex disappears."[27]

Prominent Women in the Bible

The simplest method of arguing for women's leadership from the Bible is to show women had *always* exercised authority. Grimké cites several women of wisdom and prophecy as proof that God did not silence women from speaking in public. Prophets Miriam, Deborah, and Huldah present models of power in the Hebrew Bible, as does Anna in the New Testament. Women preachers and deacons including Priscilla, Phoebe, and Philip's daughters populate the Pauline letters. That there are fewer women in the Bible overall is because of sexism (although that word did not exist before the 1960s), "that from the days of Eve to the present time, the aim of man has been to crush her."[28]

The prophet Deborah presents an intriguing challenge to the "separate spheres" ideology of private and public in Victorian society, as she assumed a public character as judge and general, in addition to being a wife and "a mother in Israel."[29] Julia McNair Wright (1840–1903), a writer who was active in education and temperance work, calls her part of a line of "warrior women who shine on the historic page." When William Ellery Channing, a leading Unitarian, questioned women's theological abilities, she quipped that the "good doctor is not the only man who has been wiser than God" and notes that Channing would have denied Miriam's prophesying, Deborah's salvation of the people, and Priscilla's teaching.[30] For some contributors to *The Woman's Bible*, Deborah is evidence for the idea that society was once matriarchal, and that women enjoyed more rights in ancient Judaism, while Christianity had systematically deprived women of equal status and rights.

The prophet Anna, who appears in chapter 2 of Luke's gospel praising God and recognizing the infant Jesus as chosen, provides an example of women's spiritual superiority for Sarah Hale (1788–1879), an American writer and editor of the popular *Godey's Ladies Book.* She compares Simeon (who greets the baby Jesus as the fulfillment of prophecy when he visits the Temple) to Anna, who seems to live in the Temple,

> Thus we find the advent of our Lord was made known, spiritually, to woman as well as to man. The good old Simeon had no clearer revelation than the aged devout Anna. Both were inspired servants of the Most High; but here the characteristic piety of the woman is shown to excel. Simeon "dwelt in Jerusalem," probably engaged in secular pursuits; Anna "departed not from the temple, but served God with fasting and prayers night and day."[31]

Phoebe Palmer (1807–1874), a leader of the Methodist Holiness movement, defended women's spiritual equality and right to preach publicly, even as she claimed not to suggest "a change in the domestic or social relation." She shows that God calls women to preach, as when Mary and the other women disciples received the tongue of fire in answer to the Promise of the Father" in Acts 2:4,[32] and the Samaritan woman in John 4:39, who preached as an apostle in Samaria.[33]

Moving beyond mere catalogue, Willard, like Palmer, explores the possibility of women's discipleship, an approach that anticipates contemporary feminist scholarship.[34] She notes actions of women that are equivalent to discipleship, even if the women were not formally called by Jesus: Mary Magdalene as the witness and declarer of Jesus's resurrection in all the canonical gospels, the special commission to the Samaritan woman in John 4, women's following and ministering to Jesus in Luke 8, and Martha declaring Jesus Messiah in words nearly identical to Peter's in John 11:27. Women were part of the larger group with the Eleven who receive the Spirit at Pentecost.[35] Being formally called is not altogether desirable, anyway; it sounds "churchy," and applies to Judas Iscariot, too.[36] Herself a woman who spoke all around the country for temperance, leading an army of women speakers and activists, Willard points out, "there are thirty or forty passages in favor of woman's public work for Christ and only two against it, and these not really so when rightly understood."[37]

Willard shows an elastic view of gender as she considers the idea of Jesus himself as embodying both sexes, the "dual-natured founder of Christianity," who chose male apostles only because his "barbarous age demanded it."[38] Clericalism has robbed Christianity of its gentle and loving side, "it is men who have given us the dead letter rather than the living gospel. The mother-heart of God will never be known to the world until translated into terms of speech by mother-hearted women . . . Why should the pulpit be shorn of half its power?"[39] Willard turns the "separate spheres" doctrine and romantic ideas of motherhood to her own purposes, speaking of madonnas and the sacred cadence of a mother's voice, but attributing the silencing of women to the devil's designs.

Contributors to *The Woman's Bible* fail to mention some potential feminist heroines like Miriam, but praise Deborah for her prophetic powers and military leadership, Huldah for learning, and Esther, "who ruled as well as reigned." Esther appears as risking her life on behalf of her people, imbued with God's spirit. Vashti, who is mentioned only briefly in the book of Esther, evokes praise from two contributors, including Stanton, for her refusal to obey her husband's command to display herself to court and because she "scorned the Apostle's [Paul's] command, 'Wives, obey your husbands.' She refused the king's orders to grace with her presence the reveling court."[40] Given the alliance of temperance and suffrage at the time, it is no surprise that Vashti becomes a symbol of resistance to drunken and dictatorial husbands, and a popular model for Black women who had been enslaved. God is on the side of women, *Woman's Bible* contributor Lucinda Chandler argues, as she too invokes the idea of devilish opposition and progressive revelation, "Women as queenly, as noble and as self-sacrificing as was Esther, as self-respecting and as brave as was Vashti, are hampered in their creative office by the unjust statutes of men; but God is marching on; and it is the seed of woman which is to bruise the head of the serpent.

It is not man's boasted superiority of intellect through which the eternally working Divine power will perfect the race, but the receptiveness and the love of woman."[41]

Paul, as always, presents a challenge to feminists. Commentators in *The Woman's Bible* point to Paul's praise of certain women as fellow workers in spreading the gospel and building the church. Romans 16 mentions Phoebe as a deacon, as well as Priscilla and other women. Stanton notes that, as in her time, women provide many different kinds of service to the church in fundraising and hospitality but are not given a voice. Instead, they are reminded of their "divinely appointed sphere." When seeking authority in creeds and church discipline, "then the Marys, the Phebes, and the Priscillas are ordered to keep silence and to discuss all questions with their husbands at home, taking it for granted that all men are logical and wise."[42] The declaration of equality in Paul's Letter to the Galatians 3:28, "there is neither Jew nor Greek, there is neither bond nor free, there is neither male nor female; for ye are all one in Christ Jesus," is laced through the second part of the work on the New Testament, but does not receive its own commentary.

These references to early biblical role models do not move much beyond proof-texting, the simple citation as evidence of women wielding authority. A more emotionally charged and literary use of biblical women's examples appears in the poetry of Frances Harper, where the experiences of suffering Black women in the nineteenth century are fused with biblical figures.

Frances Ellen Watkins Harper

"We had rather an exciting time," reports Frances Harper of her conversation with a former dealer in enslaved people as they rode in a rail car in South Carolina in 1867 as a small audience gathered. She notes, however, that "it was not worthwhile to show any fear."[43] Frances Ellen Watkins Harper, a freeborn Black woman of letters, traveled extensively through the Southern states just after the Civil War, enduring peril and discomfort to speak publicly about the condition of her race.

Speaking in churches, schools, and outdoor spaces to both Black and white hearers, she would engage any and all in conversation.

Harper belongs to the category of interpreters who saw themselves in the experiences of biblical figures, but as a woman of letters her writing is so extensive and her methods so much more literary than most other activists that she merits special treatment. Harper wrote poetry, novels, essays, and speeches, becoming a member of Baltimore's intellectual elite and one of the earliest and best-known African American women to be published in the United States. Truly intersectional in her thinking and activism, she embraced abolitionism, women's suffrage, and temperance. She championed the needs and talents of Black women in particular, assuming they would flourish when these causes succeeded.

Poetry

Black women—their suffering, their industry and intellect, their limitations under male authority—were Harper's abiding concern. Her poetry holds up biblical models of women's bravery and integrity in the face of suffering the loss of their children. The unique suffering of mothers under enslavement occupies a number of her poems, including "The Slave Mother" and "The Slave Auction." Folded into the collection is "The Syro-Phoenician Woman," about the forthright outsider in Mark 7:24–30.[44] She begs Jesus to heal and save her child from death and, after his initial rebuff, convinces him by her "word" that teaches him the reach of his own ministry.

> *"Woman," said the astonish'd Lord, "Be it ever as thy*
> *word! By thy faith that knows no fail, Thou hast*
> *ask'd, and shalt prevail."*

She is every mother whose life is bound up with her child's. This poem appears in the 1854 collection just before the wrenching "The Slave Mother," where the child is torn away by being sold.

Tales of suffering mothers who lose children to separation and death appear in Harper's poetry written before 1865, when women and men were still enslaved in the South. The brief but excruciating biblical story of Rizpah, who sees her two sons impaled and guards their bodies from degradation by animals of prey, notes the reality of a son's death and the denial of the dignity of proper burial to so many under enslavement.[45] Her grief and love are all that is left, but she remains dignified, "oh grief like hers has learned no tone—a world of grief is all its own."[46] Naomi, who loses both husband and sons, is left a woman of woe to be comforted by her daughter-in-law, Ruth.[47]

Harper's extended poem in blank verse, "Moses: A Story of the Nile" (1869), speaks to the longings of mothers and the pain of partings.[48] It begins with the protests of Pharaoh's daughter, who raised Moses, dismayed by his farewell as he comes to offer thanks to her. Her argument in vain invokes "the radiance, Of our throne as in the shadow of those, Bondage-darkened huts." Moses conjures up the image of his birth-mother's parallel loss and longing, "within those darkened huts my mother plies her task." The princess then is caught up in an extended reverie as she recalls finding the beautiful child, "he wakened with a smile and reached out his hand, to meet the welcome of his mother's kiss." Readers may rightly wonder, "which mother?" The grieving princess then remembers her pitched argument with her father to keep the child and save him from Pharaoh's decree of execution of the Hebrew male babies.

Vashti, a minor character in the book of Esther, becomes a symbol of Black women's resistance to male power. The Persian king orders her to appear before him, arrayed in finery, "to display her beauty to the peoples and the officials."[49] She refuses and infuriates the king, whose advisors argue that such wifely rebellion will cause widespread disrespect for husbands and their authority throughout the kingdom. The text does not tell us what happens to her, except that she is removed as queen. For African American women, who had been subject to the sexual whims of their enslavers in the South and continued to battle the stereotype of being over-sexed Jezebels, Vashti's courage to resist

sexual exploitation makes her, not Esther, a role model. Harper's poem,
"Vashti" (1870) includes

> *Then, gracious King, sign with thy hand*
> *This stern but just decree,*
> *That Vashti lay aside her crown,*
> *Thy queen no more to be."*
>
> *She heard again the king's command,*
> *And left her high estate,*
> *Strong in her earnest womanhood,*
> *She calmly met her fate,*
>
> *And left the palace of the King,*
> *Proud of her spotless name—*
> *A woman who could bend to grief,*
> *But would not bow to shame.*[50]

"We Are All Bound Up Together"
Speech by Frances Harper

The contributions of African American women to the suffrage movement had been nearly erased from white women's histories of the movement, in particular the six-volume *History of Woman Suffrage*, edited by
Stanton, Anthony, and others from 1881 to 1922.[51] Racism and nativism
tainted the suffrage movement. Black women were excluded and not
recognized for their efforts, founding their own suffrage groups by the
end of the nineteenth century.

Harper, well aware of racist, exclusionary elements, attended the
National Women's Rights convention in 1866 in New York City, with
leading lights Lucretia Mott, Elizabeth Cady Stanton, and Susan B.
Anthony in attendance as she gave her speech, "We Are All Bound
Up Together."[52] The speech, though brief, addresses interlocking kinds
of injustice—sexism, racism, classism, suppression of free speech, and

suppression of a free press.[53] Two biblical characters appear: Ishmael and Moses, both representatives of outsider status and enslavement. Ishmael is the first-born of Abraham who suffers banishment because of race and enslavement. His mother Hagar is Egyptian, so non-Israelite, and an enslaved woman. Moses is a foreigner in Egyptian society, the one chosen to liberate the enslaved Israelites from bondage.

Harper leads with her own suffering of injustice as a woman. Suddenly widowed when her husband was in debt, she lost her home and all her possessions (save a mirror!) and was driven from her home. She asks, "had I died instead of my husband, how different would have been the result." No administrator would have taken apart her husband's home and left him with no means of support. Forced to leave town, she blames it on women's legal inequality, "I say, then, that justice is not fulfilled so long as woman is unequal before the law." When her race is added to her sex, she suffers more mistreatment. Teaching her white sisters, she says, "you white women here speak of rights. I speak of wrongs. I, as a colored woman, have had in this country an education which has made me feel as if I were in the situation of Ishmael, my hand against every man, and every man's hand against me." She describes experiences of her own and other Black women in Washington and Philadelphia, who, when attempting to ride trains and streetcars, were sent to the smoking cars or to the open platforms with the drivers or were not allowed to ride at all. Her final example is of the mistreatment of Harriet Tubman, the Moses of her people, who acted out the Exodus, having "gone down into the Egypt of slavery and brought out hundreds of our people into liberty." When Harper had last seen Tubman, her hands were swollen from a brutal exchange with a conductor who tried to eject her from public transport.

Within the brief speech, she condemns the racism that says Black men were good enough to be soldiers in the Civil War but not good enough to vote. The brutal treatment of her race has hurt the white nation, too. She also condemns the ill-treatment of the poor white men by rich white men, the trampling of the underprivileged, the suppression of constitutional freedoms. Society's neglect of any group affects all its members. White women need the vote, not only to address injustice, but to force them to confront society's ills, "Talk of giving women the ballot-box? Go on. It is a normal school, and the white women of this country need it. While there exists this brutal element in society which tramples upon the feeble and treads down the weak, I tell you that if there is any class of people who need to be lifted out of their airy nothings and selfishness, it is the white women of America."[54]

Harper has been accused of choosing the voting rights of Black men over women's rights; a third party at the 1869 AERA meeting, the site of the Great Schism, reported in Stanton and Anthony's paper *The Revolution* that "when it was a question of race, she let the lesser question of sex go."[55] Yet Harper's letters and stories of this period show she did not abandon the cause of either race or gender equality, notes C. C. O'Brien. The two were inextricably "bound together."[56] Indeed, in this speech and in her poetry, Harper continuously addresses multiple social categories and forms of injustice as they interacted with one another.

The Bible as the Enemy of Women's Rights
The Woman's Bible and Matilda Joslyn Gage

As the women's rights movement experienced a period of the doldrums in the late nineteenth century, Stanton was determined to go after a large chunk of the institutional "wall" of religion that Lucy Stone decried: the Bible. Raised a Presbyterian, Stanton claimed a brief experience with the evangelicalism of Charles Finney but embraced science, rationalism, and some of the historical-critical currents of biblical scholarship. Stanton drew from many wells of thought, including Comte's positivism and the Free Thought currents of the day, developing her own view of God as the great spirit in nature. Despite a generally skeptical and negative evaluation of the Bible and its effect on culture in the commentary, some contributors admired the women who populate the biblical text.

Stanton planned to assemble a large group of commentators—scholars, lay people, Protestants, Catholics, Jews, and evangelicals. Many turned her down, so Stanton did much of the work herself, though some faithful coworkers like Clara Colby and Lillie Devereux added their own New Thought, esoteric-inflected interpretations. Some no doubt considered the project a political mistake, but many, like Frances Willard, also did not share Stanton's view of the Bible as irredeemably anti-woman, rather considering its use to subjugate women a *mis*-use. Stanton, at the end of her life, was out of patience with forced interpretations, whether from esoteric thought or from biblical criticism. None "could twist out of the Old or New Testaments a message of justice, liberty or equality from God to the women of the nineteenth century."[57]

Some contributors relied on the principle that God created the sexes for equality, while subordination of women is part of the contamination of culture that infects the biblical text. A notion of "pure" religion and a "God of nature" over against institutions like church, the clergy, and text allows women's rights advocates to separate out some parts of the biblical text as legitimate and divinely given versus other parts as the result of the heavy hand of a patriarchal culture. Colby, for example, targets what some call eisegesis, reading one's own ideas into the text: "Too often instead of searching out the Bible to see what is right, we form our belief, and then search for Bible texts to sustain us, and are satisfied with isolated texts without regard to contexts, and ask no questions as to the circumstances that may have existed then but do not now." Translators similarly are not inspired and infuse the text with their own views, using "obey" for a wife to a husband, but "defer" for the same word elsewhere.[58]

Stanton uses the first creation story (Gen 1:1–2a) to indulge in her own brand of positivist, nature-based religion. The simultaneous creation of male and female suggests to her a different kind of Trinity, father, mother, and son. "If language has any meaning, we have in these texts a plain declaration of the existence of the feminine element in the God-head, equal in power and glory with the masculine. The Heavenly Mother and Father!"[59]

Few narratives or individuals, including God, fare well in the commentary. Abraham and Sarah come in for severe criticism; Sarah's cruelty to Hagar and Abraham's failure to save her and his own son

Ishmael go against "common humanity." Even more reprehensible is God's approval of their actions. Rebecca and Jacob make out only slightly better. Rebecca's role in convincing Jacob to steal the birthright means she is not a worthy model for womanhood, says Stanton, "One must read the whole story in order to appreciate the blind confidence Isaac placed in Rebekah's integrity; the pathos of his situation; the bitter disappointment of Esau; Jacob's temptation, and the supreme wickedness of Rebekah in deceiving Isaac, defrauding Esau, and undermining the moral sense of the son she loved."[60]

These stories are mainly dismissed as tales of "the undeveloped religious sentiment of the early Hebrews,"[61] probably not from God, but "a very cunning way for the Patriarchs to enforce their own authority, to do whatever they desired, and say the Lord commanded them to do and say thus and so."[62] In other words, progressive revelation, along with a whiff of antisemitism, allows the tales to be dismissed as the heavy hand of patriarchy. Stanton and Colby's God was a Great Spirit, evident in nature, not in hoary stories.

The New Testament emerges only slightly better than the Old. Contributor Ellen Battelle Dietrick gives Paul credit for recognizing women as equal partners, as disciples, and teachers, even as commentators of her own time read in their own prejudices about women. Priscilla was a teacher of Apollos, and with her husband, Aquila, probably a founder of the Roman church. Phoebe, called a deacon by Paul, is rendered a bishop at Cenchrae by Dietrick. Compared to her own contemporary interpreters, who explain away women's power, Paul affirms it. "Paul was not a great Apostle at all, in those days, but a simple, self-sent tent-maker with a vigorous spirit, who gladly shared the 'Apostolic dignity' with all the good women he could rally to his assistance. . . . The fact stares him [the commentator] in the face that she was the teacher of the man whom Paul specially and emphatically pronounces his own equal. (Compare Acts 18:26, with 1 Cor. 3)."[63]

Stanton, like Willard, is aware of critical biblical scholarship coming out of Germany at the time. Its theories of multiple authors and documents, the foundation of source criticism, allow Stanton to simply jettison objectionable portions without much explanation. She also identifies the effect of a patriarchal culture in the inclusion of the second creation story in Gen 2–3. Unlike Grimké and Willard, who can explain the text as misused or misunderstood, Stanton argues it is neither from God, nor authoritative:

> It is evident that some wily writer, seeing the perfect equality of man and woman in the first chapter, felt it important for the dignity and dominion of man to effect woman's subordination in some way. To do this a spirit of evil must be introduced, which at once proved itself stronger than the spirit of good, and man's supremacy was based on the downfall of all that had just been pronounced very good. This spirit of evil evidently existed before the supposed fall of man, hence woman was not the origin of sin as so often asserted.[64]

The second story, then, originates not in divine decree but in the imagination of an untrustworthy editor. Dietrick is more specific, implicating Judaism as a whole. Since both accounts cannot be true, she opines, "My own opinion is that the second story was manipulated by some Jew, in an endeavor to give "heavenly authority" for requiring a woman to obey the man she married. In a work which I am now completing, I give some facts concerning ancient Israelitish history, which will be of peculiar interest to those who wish to understand the origin of woman's subjection."[65]

Progressive revelation, the idea that society was moving from primitive to more enlightened forms of religion, paired with Orientalism, allowed some to dispense with objectionable parts of the Bible but opened the door to antisemitic readings of history. Its premise is that more ancient peoples were more primitive, so the Old Testament must be more primitive than the New, and the Hebrews less enlightened than other peoples. Grimké, for example, throughout her letters denounces "the Jews" or "the Hebrews" as well as many ancient non-Western societies for treating women as slaves and ornamental dolls, all to be improved by the coming of Jesus Christ. Although Stanton indulges in similar ideas at times, her distrust of all religion prevents simplistic approaches. Yet she could not prevent others taking the easy route. When she tried to introduce a resolution citing institutional religion as the source of women's subjection, the convention turned it into a condemnation of Jews and Judaism. She objected, saying they were "handing over to the Jews what I had laid at the door of the Christians."[66]

The Woman's Bible earned notoriety as a work of Satan, often from people who had not read it. Some women said they needed no special Bible, as the current one suited them fine. In fact, the commentary is highly flawed, episodic, marred by antisemitism, and a platform for a variety of esoteric, positivist, and other views. One critic found it "superficial and flippant" and even Anthony privately said it was far from Stanton's best work.[67] When Stanton wrote and compiled the commentary, she was elderly and no longer at most conventions of the movement. The next generation was more conservative and strategic, narrowing their focus to the vote for women over Anthony's and Stanton's broader reforms of society. Viewing the *Woman's Bible* as a distraction and liability, the coalition of the two wings of the movement, now the National American Woman Suffrage Association (NAWSA), officially distanced itself from the work at the 1896 convention.

Matilda Gage, a radical suffragist and activist for multiple causes, including Native American rights, agrees that the Bible is one tool in the subordination of women but targets a broader set of injustices. The institution of the Church allied with the State has worked to suppress and destroy women and the feminine aspects of culture throughout history. In *Woman, Church, and State,* Gage argued that many ancient societies were respectful of women's power, if not outright matriarchies. The argument of Eve's sin was one of many pretexts to limit women's possibilities, encouraging celibacy, self-sacrifice, and witch-hunting. Gage reverses the typical pieties of progressive revelation, seeing Christianity as introducing and promoting ideas of women's subjection, while claiming to elevate their lot. Ancient Hindu, Egyptian, Native American, and other societies recognized women's authority, including women's priesthoods and matriarchates, while Christianity restricted women's liberties, in large part by promoting celibacy. Rejecting marriage meant denigrating the feminine principle in the Divine and primal man, "inasmuch as it was a cardinal doctrine that the fall of Adam took place through his temptation into marriage by Eve, this relation was regarded with holy horror as a continuance of the evil which first brought sin into the world, depriving man of his immortality."[68] Teachings from the Bible provided cover and content for such ideas, crowding out other beliefs in androgynous primal humanity, or a Godhead of masculine and feminine elements. Even when Protestant churches allowed married clergy, they "did not change priestly teaching that woman was created solely for man, and they found apologies in the Bible for illicit conduct."[69]

The Bible as Bystander
Ernestine Rose

Ernestine Rose, a declared atheist who was also the daughter of a Polish rabbi, considered the Bible irrelevant to the discussions of women's rights, which rested on earlier and more profound truths. When Reverend Antoinette Brown introduced a resolution at a women's rights convention in Syracuse in 1852 that showed via extended proof-texting that the Bible supports the rights of women, Rose blocked it. She argued, "Here we claim human rights and freedom based upon the laws of humanity and we require no written authority from Moses or Paul, because those laws and our claim are prior even to these two great men . . . It has done mischief enough. A book that is so ambiguous as not to convey any definite idea, can furnish no authority to this convention."[70] Rose's proposal to table Brown's resolution passed unanimously, earning agreement even from Lucretia Mott, then president of the association, who said that the discussion of the Bible was a distraction. Mott counseled that they avoid the pitfall of early abolitionism when there was too much preoccupation with the Bible. Women's rights were self-evident from reason and universal human rights.

Jesus, Paul, and the Problem of Antisemitism

Threaded through all of our interpretations are constant references to Jesus and Paul. But women's rights advocates had the same two problems as abolitionists: Jesus's silence and Paul's statements. Although several writers here see an anti-woman strain throughout Christian society and institutions, the chief culprit for many of them has been Paul. Stanton fantasized about interviewing him in the afterlife and disputing with him about his teachings, including "his gross ideas on marriage."[71] Kern suggests that Paul became a cipher for Stanton's opponents.[72] Jesus, however, is always deemed innocent of prejudice against women. Willard calls Jesus "her [woman's] Emancipator" and "Woman's Liberator, possessing both motherly and fatherly qualities."[73] Stanton was unusual in observing correctly, "He never expressed any opinion on the question, as there were no republics in his day."[74] She devotes little space in her commentary to the figure of Jesus, but an anonymous contributor does cite him as "the great leading Radical of his age" opposed by "the Conservatives" whose power and order he challenged, clearly a nod to the authorities of her own day.[75] The attempt to separate Jesus from both his Jewish matrix and later institutional Christianity corresponded to the scholarly enterprise of the time, later called the first quest for the historical Jesus. Strauss's *Das Leben Jesu,* in which he tries to peel away layers of accretion to discover the historical figure of Jesus, was translated into English and accessible to all in Unitarian newspapers.

Paul was as problematic for women as he had been for abolitionists. He forbids women speaking in churches and, in a somewhat confused argument, says women should cover their heads.[76] Lucy Stone came up against the latter injunction when she made her case to the Ladies Board at Oberlin to remove her bonnet during church services as it exacerbated her headaches.[77] Paul's statement recommending women's silence in the Corinthian church was elevated to a general principle by some nineteenth-century readers that women should not speak publicly at all. Stone faced this argument too when she wanted to study rhetoric at Oberlin, then faced her parents' opposition for the same reason when she became an agent for the American Anti-Slavery Society.[78] Other voices counterbalanced, as when she heard Theodore Parker in the offices of *The Liberator* exclaiming, "Whether we like it or not, little woman, God made you an orator!"[79] Stone's daughter, Alice Stone Blackwell, who generally defended the Bible as elevating women and mothers, still excepted Paul.[80]

Progressive revelation ill conceals the antisemitism of its claims of the Hebrew Bible as a primitive stage in the march of human progress or its barbs at "the Jews" as authors of ancient trickery to subordinate women. Yet antisemitism shows itself most plainly in the interpretations of Paul's and the Deutero-Pauline letters. The latter, works like Ephesians and Colossians, as well as the pastoral 1 Timothy, are attributed to him by our writers and most nineteenth-century readers, even though later critical scholars have concluded they were probably written by others. To exonerate Christianity of anti-woman prejudices, Paul is split in two. Paul the Jew keeps women subordinate, while Paul the "Christian" liberates them. Even Gage, who had little use for Christianity and was not seeking to exonerate it, nevertheless took the well-trodden route of blaming Judaism for the anti-woman tenor of Christianity, and blaming Paul in particular,

> for this double code the church is largely indebted to the subtle and acute Paul, who saw in the new religion but an enlarged Judaism that should give prominence to Abraham and his seed from whom Christ claimed descent. His conversion did not remove his old Jewish contempt for woman, as shown in his temple [sic] service, the law forbidding her entrance beyond the outer court. Nor could he divest himself of the spirit of the old morning prayer which daily led each Jew to thank God that he was not born a heathen, a slave, or a woman.[81]

Anachronistically, Gage calls Paul "the first Jesuit." Both
Christianity and Judaism stand condemned in the centuries of suppression of women's powers. Judaism supplied the offending ideas, but the
power of Christianity, in tandem with political power, brought them
into society.

To Augustine is the world indebted for full development of
the theory of original sin, promulgated by Paul as a doctrine
of the Christian Church in the declaration that Adam, first
created, was not first in sin. Paul, brought up in the strictest
external principles of Judaism, did not lose his educational bias
or primal belief when changing from Judaism to Christianity.
Neither was his character as persecutor changed when he
united his fortunes with the new religion. He gave to the
Christian world a lever long enough to reach down through
eighteen centuries, all that time moving it in opposition to a
belief in woman's created and religious equality with man, to
her right of private judgment and to her personal freedom. His
teaching that Adam, first created, was not first in sin, divided
the unity of the human race in the assumption that woman was
not part of the original creative idea but a secondary thought,
an inferior being brought into existence as an appendage to
man.[82]

Grimké, in legitimating the Bible as a source for women's equality,
similarly blames Paul's suppression of women's voices on his Jewishness.
She relies on Clarke's commentary that explains the command of
women's silence in the churches as "a Jewish ordinance," and cites a
saying attributed to Rabbi Eliezer, "Let the words of the Torah be
burned, rather than they should be delivered by women." Considering
the other passage commonly cited as evidence of Paul's prejudice, 1
Timothy 2:11–12, she suggests that, because the punctuation and verse
and chapter divisions were not original, the meaning is unclear. Given
that Joel 2:28b says, "your sons and *daughters* will prophesy," and that

Paul talks about women praying and prophesying in 1 Corinthians 11, she reasons that Paul either grossly contradicted himself, or his silencing of women in public was only about reference to some peculiar local customs, which were then common in the religious assemblies. She finds a quirky way to further implicate Judaism, suggesting that the Corinthian women got overexcited and went wild when freed from "the restraints imposed upon them by Jewish tradition and heathen custom."[83] The undercurrent of antisemitism in feminism would prove hard to eradicate. Evident in Grimké, Gage, and the *Woman's Bible*, it is part of Free Thought, as one editorial complained about the Hebrew Bible and "the nastiness of the old Jew book."[84] Along with nativism and racism, antisemitism proved a hardy and unsavory aspect of the women's rights movement.

Not all women's rights writers rejected Paul or Judaism. Willard avoids antisemitism, and uses Paul as a resource, piling up his statements that show women as dignified and equal members of Paul's communities. He mentions women prophesying and working with him as partners in spreading the gospel.[85] She brings Romans 11:11, which shows men and women in a relationship of mutual dependence, as well as the favored formula of Galatians 3:28, probably originally a baptismal formula, "there can be no male and female . . . for ye are all one *man* [sic] in Christ Jesus."[86] Combined with verses from the Old Testament and New Testament that show women as prophets and teachers, and verses that indicate equality, Willard overwhelms the impact of Paul's alleged anti-woman comments by the sheer number of opposing statements. She even suggests that early manuscripts may have been tampered with to minimize women's importance, giving an example from a missionary to China of her own acquaintance, who left out such verses to avoid offending his patriarchal Chinese hearers. Translators are as equally suspect as the early writers, and she argues we will never have the true version of the biblical text until men and women translate it together.[87]

A few women identified with Paul as a lonely prophet. Anna Howard Shaw, ordained in the more liberal Methodist Protestant church, saw Paul and Jesus as fellow reformers, "No one of God's children has ever gone forth to the world who has not first had revealed to him his mission in a vision. They must live without sympathy; their feelings will be misunderstood; their efforts will be uncomprehended. Like Paul, they will be betrayed by friends; like Christ in the agony of Gethsemane, they must bear their struggle alone."[88] Similarly, Black abolitionists and civil rights leaders also saw Paul as a fellow sufferer and striver for justice.

The Bible and Women's Rights
Mixed Responses

Women's rights thinkers differ from the abolitionists in the scope and variety of their attitudes. Abolitionists who used the Bible generally assumed and proved that it was on their side.[89] But women activists like Stanton, Gage, and Rose were ready to call the text out for its complicity in harming women's rights. Others like Grimké and Willard insisted the text was on their side. Women's lives in the nineteenth century were shaped by attitudes founded on biblical justifications more than any other group examined in this book (with the possible exception of abolitionists, with whom they are deeply linked). The creation stories in the Hebrew Bible and a few verses from Paul and others in the New Testament propped up social attitudes that limited women's access to education, most professions, public life, and the vote. Perhaps that is why the women examined in this chapter and others like them countered with a thorough-going examination of the text, an agility in interpretation, and a range of literary expression unmatched by other movements. They learned biblical languages: Grimké, Stanton, and Stone learned Greek, Latin (Stone), and possibly Hebrew.[90] Some familiarized themselves with historical-critical methods of studying the Bible emerging from Europe, a set of approaches that tried to reconstruct the Bible's composition and historical settings, thus rejecting literalist interpretations. Stanton and Willard knew these new methods by way of their acquaintance with scholars and reading periodicals.[91]

Many more women and men were exposed to these currents in biblical scholarship through newspapers and magazines like *The Independent* and *Harpers*. The late nineteenth century also hosted many competing strains of thought that encouraged direct access to God outside of institutional structures—Protestant revivalism, the Holiness movement, Free Thought, transcendentalism, and interest in the occult—some of which appear in *The Woman's Bible*. Women's rights advocates had many tools to chip away at the "wall" of literalist and particularist biblical interpretation that institutions had erected as an obstacle to their equality.

CHAPTER 3

The Bible and Temperance

TEMPERANCE WAS THE largest reform movement of its time and one of the longest in US history, at home in middle-class Protestantism, but bringing in people of different sexes, classes, races, and political persuasions.[1] Peopled by "improvers," who saw themselves as healing society and responding to human misery, its membership overlapped with abolitionist and women's rights groups, bringing women into the public eye as speakers, writers, and activists. At its height, The Women's Christian Temperance Union (WCTU), under the leadership of Frances Willard, encompassed a wide variety of initiatives to improve society, including establishing child labor laws, free kindergarten education, soup kitchens, and raising the age of sexual consent. Many African Americans promoted temperance as part of a program of moral improvement, while decrying the nativism and exclusion of Blacks by some groups. Frederick Douglass, Maria Stewart, Frances Harper, and Ida Wells agreed with temperance and considered liquor trafficking a scourge on the Black community. Wells, who clashed publicly with Willard on other matters, called the liquor industry "one of the principal stumbling blocks to race progress."[2]

Alcohol had flowed freely in colonial America and was part of everyday life, as it had been in Europe. On board the famous Arabella, where John Winthrop memorably called the Massachusetts Bay Colony "a city on a hill" in 1630, supplies included 10,000 gallons of beer and 12 gallons of distilled spirits. Religious and moral leaders distinguished everyday drinking from "drunkenness," which they condemned along with other forms of excess.[3] Local and state groups began to form in the early nineteenth century to combat drunkenness. The first national American Temperance Society formed in 1826 by clergymen in Boston initially focused on "ardent spirits" or distilled liquor. Its influence spread quickly and by 1836 the group held its national convention in Syracuse, NY, changing its name to the American Temperance Union and moving toward teetotalism, the abstinence from all forms of alcohol, including wine and beer.

The movement to control alcohol consumption unfolded in phases, broadly moving from moral suasion to coercion, from promoting moderation in consumption (at times distinguishing wine and beer from distilled spirits) to teetotalism, from seeking individual voluntary pledges to abstain to a constitutional amendment prohibiting the manufacture, sale, and transportation of alcohol. Unlike abolitionism and the women's rights movements, temperance and its successor prohibition did not win the day in permanent legislation, nor in a legacy of positive regard by most Americans. In its day, however, it enjoyed wide popular support with an estimated 150,000 members of the WCTU in 1890, taking its place alongside abolitionism (estimated at 250,000 in 1838) and suffrage (8,981 members of the National American Women's Suffrage Association in 1901, a period of low ebb for suffrage).[4]

The preeminence of the Bible in Protestant Christianity meant it had to be brought over to the side of temperance. Alongside the growth of local and national temperance, a set of intellectual arguments from the Bible were developed to support the movement. This chapter looks at three moments in the history of temperance where the biblical presence looms large. Temperance had multiple phases, but it was with the founding of the Women's Christian Temperance Movement in 1874 that it became especially visible and committed to many kinds of social reform, a true progressive movement.[5] It followed the brief but noteworthy Woman's Crusade of 1873–1874.

In the Temperance movement, the Bible was both a prop and a problem. Culling its depths, one can find verses condemning drunkards and drunkenness but hardly a blanket condemnation of alcohol.[6] On the contrary, wine is one of God's gifts to humanity, "to gladden the human heart," and God approves of its consumption.[7] Wine was part of the drink-offering in the Jerusalem Temple.[8] The metaphor of God's people as a vineyard is ubiquitous in the Hebrew prophets and in Jesus's parables.[9] At the Last Supper, Jesus blesses bread and wine, and at Cana, he turns water into wine.[10] Despite the potential problem these examples posed for the arguments of temperance advocates, the Woman's Crusade employed the Bible as a highly visible physical presence and symbol of their cause.

The Woman's Temperance Crusade, 1873–1874
The Bible as Material Presence

Woman-like, they took their knitting, their zephyr work or their embroidery, and simply swarmed into the drink-shops, seated themselves and watched the proceedings. Usually they came in a long procession from their rendezvous at some church where they had held morning prayer-meeting; entered the saloon with kind faces, and the sweet songs of church and home upon their lips, while some Madonna-like leader with the Gospel in her looks, took her stand beside the bar, and gently asked if she might read God's word and offer prayer.[11]

The Woman's Crusade in the winter of 1873–1874 was ignited by the lectures of Dr. Diocletian Lewis, a homeopathic physician who advocated women's health and autonomy, who spoke in Fredonia, New York and Hillsboro, Ohio, in December, 1873, on the duty of women in the temperance cause. Although women had confronted alcohol sellers before, they now organized into a mass movement to shut down the sale of alcohol.

These crusaders employed the physical presence of the Bible in their actions in much the same way that physical props enhance theater productions. In the hands of temperance marchers, Bibles stirred emotions and projected images of home and family and a purer life. Pictures from an action in Xenia, Ohio in 1874 show a group of women with open books, no doubt Bibles or hymnbooks, outside a bakery that sold intoxicants.[12] Descriptions of the Crusade in the winter of 1873–1874 make clear the presence of the Bible in their actions. Contrary to the image of the hatchet-wielding Carrie Nation, a later and somewhat idiosyncratic figure, members of the Woman's Crusade asked permission to enter saloons, remaining outside if it was denied. If granted, they would proceed by opening their Bibles and reading from them, singing hymns, and attempting to cajole the barkeep or saloonkeeper to change his ways. A hostile observer in Ohio suggests the women are not above some tears, "sweet talk," and flattery:

> she also told him he was good-looking, and from all appearances a man of intelligence and culture, well educated; and she didn't quite say it, but came pretty near it, that if he would quit the business he was engaged in he would, at some future time, make a pretty little angel away up in heaven and have a tin horn and a jew's harp. Now wasn't this putting the thing pretty strong, when the man was neither pretty, handsome, nor good-looking, but was ugly, extremely ugly? And we doubt whether he has any education worth speaking of.[13]

Some saloonkeepers would "surrender," as the ladies called it, agreeing to follow a different way of life, perhaps handing over liquor to be poured out in the street or sent back to a supplier. One who surrendered might be gifted a Bible. A saloonkeeper who resisted the women's ministrations would find himself visited by succeeding bands of women, as many as six or seven more visits. Mother Eliza Stewart admits it was an "ordeal" for the man;[14] no doubt it was meant to be.

Crusaders who were refused entrance met outside on the street in front of a saloon, attracting onlookers as they engaged in the same activities, singing, praying, and reading from the Bible. Potentially more problematic for the establishments, the women's presence outside may have garnered sympathy and made it harder for patrons to enter. Stewart reports a Sister Philips who read the Bible while pacing back and forth in front of the saloon door. Several men got so interested in her readings that they used up too much of their lunch hour and instead of stopping for a drink, ran home for their dinner.[15] A Sister Wirtz read outside from a German Bible, prompting a man to approach her saying, "that verse was meant for me."[16]

The Bible reading and its physical presence seemed to stir the emotions of onlookers. Even when outside, Stewart notes the affective, nostalgic quality that Bible readings evoked, "I was often struck with the respect and reverence manifested for the Scriptures. Even after the novelty of the Crusade visitation had in a degree passed off, the reading of God's word would fasten the attention of men who had rarely read or heard it since the old family Bible was read by father at the altar in the old home, or the thrilling stories were taught by mother as they stood by her knee."[17]

The Bible served as a salient physical presence in nineteenth-century Protestantism, a "material Protestantism that depended on the physical senses to produce religious emotion."[18] More than a book, it was a composite representation of the family, containing birth and death records, locks of loved one's hair, and pressed flowers. As a "domestic object," it stirred both personal sentiment and nostalgia for real and imagined domestic scenes. Engravings displayed in *Godey's Lady's Book*, a popular women's magazine, and other drawings of the Victorian era show a father reading a Bible aloud as his household is gathered around. Others are more intimate ones of a mother and child reading a Bible while sitting close together, resembling paintings of the Madonna and child.[19]

Evocations of home and motherhood remained part of temperance, as the WCTU under Willard adopted the slogan "Home Protection" for its work, carrying on the theme of drink as a threat to families. Banners for the WCTU proclaimed "For God, and Home, and Native Land" (or sometimes 'Humanity')." Willard called the movement, "the home going forth into the world." Using such rhetoric upheld the ideal of Christian domesticity, while it simultaneously gave sanction for women's public activism, helping to erase the boundary between home and public life and undermined the "separate spheres" ideology that ascribed high moral standing and suasion to women in the home but judged political and public issues as too unseemly for their participation.

The Women's Christian Temperance Union

Forty-four hundred people, including some of society's elite, filled the newly built Metropolitan Opera House on October 19, 1888. They listened as the neat figure with the musical voice addressed them for more than an hour. Frances Willard, the president of the Women's Christian Temperance Union, spoke of a wide plan of reforms to an appreciative audience. When she was reelected president a few days later, the *New York Times* reported that "the house went wild with enthusiasm, thousands of white handkerchiefs fluttered excitedly up and down."[20]

The Woman's Crusade was short-lived but had established alcohol reform as a women's battleground. On its heels, broadening and deepening the issue, the Women's Christian Temperance Movement formed in 1874 in Cleveland, becoming a massive, well-respected force in US society. Its second president, Frances Willard, was a force of nature and international celebrity, promoting a panoply of progressive social reforms under her policy of "do everything." She and her organization worked for not only temperance, but for establishing child labor laws, raising the age of sexual consent for girls, prison reform, free kindergarten, soup kitchens, combating domestic violence,[21] women's suffrage, and abolitionism. Toward the end of her life, she addressed the fundamental economic inequality at the heart of so much suffering by arguing for "Christian socialism" in her Fourteenth Presidential Address, anticipating the Social Gospel movement. Despite her progressivism, her legacy is marred by racism and nativism.[22] Her support for abolitionism and for the WCTU's policy of welcoming both Blacks and whites was real; so were her troubling remarks on Black men's sexuality and lynching and her uncritical admiration of Southern white culture.[23]

Gender politics were complex in the temperance movement and in the WCTU.[24] In cartoons, temperance novels, and other propaganda, drunkenness was a man's vice, to be countered by the nobility of women. Men were not let in as voting members nor stockholders in the Temple and all the editors of the movement's newspaper, *The Union Signal*, were women. Willard explains that "they felt that if men had an equal place in its councils their greater knowledge of Parliamentary usage, and their more aggressive nature would soon place women in the background, and deprive them of the power of learning by experiences so that in some future day they might be true co-partners with their brothers in an organized effort to help the world to loftier heights of purity in conduct and character."[25] Willard herself was something of a contradiction. Her movement affected a domestic agenda of "the home going forth into the world" and its slogan was "home protection," implying that alcoholism particularly threatened wives and children. Willard recommended a persona of "womanliness first" for her speakers. Hearers praised Willard herself for her pleasing, musical voice and womanly appearance. On other hand, the WCTU was a respectable conduit for women to organize and speak publicly, weakening the wall between domestic and public lives. Willard quickly aligned herself and the movement officially with suffrage, and wrote *Woman in the Pulpit*, making the case from biblical texts for women clergy and equal rights in the Methodist church.

The Bible as Ally

Because an intellectual defense of temperance from the Bible was playing out in seminaries, colleges, pamphlets, and church presses, Willard and others did not need to "prove" the text's alliance with their movement; it was assumed. Many writings simply elided the temperance cause with the story of biblical redemption without providing a rationale or proof from texts. The temperance army was God's army; its struggles to save humanity matched those of the Bible's heroes.

In Willard's 1888 speech in New York City, she spoke of the "new" movement to study the Bible in colleges and seminaries as more pressing than teaching the "heathen classics." She recommended teaching the principles of ethics found in Scripture in all public schools. Since the WCTU claimed no creed or sectarianism, she suggested teaching principles of ethics that are drawn from Scripture, broad enough so as to be "questioned by no sane mind, whether Jew or Gentile, Catholic or Protestant."[26] She quickly skipped from such teaching to temperance instruction in the schools. Claiming no system of ethical instruction in the public schools has been put in place, *except* by the WCTU, she notes that many do not know that in thirty-three states and territories "the white ribbon women [temperance advocates] have secured laws making obligatory the instruction of all the children in scientific temperance with special reference to the effect of alcohol on the human system." Biblical ethics has merged with the teaching of "scientific temperance." She equates the two because "God's laws written in our members are to be sacredly obeyed," and the study of human health and hygiene (where temperance is paramount) is "another name for the religion of the body."[27] Whether naïve or disingenuous about her exclusivist religious view, Willard can claim that "Christ is central" in ethical teaching, while still arguing for a nonsectarian union and recommending the appointment of "a committee of all faiths" at the convention because "real womanhood has a broad free life and outlook on the world." Sections of the Bible to be taught in schools would be those that "people of all faiths can agree on, such as the Lord's Prayer."[28]

The Union Signal

The official newspaper of the WCTU, *The Union Signal* also assumed the Bible and the temperance movement shared identity and aims. Any biblical verse, whether from the Hebrew Bible or the New Testament, even with no explicit reference to temperance, could do double duty as a defense of the movement. For example, the story of the spirit coming upon Jesus's followers at Pentecost in Acts 2:1–13 and the mistaken claim of onlookers that some were simply drunk was because "alcohol was the devil's counterfeit of God's Holy Spirit." The particular mission of women in the temperance fight is indicated by the correct observation in Acts 1:14 that "women too were endowed with the spirit."[29]

Examples from the Hebrew Bible were culled broadly from the more obvious examples like the Nazirite vow, which includes abstention from alcohol, from general admonitions to sons not to shame their fathers by riotous living, and from much less defensible ideas like "Joshua believed in the pledge" because he admonished the people of Israel into pledging "the Lord our God we will serve and his voice we will obey."[30] A particular focus on teaching temperance to children appears often, citing as proof-texts verses like Matthew 19:14, "But Jesus said, Suffer little children, and forbid them not, to come unto me: for of such is the kingdom of heaven," and Mark 9:37, "Whosoever shall receive one of such children in my name, receiveth me: and whosoever shall receive me, receiveth not me, but him that sent me."[31] A regular column appears in *The Union Signal*, "Temperance Lessons for the Sabbath School" where general admonitions and examples are transmuted into temperance issues. A column for children by "Captain Deborah" called "Around the Campfire Talk" teaches temperance lessons via Bible stories.

Do Everything
A Handbook for the World's White Ribboners

In 1895, Willard published a handbook that addressed the burgeoning international temperance movement, a movement that claimed supporters on five continents as a result of missionary efforts. By this time, she notes the evolution of the movement to include a raft of social reforms, including raising the age of sexual consent, better legal protection for women, anti-cigarette campaigns, opposition to opium traffic, and opposing the laws around prostitution that allowed forced examination of prostitutes. She defends the broadness of their programs as a natural evolution of the movement, supported by gains in science, legislation, and political activity.[32]

This document shows fewer quotations of biblical verses, perhaps because Willard has moved to a more capacious sense of religion, arguing in one place for natural law. She worships Christ, while others may use language of "the First Great Cause," but both refer to "the Author of Law."[33] Instead of using specifically Christian language, she frequently invokes the idea that they are all God's warriors, imbued with his spirit and thinking his thoughts. Their fight to preserve the health of humanity is "the holiest fight this side of Jehovah's throne."[34] Like the biblical women leaders, WCTU women fight as they did in ancient times, "when Miriam sang, Deborah ruled, and Anna prophesied."[35]

The Anti-Saloon League

While the WCTU enjoyed celebrity and influence, other temperance organizations continued to meet and flourish. A separate political party formed to put their "dry" candidates into office. In 1869, the Prohibition Party formed, later being renamed the National Prohibition Reform Party. Like the WCTU, it folded a number of progressive causes like women's suffrage into its platform, considering itself a "broad gauge" party. Willard and her organization endorsed it in 1884 at their national convention and continued their support until her death. Both organizations were ultimately eclipsed, however, by a politically savvy and single-focus group, the Anti-Saloon League. Founded in 1893 and dominated by Protestant clergymen, it left behind other progressive causes and narrowed its gauge to a single issue: the creation of national legislation to make the United States an alcohol-free nation.[36]

The League broke no new ground in biblical arguments for temperance. However, its publications arm, the American Issue Publishing Company, distilled and distributed the fruits of arguments that had taken place in academic circles, publishing tracts, pamphlets, books, and the comprehensive *Standard Encyclopedia of the Alcohol Problem*. The broader public could read answers to its questions about Jesus's use of wine and the other appearances of alcohol in the Bible, absorbing the intellectual supports for temperance.[37]

Undermining Literalism, Claiming Biblical Authority

In tandem with the political activism promoting abstention from alcohol, a set of intellectual arguments emerged that provided the underpinnings of the movement. Scholars and preachers martialed considerable erudition to solve the problem of the Bible's apparent affirmation of wine's value versus their own conviction that it was the poisonous work of the devil. These arguments were rehearsed in pulpit and pamphlet around the country. Ironically, they waded into areas of historical contingency that were more in line with emerging biblical criticism than evangelical literalism.

Two-Wine Theory

Because two Hebrew words for wine appear in the Hebrew Bible, *yayin* and *tirosh*, some argued that two kinds of wine existed, one fermented and alcoholic, the other unfermented and nonalcoholic (grape juice). The stage for this theory was set when Moses Stuart, a professor at Andover Seminary and a leading biblical scholar of the time, wrote an essay in 1830 distinguishing between spirits and fortified wines. He argued that the Bible forbade spirits but not the more common and less alcoholic wine consumed by Jesus and other biblical heroes.[38] John Maclean, professor of ancient languages and literature at the College of New Jersey (later Princeton), in an article in the *New York Observer*, objected and argued against Stuart on philological grounds that nothing in the Bible forbade either spirits or wine. He did not advocate use of either to the level of intoxication but rejected Stuart's attempt to split the two as intellectually unsustainable.[39]

George Duffield was the earliest one to tout the two-wine theory in "The Bible Rule of Temperance," published in *The Philadelphia Observer* in May 1835.[40] It dovetailed with Stuart's ideas and Stuart adopted the more restrictive principle in his later essay, *A Scriptural View of the Wine Question*.[41] In a section entitled "Fermented Wines Condemned in the Bible," Duffield maintains: "In the original Hebrew there is a distinction carefully maintained between fermented wine which is intoxicating and another product of the vine, which is not. To the English reader, this is not apparent in our translation." Fermented wine, indicated by the Hebrew word *yayin*, is condemned for many reasons, which he cites with references. To note a few, it "excites and exhilarates," "inflames the blood," and "promotes disorder, riot, quarrels, and blood-shedding."[42]

Philology also comes into play in *The Temperance Bible Commentary*, published in Britain in 1868, and in an American edition with new preface by Tayler Lewis in 1870.[43] It distinguishes ten different words for wine or the fruit of the vine. In considering the Last Supper, for example, it examines the many appearances of the word "wine" and rejects the idea that it always means fermented wine. Where the word "wine" appears, they often render it "vine-fruit."[44] An appendix lists a series of preferred renderings of familiar verses. For example, "and the mountains shall drop sweet wine" is better put as "the mountains shall drop fresh juice."[45] The command to take care of others in Matthew "and whosoever shall give to drink unto one of these little ones a cup of cold water only in the name of a disciple, verily I say unto you, he shall in no wise lose his reward" becomes "and whosoever shall give to drink unto one of these little ones a cup *only* [emphasis mine] of cold water."[46] Moving one word has utterly changed the sense of the command.

Advocates repeated this claim of two kinds of wine throughout the nineteenth century. All wine referred to approvingly or used by biblical heroes was put into the category of unfermented wine. Wine used by Jesus was obviously unfermented. Especially relevant was the Last Supper, the template for communion, leading to the argument that the churches should only use grape juice for communion. In an interview with Mordecai Noah, a well-known, if not especially learned Jew of the day, one writer reported that Jews used raisin wine at Passover. This allowed some temperance leaders to say that Jews always used raisin wine, going back to the time of Jesus. Noah had not meant to endorse temperance or argue that the Bible forbade alcohol, but his statement allowed temperance leaders to claim Jesus drank unfermented wine, and that was the only thing they were interested in.[47] Wilbur and Sara Crafts, revisers of *The World Book of Temperance*, another encyclopedic work, quoted "learned Hebraist Dr. Cunningham, 'No Jew with whom I have conversed, of whatever class or nation, ever uses any other kind.'"[48] Jews have used wine made by soaking raisins in water and adding sugar, especially for Passover. Jonathan Sarna suggests several possible reasons for this custom, the most likely one that kosher wine was not widely available in the United States before the Civil War.[49]

Other dubious arguments from Jewish custom ensue, one that all fermented things are forbidden during Passover so fermented wine is forbidden (in fact, only grain products are included) and another that most people actually could not drink the four cups of wine commanded for the Passover seder if they contained alcohol.[50] Jesus hated fermentation because he said, "Watch out! Beware the yeast of the Pharisees and the yeast of Herod."[51] Jews themselves were not enthusiastic about temperance for many reasons, according to Marni Davis. Wine formed part of religious rituals and Jews prided themselves on their own moderation in using alcohol. Jews were producers and merchants of wine and spirits in Europe and brought their profession to the United States. The overwhelmingly Protestant and sometimes nativist flavor of the temperance movement was not welcoming to them and threatened the ideal of a nonsectarian society. Finally, women's public activism in the temperance movement did not fit some group's notions of Jewish women's modesty and dignity.[52]

Temperance gathered and advanced many other biblical, religious, and scientific arguments in *The Temperance Bible Commentary*, *The World Book of Temperance* published in the Washington, DC in 1908,[53] and the *Standard Encyclopedia of the Alcohol Problem*, published in 1925–1930, to dispose of the problem of Jesus and wine, and bring many more examples to shore up their arguments. Many texts that are not about alcohol *do* promote abstinence, according to the temperance commentators: the story of Jacob and Esau (where Esau is undone by excessive appetite), Isaac blinded by wine, or God's gift of water in Exodus 17 (showing it to be the superior drink). A patina of scholarship in the form of philology, history, and social commentary on how things were different in the ancient world legitimates the arguments. Little of temperance writing embraced biblical literalism. It could not afford to.

Some writers relativized the Bible's references to drinking and made much of the distance in time and place from ancient Palestine.

James Wallace, a classics scholar, suggested rules for interpretation. In his essay "Have We Bible Warrant for Wine Drinking?" he says, "all scripture must be interpreted with reference to the time and country in which, people for whom, and the immediate object for which it was written."[54] Things were different then, says Wallace. Distilled spirits did not exist, and Jews did not know anything about making or drinking beer. Drunkenness was not a problem back then due to a more hospitable climate and ancient Jews had little proclivity for intemperance.[55] These claims, of course, are impossible to prove, and in some cases contradict more recent evidence. Vessels for drinking beer have been discovered in ancient Israel and evidence for beer production is all over the ancient Near East.[56]

Furthermore, says Wallace, not all biblical ideas are equally valid, "what is local and transient must be distinguished from what is general and permanent."[57] Temperance, he argues, is a permanent value. Although the writers do not acknowledge it, the idea of historical contingency undermines the idea of timeless truths and more absolutist views of Scripture associated with evangelicalism. The preface to the original British publication of *The Temperance Commentary* reveals the enlightened social values of much of the temperance movement in its rejection of slavery and young earth creationism (though accompanied by some anti-Catholicism), claiming that not the Bible, but its *mis*-use, has produced "various fallacies professedly extracted from the Scriptures. In physical science, the fixity and recent creation of the earth; in political philosophy, the right of arbitrary government and Negro slavery" and more. What has changed is not Scripture, but how it is interpreted, and temperance belongs to the more enlightened method of interpretation.[58] The preface to the American publication by Tayler Lewis picked up these ideas, citing the anti-temperance interpretation as "the same error of interpretation that so long perverted and confused the slavery question. It was the error of applying ancient words and ancient ideas expressed by them, to modern things, modern relations, and modern practices, which though covered by the same general language, had undergone a change so great, as to amount to almost a radical difference." So just as the loyal servants of the tribal chief Abraham bore no relation to slaves in the United States, so too harmless, low-alcohol wines in ancient Palestine bore no relation to "vile and noxious compounds" of the nineteenth century that go by the same name.[59] By analogy, say the authors, such "one-sided exegesis" leads some to argue wrongly (but perhaps innocently) that consuming alcohol is encouraged by the biblical text.

Literal interpretation of the text became a vice. Wallace, for example, pushed against absolutism, a word for literal interpretation: "If Christ were among us, there is no doubt he would send forth the forked lightnings of his wrath against those modern, literalistic Pharisees."[60] General biblical principles prevail over examples. If examples of imbibing wine appear in the Bible, they are neutralized by larger principles, for example, the charge to not put stumbling blocks before the vulnerable.[61] Jesus enunciates the same truth. Similarly, those who quote examples of biblical toleration of wine-drinking are likened with Jesus's ancient opponents, Pharisees, "who by misinterpretation, make the law of God of no effect."[62] The larger principle of not being a cause of stumbling for others, "as Jesus and Paul plainly taught," therefore equals total abstinence.

Finally, like the earlier movements, temperance writers invoke the popular "progressive revelation" concept, which relegated the world that produced both testaments to a period of more primitive ethical development and posited steady moral development in culture over time. Gerrit Smith, the well-known abolitionist, goes so far as to say that, in drinking wine, Jesus did not know any better.[63] The Crafts argue from this same case: "Let us not put more into our Bible lesson today than belongs there. The virtues of total abstinence and prohibition had not yet been fully revealed. For clear teachings on those virtues we must look into later portions of the Bible and into the newest testament of modern history, in which God is still speaking to men."[64] Wallace too notes that slavery, polygamy, and divine right of kings were tolerated in biblical times, but no longer. In something of a contradiction, some argue that drunkenness is a bigger problem now because alcohol is cheaper and more accessible. The article on "Drunkenness" in Hasting's *A Dictionary of the Bible* of 1898 typically examines Hebrew and Greek words in the Bible but makes an economic argument with assumptions about the proclivities of the lower classes:

> Anyone who will carefully study all the passages in the Bible which speak of this matter will note that, in a large majority of them, drunkenness is explicitly spoken of as the vice of the wealthy . . . In modern times, on the contrary, drunkenness is supposed to be much more prevalent among the poor than among the well-to-do. This difference is not an accident. It is mainly the result of the cheapening of intoxicants, through improved prices of distilling and brewing introduced within the past two or three centuries. When the price of enough wine or beer to make a man drunk was equal to half a month's wages, and no other intoxicants were to be had, it was impossible for most men to become sodden drunkards. The case is different when an hour's labour will pay for an intoxication quantity of cheap liquor. In the older time, habitual drunkenness was possible for thousands where it is now possible for hundreds of thousands.[65]

Whether consciously or not, these arguments relativize the authority of the biblical text and, in embracing historical contingency, dovetail with historical-critical scholarship emerging in the nineteenth century. The notion of slow moral development or "progressive revelation" also allows distancing from uncomfortable references to imbibing alcohol. Distancing their own time from the ancient past allows interpreters to say that the ancients were both worse and better than contemporaries because they were less developed ethically, but also not as prone to drink because it was less available or less potent in the ancient world. Historical contingency and relativizing of the biblical language mixed it with literalism only when it seemed convenient. More often than not, literalism was the enemy.

The Bible proved as slippery an ally for temperance as it did for abolitionism and women's rights, the other progressive movements that nourished temperance. Many major figures in both abolitionism and women's suffrage also espoused temperance, although others pulled away from it. Elizabeth Cady Stanton and Susan B. Anthony had founded the Women's State Temperance Society in New York in 1853, but shortly after, Stanton wrote to Anthony not to waste any more energy on the Woman's State Temperance Society, because they had "bigger fish to fry."[66]

An essential part of nineteenth-century piety and rhetoric, the Bible evidence could hardly be put aside, but wrestling with it to render it alcohol's foe took ingenuity. Temperance advocates saw themselves as fighting God's battles and simply absorbed the Bible into their arsenal of weapons, but advancing arguments that rendered the text anti-alcohol meant embracing some fairly liberal methods of interpretation. Other arguments about the dangerous nature of alcohol, its ruinous effects on families and society, became more compelling. Stories in magazines like the *New Harpers' Monthly* were often maudlin tales of families destroyed when husband or wife tries a small amount of alcohol which sets them on a ruinous course.[67] Appeals to the good of society, personal improvement, and stability of families supplemented and eventually overtook the biblical arguments.

CHAPTER 4

The Bible and Civil Rights

THE BIBLE'S ROLE in the mid-twentieth-century civil rights movement was more than the occasional rhetorical flourish or majestic metaphor. Teachers, preachers, and organizers wove its words and images into their own story and developed a sense of themselves as part of a cosmic, apocalyptic battle against evil. They participated in a long-running tradition of interpretation that reached back to the days of enslavement and Reconstruction and looked forward to a dramatically altered society.[1] Biblical ideas provided scaffolding for a set of ideas poised to subvert white supremacy, a founding myth of American society.[2] Harnessing the authority of Scripture and identifying with an alternative narrative of peoplehood allowed leaders to take a radical stance against mores and laws that denied their full humanity. Just as the apostle Paul battled an array of persecutors, from the human to the demonic, they similarly faced multiple "principalities and powers."[3]

Not everyone in the movement looked to the Bible, and no one used it in isolation. The "integrationist" strain of thought, exemplified by the three people discussed in this chapter, Septima Clark, Fannie Lou Hamer, and Martin Luther King, also trusted in the principles of justice embedded in the nation's founding documents, the Declaration of Independence and the Constitution. These values were complemented by biblical principles of equality and prophetic calls to social justice. The second, "nationalist" strain, exemplified by Malcolm X, saw American society as fundamentally corrupt and permanently opposed to full citizenship for Blacks. He famously said, "We didn't land on Plymouth Rock. The Rock was landed on us."[4] In this second view, biblical ideas promoted passivity and were part of the bill of goods sold to African

Americans. James Cone notes these two strains of thought have pedigree in the intellectual history of Black Americans and suggests that we should not see them as antitheses, but mutually dependent correctives of one another.[5]

A third approach was pioneered by Albert Cleage, Jr., founder of the Shrines of the Black Madonna, also known as the Pan African Orthodox Church.[6] Embracing the liberationist message of Christianity, he spoke of the need to give Black youth a sense of belonging to a "nation within a nation," apart from white society. Like Malcolm X, he had no confidence in the integrationists' attempts to waken the moral conscience of white society. Cleage drew from the person and ethics of Jesus, and his embeddedness in the story of national redemption that is Israel's scriptures. Jesus, as a descendant of the nation Israel formed out of their experience among many non-white peoples in Egypt, was Black. His message was a collective one to a nation suffering under Roman occupation; his messiahship, like King David's, was to secure and liberate a people. Cleage drew on the nationalism of Israel's story and its rootedness in this world, fashioning a message of liberation and identity for Black youth, "the Bible becomes something new when you understand that it is talking about a black people and a Black Messiah. This faith in our future we give our youth."[7]

A major, necessary corrective to any review of male thinkers brings to the fore the women leaders and activists in the movement. The standard narrative of the civil rights movement springing solely from the cradle of the Southern Black churches in the middle of the twentieth century is too late, too churchy, and too male. If the church was dominated by male clergy, the schoolhouse was the domain of women. Septima Poinsette Clarke (1898–1987), for example, challenged the all-white school board to get Black teachers into the segregated Black schools in 1918, the same year she joined the NAACP. Her career teaching citizenship and literacy to both children and adults spanned most of the twentieth century and was a continuous act of resistance to white supremacy.

The role of some Southern churches in rousing people to action is well-known; less often recognized is the role of the schoolhouse in fostering literacy, citizenship, and a sense of identity. Far less dramatic than a soaring speech is teaching someone to write a name, and how to register to vote.[8] African American women formed the core of the voting rights initiative from the beginning, including Clark, Hamer, Clark's cousin Bernice Robinson, Ella Baker, Dorothy Cotton, and many more.[9] Clark reported that there were fifteen women coordinating the Citizenship Education Program out of the Atlanta office of SCLC, copying teaching materials and keeping records of students and schools.[10] This parallel development has been underappreciated, probably because of the sexism of the early civil rights movement and the relatively less dramatic nature of teaching versus oratory.[11] In their quotidian work of literacy and citizenship education, the women teachers represent a second strand in creating a movement, a clear form of resistance in a time when schools for African Americans in the Jim Crow South were underfunded in deliberate attempts to keep Black education separate and unequal and to reduce the Black vote. Clark said during her time growing up in Charleston's Black community, "nobody thought of voting."[12]

Septima Poinsette Clark

In stories about the civil rights movement you hear mostly about the black ministers. But if you talk to the women who were there, you'll hear another story. I think the civil rights movement would never have taken off if some women hadn't started to speak up.[13]

Septima Clark was a teacher, not a preacher. She spent her life figuring out how to get people the liberating knowledge they needed to participate in American society. Born into the segregated city of Charleston, South Carolina, in 1898 to parents determined to secure her a good education, she was ready for her first teaching post at age eighteen. She stepped onto a gasoline-powered boat for an eight-hour journey to Johns Island, one of the seacoast islands on the South Carolina coast, then accessible only by inland waterways. It was September 1916.

Isolated from the mainland, its inhabitants, many the descendants of free, formerly enslaved peoples, spoke Gullah or Geechee, a creole dialect of English and African loan words, and maintained a distinct culture. Although Clark labored in a dilapidated schoolhouse, without textbooks, teaching children of different ages, she also developed deep relationships and learned the value of "meeting people where they are." The teacher was a respected and trusted community figure, part of the lives of families on the island, so it was natural for her to initiate teaching literacy to adults, as well as tutoring adults in speech-giving, and helping them fill out forms and write letters.[14] Clark's first teaching assignment on Johns Island, SC, taught her the importance of forging bonds with the community, attending to local culture, and the liberating quality of the basic skills of reading, writing, and mathematics.

After two years, she returned to teach in Charleston, and in the summer of 1918 she joined the NAACP, then a young organization. After marrying, having a child, and becoming a widow, she settled in Columbia, SC, and later back in Charleston, teaching in the public schools by day, pursuing her own education at night. Not only did she earn a master's degree, she also found time to tutor adults in literacy and citizenship, carrying on the legacy of the Black women's club movement, formed to protect and improve women's lives and serve the African American community.[15] After a long career in the Charleston public schools, Clark's contract was terminated in 1956 because of her membership in the NAACP. Although she had been a member for decades, the red baiting of the Cold War era and the white supremacist backlash to *Brown v. Board of Education* led many Southern locales to clamp down on any organization that promoted racial equality and integration. Shortly after her dismissal, she was hired by famous educator Myles Horton to teach and organize at the Highlander Folk School in Monteagle, Tennessee, a racially integrated center for adult education and social change.

At Highlander, Clark and her cousin Bernice Robinson set up a curriculum for Citizenship Schools to teach both literacy and citizenship. Literacy tests and lack of education on representative democracy were two ways white supremacists conspired to keep down the Black vote, thwarting the Fifteenth (1870) and Nineteenth (1920) Amendments that granted the vote to African American men and to all women, respectively. Clark and Robinson presented a series of workshops to train local leaders to go back to their communities to teach literacy, to organize, to encourage people to register to vote, and to help them navigate the roadblocks set up to African Americans for voting. One of their attendees was Rosa Parks, whom Clark recalls as painfully shy. It was three months after her course in community organizing at Highlander that Parks refused to give up her seat on a Montgomery bus to a white man, sparking the Montgomery bus boycott. Although Parks had been an activist before Highlander, Clark took some pride in her action, "Rosa? Rosa? She was so shy when she came to Highlander, but she got enough courage to do that."[16]

Women-Centered Activism

In January of 1957, Clark and Robinson started an adult course for literacy on Johns Island, where Clark had begun her teaching career forty years earlier. Clark recruited Robinson, a beautician, for her "good ear" or ability to listen,[17] to work with Esau Jenkins, a local bus driver who did rolling voter education as he drove passengers back and forth over a bridge to the mainland. They bought a building with a store in front and two back rooms for classrooms. The schools taught people whatever was needed, to read and write, the Constitution, local laws on voting, taxes, social security, but also crocheting and sewing. The result was increased voter registration. Soon people on neighboring islands clamored for their own schools in the same model and soon they were set up on Wadmalaw and Edisto islands.

The pedagogy developed by Clark and Robinson began with the adult students. Robinson asked them what they wanted to know. They asked for help to read the Bible and newspapers, to write letters to family, to fill out catalog and money orders, to pass the literacy test, and to register to vote. Political messages about the importance of exercising voting rights, mixed at times with a small dose of religion, were slipped in with literacy education.

Highlander Folk School, which oversaw these schools, had always been under suspicion because it was racially integrated. It was raided on a summer night in 1959, and Clark and others spent the night in jail, before it was shut down for good in 1961. Clark's Citizenship Schools program came under the aegis of the Southern Christian Leadership Conference (SCLC), headed by Martin Luther King, setting up in Dorchester Co-operative Community Center in McIntosh, Georgia. The program was slightly renamed as the Citizenship Education Program, headed by Dorothy Cotton and Clark. Clark continued doing the same things she had at Highlander, holding workshops, traveling and fund-raising, and sending teachers and organizers into communities. Between 1962 and 1964, SCLC joined with CORE and other groups, training 10,000 teachers for its programs. In 1972, the first two African Americans from the Deep South were elected to Congress since Reconstruction, Andrew Young and Barbara Jordan.

Biblical Underpinnings

In an article written at the end of her remarkable career, Clark reveals the basis of her life's work in the gospel preaching of Jesus. In "Citizenship and Gospel," she sees her work as part of the mission set out by the prophet Isaiah, crystalized in Jesus's ministry, citing Luke 4:18–19, a verse familiar in African American hermeneutic,

> The Spirit of the Lord is upon me, because he hath anointed
> me to preach the gospel to the poor; he hath sent me to heal
> the brokenhearted, to preach deliverance to the captives, and
> recovering of sight to the blind, to set at liberty them that are
> bruised. To preach the acceptable year of the Lord.

This verse, attributed to the prophet Isaiah,[18] appears in Trito-Isaiah, a set of hopeful materials from the period of restoration after the return of exiles from Babylon in the sixth century, BCE. Luke's gospel situates the verses at the opening of Jesus's ministry, transferring the same authority of prophet as bringer of God's deliverance to the oppressed to Jesus. In Clark's work, she takes on the same mantle of the prophet as repairer of society, placing herself in the chain of tradition.

In her integrationist view, she characterizes the civil rights struggle as "part of a dream which is both Christian and American. But beyond America a much larger stage beckons, as two grand narratives come together. The civil rights movement's struggle for equality and justice is God's taking the part of the oppressed in the millennia-long struggle against evil."[19] For Clark, their work of teaching instantiates Jesus's mission of care for the poor and underprivileged. "Love and concern for others must be made concrete," in teaching people agricultural methods, providing health care facilities, and establishing schools. But a more ambitious goal beckons, namely, "to redeem the system which keeps them in captivity." The citizenship schools fight for full citizenship will undo the continuing educational, economic, and political disadvantages that are subtler forms of continuing oppression. She wrote this in 1980, noting some Blacks had made it into the middle-class. But tokenism should not satisfy Christians. "They must continually remain sensitive to the will of God for the redemption of 'the saints of rank and file,' the people of the land around whom Jesus centered his earthly ministry."[20]

One of the reading booklets Clark and Robinson prepared was "The Bible and the Ballot." It was a little Bible and a lot of ballot, but for her the two were inseparable. Nor did she need to do more than nod to familiar biblical narratives, so much a part of Southern Black culture, to remind her hearers of the larger canvas of history, "we cannot be spectators on the stage of history. We are under orders as Christians to become involved in the total life of the world. We are under orders to work for all those things which make for life that upholds human values and for conditions in which man can grow towards wholeness and life abundant." She decries the intimidation, discrimination, despair, and lack of training that stand in the way of African Americans voting. Exhorting her readers, she weaves in the Bible, the Constitution, and the drives for voter registration, noting the work by SCLC, National Council of Churches, and Presbyterians in Hattiesburg who have already worked to sign up voters. She then asks the churches' help in providing facilities, promoting programs, and giving financial support.[21]

Just as Jesus is presented as the heir of Isaiah, so Clark saw their struggle as the inheritance of Jesus' ministry and mission. In *Echo in My Soul*, she reflects on her lifetime of teaching and offers an explicit parallel,

> I'd prefer to be looked at as a worker, a woman who loves her fellow man, white and Negro alike, and yellow, red, and brown, and is striving with her every energy, working—not fighting—in the true spirit of fellowship to life him to a higher level of attainment and appreciation and enjoyment of life. I hope that I have—surely I wish to possess and I do strive to attain—something of the spirit of the lowly and glorious young Man of Galilee, who, as I read him and understand him and worship him, saw no color or racial lines but loved with a consuming devotion all of the children of God and knew them all as his brothers.[22]

In a talk at a church on Wadmalaw Island, she promoted the NAACP and tried to rally some people from the community to attend a seminar on the United Nations at Highlander. She rooted the work in the gospel, "The whole idea of the worth and dignity of man and the right of each individual to the good life comes from our Christian gospel, from the demands of the prophets for justice for all from the teaching of Jesus that all men are brothers and all are equally loved by God."[23] Thus, the rights guaranteed by the Universal Declaration of Human Rights, adopted by the United Nations (UN) in 1948, undergirded the drive for voter rights in the United States, and flowed from biblical precepts.

Much of this material is second nature to many Christians today, especially those raised on principles of social justice. Yet it ruffled the feathers of some ministers and rank-and-file Christians who resisted attempts to link religion to social change of any kind. Some ministers, Black and white, defined their call to save souls, not to change society. Mixing politics and religion is a bad idea, they said, or society was not ready. Anne Moody recalls canvassing for voter registration for the Student Non-Violent Coordinating Committee (SNCC) in Mississippi. After getting doors slammed in their faces, they went to churches only to find that some Black ministers asked them to stop coming because they scared off their congregants. Anne was similarly frustrated at a church of middle-class Blacks in Canton, Mississippi, pastored by "the biggest [Uncle] Tom," who influenced all the other ministers. However, she and her fellow workers went to some of the prominent church members and succeeded.[24] Hamer also called out preachers who said, "'I don't like bringing politics into the church,' saying 'If this man don't choose to be a shepherd, he can be a sheep and follow the shepherd.'"[25]

Biblical groundedness took away Clark's fear. Like King and Hamer, Clark frequently mentions that she was not afraid; she did not back down when others did. When dismissed from a long-held teaching position because of membership in the NAACP, she said, "I was not nervous and not afraid. I was somewhat surprised, of course, and considerably hurt. But I was not frightened. I felt then—and I feel now—that a kind Providence directs us when we strive to do what we think is right, and I have sought all the years since as an eighteen-year-old girl I went over on Johns Island, to do what is right, not only for my own people but for all people." Providence, she continues, took her to Highlander.[26] Similarly, her safe passage through dangerous waters of white supremacist violence and accidents on her travels, she attributed to her being in God's care. This included a plot to blow up the house she was in that was thwarted in time.[27]

Clark sees God at work in the success of their movement, citing events like James Meredith enrolling at the University of Mississippi in 1962 and Senator LeRoy Johnson, the first Black to be elected to the Georgia state legislature in fifty years. In a piece titled "Why I Believe in God," she relates her quest to provide rational grounds for her beliefs. When discouraged by the seeming triumph of injustice, she found reassurance in the Bible and the longer arc of history: "what the Bible says about the nature and destiny of man and institutions not only come to my rescue but also strengthen my belief." She also affirms God's protection in her life, saying that like Paul, "he is able to keep me until this day."[28]

Fannie Lou Hamer

> I told the policeman, I said, "It's going to be miserable when you have to face God," I said, because one day you are going to pay up for the things you have done. I said, because as the Scripture says, "has made of one blood all nations."[29]

One of the graduates of the Citizen Education Program at the Dorchester center was Fannie Lou Hamer, an iconic figure in the history of civil rights, who, it is said, was unaware of her constitutional right to vote until she attended a mass meeting in August 1962 at the age of forty-four and heard sermons that linked biblical messages to voter registration.[30] After attending one of Clark's SCLC workshops, Hamer started a citizenship education group in Ruleville, Mississippi, and later led her group to register to vote, an action that cost her a job and threatened her life. Hamer was severely beaten in a Winona jailhouse after coming home from a CEP training session on Johns Island led by Clark and Robinson. Clark attended the trial in Oxford, Mississippi, of the white policemen responsible.[31]

Hamer is recalled for her plainspokenness and incisive turns of phrase, whose best-known slogan is "I'm sick and tired of being sick and tired." Unlike Clark and King, she did not have the benefits of advanced formal schooling. She grew up in a family of poor sharecroppers, farmers who rented land from a white landlord in exchange for a portion of the profits. The system was highly exploitative and Black tenant farmers were regularly cheated of most of their profits.[32] When she began her odyssey in the movement for civil rights, Hamer was a timekeeper, a middleperson who weighed and recorded cotton yields, on a Mississippi plantation in Sunflower County.

In her earliest published speech, to a voter registration rally in Greenwood, Mississippi, in 1963, Hamer displays her rhetorical agility with Scripture. Drawing from the same well as Clark and King, the shared canon of verses within the movement, she too begins with the prophetic pronouncement in Luke 4:18. "The Spirit of the Lord is upon me, because he hath anointed me to preach the gospel to the poor." As Hamer assumes the prophet's mantle, she is saying that God is still at work in their own struggle in a chain of deliverance through history. They are, she says, performing "Christ's purpose on earth" and she regards her voter drives as "working for Christ."[33]

At a more granular level, she matches the challenges of their drive to register to vote to cosmic battles of good and evil. She describes this conflict in apocalyptic terms as a sudden ripening of the times, saying "the time is out." Their battle is ultimately between God and Satan, she implies, quoting Isaac Watts's hymn about "facing Satan's rage." It is a fight, perhaps to the death in an *imitatio Christi*. "Quit trying to dodge death," she exhorts, "I don't hide that I'm fighting for freedom. Jesus died to set us free, staying till he was thirty-three, letting us know how we would have to walk." She also invokes another martyr, "like Paul, I have fought a good fight."[34]

Hamer taps into the subversive quality of the Bible. Much of the Hebrew Bible and all of the New Testament was written by subject peoples, not in control of their political destiny. The Jews of first-century Palestine from which the Jesus movement sprang were a people occupied by Rome who, like other oppressed groups, used "hidden transcripts,"[35] codes, and metaphors to resist their occupiers. Recent decades have produced considerable scholarship on this *sub rosa* resistance in the New Testament writings.[36] The apostle Paul, for example, inverts the image of the Roman triumphal parade. Normally a display of the power of the emperor, Paul reverses the order to show Jesus, the crucified criminal at the head, followed by the temporal authorities to be destroyed, and finally by death itself.[37] A similar form of subversion appears in the language in early Christian martyrologies. Although the emperor's power over life and death is meant to be inscribed on the body of the victim, early presentation of martyrdom presents it as an athletic contest whose prize is the crown of martyrdom, a defeat of the oppressor. Hamer's rhetoric similarly rejects the apparent structure of power and predicts its defeat. Like Paul, she and her fellow workers are battling "principalities and powers," a frequent term in the Pauline and Deutero-Pauline letters for secular and demonic opponents.

Like early apocalyptic thinkers, Hamer assumed God's justice would prevail. Wrongdoers would receive punishment, and God's righteous sufferers would be raised up. Hamer regularly relied on verses from all over Scripture, including in her speech in Greenwood, MS, "Be not deceived, for God is not mocked. For whatsoever a man sow, that shall he also reap" and "Whoso diggeth a pit shall fall down in it."[38] Pits have been dug for the African Americans, Hamer says "for ages," but in truth, their persecutors were setting up their own demise, "when they was digging pits for us, they had some pits dug for themselves." Heaven and earth will pass away "before one jot of my word would fail."[39] As she bore her sufferings in a Winona jail cell, she invoked one blood doctrine as she warned the policeman ordering other Black prisoners to beat her, "It's going to be miserable for you when you have to face God, because 'God had made of one blood all nations.'"[40] She declares him "pitiful," for his ignorance of Scripture's message of equality, but also of fundamental right and wrong, that he "can beat a person and not know you're doing wrong." The moral authority rests with people on the side of God and justice.

Faith canceled her fear. God protects his own, she assures, citing the 23rd psalm, "It's a funny thing since I've been working for Christ. It's kind of like in the twenty-third of the psalms, when he said, 'Thou preparest a table in the presence of my enemies. Thou anointeth my head with oil and my cup runneth over.'" Hamer escaped death when white supremacists shot sixteen times into her bedroom when she was staying with friends in Ruleville in September 1962, saying she walked through the valley of the shadow of death. She was out that night, and she exclaims, "Don't you see what God can do?"[41]

The African Americans' struggle to realize their full rights in American society belongs to a long line of divine skirmishes with worldly powers. That the name of the organizer of the voter registration project in Mississippi was Bob Moses, Hamer saw as a sure sign of God's saving power in the Exodus coming to the fore again, "He sent a man in Mississippi with the same man that Moses had to go to Egypt, and tell him to go down in Mississippi and tell Ross Barnett [the segregationist governor] to let my people go." Despite not knowing the future, she is confident because "as I walk along, I walk with my hand in God's hand." Everyone has a cross to bear, a charge to keep, must walk in Christ's way of suffering, fight the battle as Paul did, and by their efforts, "put up a light." Her signature song, "This Little Light of Mine," is from Jesus's admonition about not lighting a candle to put it under a bushel, and his charge "Let your light shine before men" (Matt 5:15–16).[42]

Hamer and others in the movement continue to employ the jeremiad, the form of prophetic critique used by abolitionists Maria Stewart and Frederick Douglass. It calls out injustice and demands reform, underscoring God's coming judgment against evildoers, and cites special people chosen to do God's work. It brings hearers to the brink of despair over the nation's fallenness before pointing to a vision of hope for redemption.[43] The African American jeremiad, exemplified by Stewart, Douglass, and King, draws on ideas of chosenness and calls out the injustice of racism.[44] Hamer stands in this tradition, pronouncing the supremacists as blind and pitiful, and exhorting her hearers to work for justice.

The events of her own journey become mythic, foundational stories that gain significance by repetition: her attempted registration to vote in Indianola in 1962, resulting in her immediate firing and expulsion from the plantation where they lived, the shooting into her bedroom in September 1962 and her fortuitous absence, and the horrific beating in the Winona jail in June 1963. These events are recounted in many of her speeches in nearly exact detail. These details include her words to the white landowner who fired her on hearing of her registering to vote and pressured her to withdraw her registration, "Mister, I didn't register for you. I was trying to register for myself."[45] They include the Winona jail beating where she recounts the details of pulling her dress down as it worked up during the beating, and the patrolman pulling it back up, her holding her hand over her left side to shield a part of her affected by childhood polio, overhearing the beating of colleague Annelle Ponder and Ponder's refusal to call the policeman "Sir" because "I don't know you well enough." By her retellings, she integrates her own trauma into a master narrative of the defeat of evil at the hands of a powerful God. They are opposed by "principalities and powers," forces both ordinary and demonic.

Throughout her speeches, Hamer calls out hypocrisy and those unwilling to live out Christ's example, "All we have to do is trust God and launch into the deep . . . God is not going to put it in your lap." Hamer criticized clergy and lay people who come out to church every Sunday with a bunch of stupid hats on but were unwilling to join the fight for the ballot, "I don't want to hear you say, 'Honey, I'm behind you.' Well move, I don't want you back there. Because you could be two hundred miles behind. I want you to say, 'I'm with you.' And we'll go up this freedom road together."[46] She does not spare other African Americans from censure. In "The Only Thing We Can Do Is Work Together" in 1967 before the National Council of Negro Women chapter and after the Voting Rights Act of 1965, she criticizes the coalition of Blacks and whites who formed Sunflower County Progress, Inc. in hopes of attracting Head Start money, and competed with her own Child Development Group of Mississippi.[47] Sensitive to class prejudice, especially from middle-class Blacks, she notes that the "Spirit of the Lord" quote is not addressed to the rich. Perhaps she was thinking of King and the other clergy, when she said, "People can say you need a Ph.D. to live. My Holy Bible tells me he was taking it from the wise and revealing it to babes," a reference to Matthew 11:25. She asks, "Do I want my child to be ashamed? I worked with children who never saw a commode. The professional Negro got with the power structure."[48]

Hamer, like King, has been softened by some in retrospect to fit her into a more convenient memory of the civil rights struggle. But using the Bible made her more, not less radical as she viewed the struggle played out on God's canvas of history. Like King, she calls 11 o'clock on Sunday, when people are in church, the most segregated hour in the week. Referring to lynchings and murders, she called America "the land of the tree and the home of the grave."[49] The title of her speech that contains these barbs, "What Have We to Hail?" is reminiscent of Frederick Douglass's famous, "What to a Slave Is the Fourth of July?"

Martin Luther King

The sheer bulk of King's oratory and writings is overwhelming. Few Baptist preachers write books, *New York Times* articles, and Nobel Prize acceptance speeches while also giving sermons, speeches publicized to the nation, and interviews with *Playboy*. To generalize about his writings is further complicated because he drew from several traditions of interpretation and addressed many kinds of audiences for different purposes. His thinking evolved as events unfolded.

Most Americans know the broad outlines of Martin Luther King's life: growing up a minister's son in Atlanta, nurtured in the traditions of the Black Baptist church, and his education at Boston University and Crozer seminary in the liberal Protestant theology of the day. He was a founder of the Southern Christian Leadership Conference and was recruited to lead the Montgomery bus boycott (1955–1956). Other momentous events include the March on Washington (1963) and the Selma to Montgomery march (1965). Known for his stunning oratory, his last speech, "I See the Promised Land," on April 3, 1968, was to support the sanitation workers in Memphis. He was assassinated the next day at the age of thirty-nine.

Like Clark, Hamer, and others in the integrationist mode, King believed in an unfolding of history that was rooted in Christianity and Scripture. The God of history was on the side of justice and took care of his own. Yet not all King's writings contained references to Scripture. His was a broad canvas, which included brush strokes from history, sociology, literature, philosophy, even popular culture. His public work was meant to awaken the conscience of white America to its endemic racism and to lead and counsel Black Americans in the struggle for racial justice. Nor did he ever give up the idea of being a pastor—in Montgomery and later in Atlanta. We can think about his methods of using the Bible in broad and overlapping categories.

An Extended Exposition Anchored in a Biblical Story or Example

King constructs his famous "Drum Major Instinct," delivered at Ebenezer Baptist Church in 1968 shortly before his death around Mark 10:35–45, beginning with verses 35–40,

> And James and John the sons of Zebedee came unto him saying, "Master, we would that thou shouldest do for us whatever we shall desire." And he said unto them, "What would ye that I should do for you?" And they said unto him, "Grant unto us that we may sit one on thy right hand, and the other on thy left hand in thy glory." But Jesus said unto them, "Ye know not what ye ask. Can ye drink of the cup that I drink of, and be baptized with the baptism that I am baptized with?" And they said unto him, "We can." And Jesus said unto them, "Ye shall indeed drink of the cup that I drink of, and with the baptism that I am baptized with all shall ye be baptized. But to sit on my right hand and on my left hand is not mine to give, but it shall be given to them for whom it is prepared."

King suggests that James and John show a natural human desire for recognition and tells his hearers to join him in considering their own desires to be first, saying, "there is, deep down in all of us, an instinct. It's a kind of drum major instinct—a desire to be out front, a desire to lead the parade, a desire to be first." He expounds on this desire at length, citing psychoanalyst Alfred Adler, the strategies of advertising, and one-upmanship that pushes people to live beyond their means. Crime, classism, and racism are driven by the need to feel superior. He relates conversations he and his fellow protestors had with white wardens while in jail. The wardens argued their cases for segregation and against racial intermarriage, but King, learning of their economic and social status, said, "You know what? You ought to be marching with us. You're just as poor as Negroes. You are put in the position of supporting your oppressor. Because through prejudice and blindness, you fail to see that the same forces that oppress Negroes in American society oppress poor white people. And all you are living on is the satisfaction of your skin being white, and the drum major instinct of thinking that you are somebody big because you are white."[50] Even wars and conflicts between nations stem from the basic impulse to be the leader, "the drum major instinct." King looks back to the Hebrew Bible and to ancient Rome to remind hearers, "But God has a way of putting even nations in their place."

Returning to the material in Mark 10, he preaches of a better way. One need not exorcize the drum major instinct, but must harness it, turn it to new purposes, and develop a new understanding of greatness. "[Jesus said] 'It's a good instinct if you use it right. It's a good instinct if you don't distort it and pervert it. Don't give it up. Keep feeling the need for being important. Keep feeling the need for being first. But I want you to be first in love. I want you to be first in moral excellence. I want you to be first in generosity.'"

King's method of wedding a biblical passage to human psychology to address spiritual renewal comes out of mid-twentieth-century liberal Protestant preaching. Harry Emerson Fosdick, a celebrated preacher at Riverside Church and champion of modernism over fundamentalism, gave a sermon "Handling Life's Second Bests" multiple times over his career. Fosdick calls the example of Paul in Acts 16, on the road to Bithnyia, but experiencing Jesus's call and going to Troas, "wanting Bithnyia and getting Troas." Fosdick recounts numerous such examples of people intending to do one thing and having to do another, drawing the lesson of making a success out of one's failures. The sermon ends with "he took a very hard thing and made of it a triumph."[51] King's drum major instinct follows just such a pattern.

Parable

Yet King's appeal to everyday human feelings and relationships by way of a story has a much older pedigree in the parables of Jesus and the *meshalim* of the early rabbis. A parable, from the Greek *parabalo,* "to throw or place alongside," is literally two things laid alongside one another. Characters are typically fathers and sons, landowners and day laborers, women keeping house, and kings and subjects. The stories are set in worldly contexts—banquets, domestic life, appearing before judges, and planting and reaping from the land. Those in authority, kings and landowners, are normally stand-ins for God. While scholars debate origins and parallels of the form, all agree that the parable flourished in early Jewish contexts.[52] A few appear in the Hebrew Bible (2 Sam 12:1–4; 2 Sam 14:5–7), they become a primary vehicle in Jesus's preaching, and they appear in rabbinic literature.[53] An example from everyday life showing human tendencies is a springboard for a religious lesson, often organized around a single image—a lost coin, a disgruntled laborer, a mustard seed—and teaching by analogy. Here the drum major provides the organizing image.

While parables might seem to be no more than simple teaching devices, analogies to bring home a point to the unlettered, they are often unsettling and open-ended. Amy-Jill Levine shows that the gospel authors, especially Luke, have domesticated parables by fitting them, sometimes uneasily, into larger gospel themes and imposing a moral by ending with a saying that may not quite fit the story. As Levine says, "we might be better off thinking less about what they 'mean' and more about what they can 'do': remind, provoke, refine, confront, disturb."[54] The effect of juxtaposing story and teaching is to jolt the reader out of habitual ways of thinking, to challenge them to think of the world, the kingdom, and their lives differently. King does so with his drum major sermon. Instead of predictably chiding the reader for wanting to be important, or instructing on Jesus's admonition to practice humility and become a servant to all, he takes it in quite another direction.[55] He encourages people to use their need to be seen and applauded, but for higher goals: "Don't give it up. Keep feeling the need to be important. Keep feeling the need for being first. But I want you to be first in love. I want you to be first in moral excellence. I want you to be first in generosity." Considering his own life and imagining his eulogy, he said, "yes, if you want to say I was a drum major, say that I was a drum major for justice; say that I was a drum major for peace: I was a drum major for righteousness."[56] Like Jesus's parables, King's juxtaposition does not tell hearers what the story means, but what it should do to transform their lives.

Isolated Verses Appear as a Signature

At times a single verse or two will appear within a speech, placed at or near the end as a signature or punctuation. King's eulogy for the four martyred girls in Birmingham, on September 15, 1963, despite its overall religious tone, refers to only one biblical verse, "A little child shall lead them," and ends with a line from Shakespeare's *Hamlet*, adapting Horatio's farewell, "Good night, sweet prince" to the four girls, or "princesses."[57] Similarly, his 1956 speech in Montgomery, "Facing the Challenge of a New Age," delivered before the First Annual Institute on Non-Violence and Social Change contains but a single biblical reference (with a change in tense) in the final line, "the morning stars will sing together and the sons of God will shout for joy."[58] Yet King dramatically demonstrates his range with additional references from Heraclitus, Hegel, the Dred Scott decision, *Plessy v. Ferguson*, William Cowper's

"The Negro's Complaint," Bob Hope, John Donne, Ralph Waldo
Emerson, Michelangelo, Shakespeare, Beethoven, Douglas Mallock,
Thomas Carlyle, William Cullen Bryant, James Russell Lowell, Josiah
Gilbert Holland, the song "Oh, Freedom!," and "My Country 'Tis
of Thee." In this instance the biblical verse serves as a punctuation or
authoritative stamp that places the movement within the flow of history
and culture.

Imitation of Jesus and Paul

King invokes the models Jesus and Paul and the prophets to make sense
of suffering and risk, and to hew to the demands of love. Accused of
being an extremist for rejecting gradualism and promoting nonviolent demonstrations, King countered, "Was not Jesus an extremist in
love—'Love your enemies, bless them that curse you, pray for them
that despitefully use you.' Was not Amos an extremist for justice—'Let
justice roll down like waters and righteousness like a mighty stream.'
Was not Paul an extremist for the gospel of Jesus Christ—'I bear on
my body the marks of the Lord Jesus.'" He adds the examples of other
extremists in history, Martin Luther, Abraham Lincoln, and Thomas
Jefferson.[59] Similarly, he recommends rejecting conformity to an unjust
society: rather, "let us be maladjusted."[60]

Identifying with Jesus the extremist is a long tradition in American
life. David Burns uncovers the utility of early biblical criticism and
historical Jesus studies for reformers of every stripe: freethinkers,
women's rights activists, socialists, and anarchists.[61] He credits Ernst
Renan's *Life of Jesus* as the wellspring for these radicals both for its
extracting a revolutionary Jesus from the biblical texts and for its imaginative dabbling in myth and emotion. Separating the Jesus of history
from later theological developments, stories, and institutional understandings allows the reader to uncover the Jew living under political
oppression and sacrificed to it. At the same time, skepticism over the
historicity of certain elements of Jesus's story allows room for creative
identifications with that Jesus.

Historical Jesus scholarship came from Germany and France, producing numerous portraits of Jesus. Several waves, or quests, tried to extract the "real" historical preacher from later ecclesiastical interpretations and to bracket supernatural elements of the gospels as myth. The first wave ended in 1906 with Albert Schweitzer's *The Quest of the Historical Jesus*, a work that more or less declared the quest hopeless. Higher criticism was familiar in abolitionist and Freethinker circles. Abolitionist Theodore Parker published an extensive summary of D. F. Strauss's *Das Leben Jesu* in the Unitarian newspaper *The Christian Examiner* in 1840. Publications like *Harper's Weekly* and *The Independent* carried discussion of the latest findings in biblical studies, so the public, in addition to students at theological seminaries, had some access to the works.

In his influential 1949 work, *Jesus and the Disinherited,* distinguished minister and civil rights leader Howard Thurman builds his theology on a historical Jesus who is an oppressed and poor Jew in Galilee, battling the unjust Roman political system. He uncompromisingly places Jesus in his own time, place, and politically precarious status, saying Jesus "cannot be understood outside a sense of the community Israel held with God." The church has distorted Jesus in its failure to recognize this as well as the heavy hand of Rome all around: "Rome was everywhere . . . the great barrier to peace of mind." Jesus's social and historical location, combined with his religious genius, however, linked him to every victim of oppression. Thurman lamented that most interpretations failed to see "what the teachings and life of Jesus had to say to those who stand at a moment in human history, with their back against a wall."[62]

Abraham Smith captures the dual sense of Thurman's thought as rooted in the historical Jesus, and free to see Jesus in every struggle for self-determination. He calls Thurman an "activist-mystic," whose resistance began with the historical Jesus, but flowed from his identification with all of life.[63] He cites Thurman, "Jesus, the underprivileged One of Palestine speaks his words of power and redemption across the ages to all the disinherited."[64] King studied

Thurman's work during the Montgomery bus boycott but surely was familiar with him before that. As noted above, Clark, Hamer, and Cleage also saw their actions in line with the worldly mission of the historical Jesus.

King, Hamer, and others also identified with Paul but not via any scholarship on the historical figure. The "heroic Paul" in the civil rights movement emerges from reading his letters and Acts directly, without distinguishing the authentic letters from the pseudo-Paulines, nor acknowledging that Acts, with its colorful stories, presents an idealized story of the beginning of the church.[65] So while civil rights activists could identify with Paul in his suffering and struggle by reading his letters, they did not worry much about him as a historical figure. In his "Letter from Birmingham Jail," King identified with Paul as one also suffering imprisonment for the sake of the gospel.[66] He invokes the prophets and Paul, "I am in Birmingham because injustice is here. Just as the eighth century prophets left their little villages . . . and just as the apostle Paul left his little village of Tarsus and carried the gospel of Jesus Christ to practically every hamlet and city of the Graeco-Roman world, I too am compelled to carry the gospel of freedom beyond my particular hometown." In "Paul's Letter to American Christians," King writes in Paul's voice and draws on Pauline themes: they belong to the body of Christ, can stand up to persecution, and that in their struggle they battle evil itself.[67]

The Jeremiad

King was the master of the form employed by many African American interpreters, calling the nation to account and urging it toward economic and social justice. Unsurprisingly, King identifies with Amos, one of the most severe of the lot, and often quotes the stunning "Let justice roll down like waters, and righteousness like a mighty stream." The original verse is embedded in a rant, where God expresses his disgust for the hypocrisy of those who rely on religious ritual to rest in God's favor, while neglecting the poor and needy. Regarding their prayers and religious rituals, Amos reports God saying, "I hate, I despise your festivals, and I take no delight in your solemn assemblies. Even though you offer me your burnt offerings and grain offerings, I will not accept them (NRSVue)."[68]

King was heir to a long tradition of African Americans using prophetic thunder to call the country back to its stated ideals, as evidenced in Maria Stewart, Frederick Douglass, and others. Howard-Pitney argues that African Americans considered themselves "a chosen people *within* a chosen people" so their jeremiad tradition addresses *two* American chosen peoples, black and white, whose destinies are woven together.[69] All who share this convention invoke prophetic themes to prick the conscience of white America. Despite their severity, these works share an optimism that white America will actually *care* and can do better.

Taken as a whole, King's work is a grand jeremiad. His *Letter from Birmingham Jail* alone contains all the parts of prophetic critique. Five elements typify the form:

1. It castigates those who claim to be righteous, but for whom it is merely cosmetic, covering over profound injustices. Like Douglass, King shames the churches for their hypocrisy, often observing that 11 o'clock Sunday morning is the most segregated hour in America.[70] Similarly, he calls out those who take the easy path of gradualism or claim to support the movement but do nothing.

2. It condemns society for its abuses. America is so "infected with racism"[71] that "extremism," or "maladjustment is the only answer."[72]

3. It sees change already in play as signs of the times augur a new age. The outbreaks of unrest in cities are "a firebell in the night," and society is "on trial in this troubled hour."[73]

4. It predicts the judgment of God and history. "Showdown for Nonviolence," published shortly after his death, spoke of "polarization" and "the destruction of basic democratic values,"

predicting society could fail and learn "that racism is a sickness unto death."[74] The title of King's last sermon which he was preparing just before his death was "Why America May Go to Hell," extant only in title and some notes.

5. It suggests some hope for reform. A diatribe is pointless unless there is some hope that it will change behavior. A theme of hope for change threads through King's work. The idea of a "dream" or the many visions of a transformed world, often buttressed with biblical images, appears throughout his writings. His last speech, in Memphis, promised, "we, as a people, will get to the Promised Land." The essay "Showdown for Nonviolence," despite its dire predictions, said there was still time to avert disaster, "to write another luminous moral chapter in American history."

Creating a Counter-narrative

While some in the larger society promoted a narrative of white supremacy and others followed a narrative of America as a beacon of opportunity, leaders like King and Hamer created an African American counter-narrative. Disparate biblical verses helped project an image of civil rights workers inhabiting a destiny. Israel's scriptures breath a sense of national destiny in the story of the people of Israel, and King uses their images of journey, of an army on a march, of battle, and of a drama playing out on a broad canvas of history. He talks of "rocky places of frustration" and "meandering points of bewilderment" evoking Israel's trek through Sinai.[75] Key phrases like "the journey," "the freedom road," and "the mountaintop" are forms of synecdoche, evoking whole biblical stories and themes. A residue of meaning adheres to images, even when hearers might not be able to name their original source. Israel had been a small and weak nation, surrounded by the great empires of the Ancient Near East. But residing with them, says the biblical story, is the God of power, who protects the powerless and takes on the cause of the righteous.

King's last, and according to Washington, most radical, SCLC address, "Where Do We Go From Here?" is rife with biblical verses and images. The first two-thirds of the speech lays out the lack of equal access for African Americans to health care, education, and employment, underscoring the continuing need for nonviolent revolution. He references economist John Kenneth Galbraith and union organizer Walter Ruether, commenting on the Watts riots of 1965 and the Castro takeover of Cuba. Not until he moves toward his conclusion does he begin to sprinkle his speech with biblical references. Affirming his commitment to nonviolence, he says, "I have decided to stick to love . . . And the beautiful thing is that we are moving against wrong when we do it, because John was right, God is love. He who hates does not know God, but he who has love has the key that unlocks the door to the meaning of ultimate reality."[76] By this point in time, King and nonviolence have come under criticism for their inability to effect change and playing into the hands of white society.

King ramps up the sermonic quality of the speech with more references, even asking, "if you will let me be a preacher for just a little bit." He cites the story of Nicodemus coming to Jesus by night as proof that isolated actions do not work. King says, "So instead of just getting bogged down in one thing [i.e. avoiding a particular sin], Jesus looked at him and said, 'Nicodemus, you must be born again!'"[77] The biblical framing allows King to move into his theme of "divine dissatisfaction." King uses a common rhetorical strategy among early Jewish and Christian interpreters of seizing on a single word and turning it upside down. He uses "dissatisfied," a word normally denoting mild discontent and unhappiness, and makes it a virtue. He punctuates a list of America's ills with "let us be dissatisfied" and calls for change. The rhythmic refrain repeats twelve times, starting with the injustices of the day, "Let us be dissatisfied until America will no longer have a high blood pressure of creeds and an anemia of deeds," mentioning poverty, segregation, and despair. He links the legal injustices of the time to a biblical vision, "Let us be dissatisfied until every state capitol houses a governor who will do justly, who will love mercy, and who will walk humbly with his God."[78] He multiplies the biblical images, "Let us be dissatisfied until from every city hall, justice will roll down like waters and righteousness like a mighty stream." "Let us be dissatisfied until that day when the lion and the lamb shall lie down together" and "every man will sit under his own vine and fig tree and none shall be afraid." "Let us be dissatisfied. And men will recognize that out of one blood God made all men to dwell upon the face of the earth."[79] He returns in the last sentence to the disagreement within his own community at the time between Black Power advocates and his own nonviolent philosophy, saying, "Let us be dissatisfied until that day when nobody will shout 'White Power!'—when nobody will shout 'Black Power!'—but everybody will talk about God's power and human power."

As he pulls verses out of their own contexts to borrow their authority and impose a coherency, King emulates other classical preaching traditions. The ancient preachers of Jewish tradition, the rabbis, created the classical form of *midrash,* fusing narrative and commentary.[80] Much of King's material comes out of preaching traditions of the African American Baptist church, which he combines with his education in liberal Protestant theology. Kenyatta Gilbert shows his debt to the preachers from the period of the Great Migration in the early twentieth century.[81] At some undefined juncture, the method makes a poetic leap, from mere exegesis to literature, from commentary to poetry. The leap from exegesis to literature was partly a function of King's dramatic oral delivery, what one scholar calls his "poetic sorcery."[82] In this speech, too, King brings his mélange of references to a hopeful climax, finally imagining "We Shall Overcome" as a reality.

A Civil Rights Hermeneutic

Biblical interpretation helped power the mid-twentieth-century civil rights movement. A counter-narrative to more dominant social narratives, with its apocalyptic and jeremiadic tropes, identification with Jesus, Paul, and the prophets, it represents a distinctive strain within reception history of the Bible, employing many of the same processes that engaged early Jews and Christians.

A Canon within a Canon

Civil rights preachers and teachers developed their own "canon within a canon." The number of verses and images from the biblical text that continually surface is relatively small, appearing in the work of all three of the people of this chapter—Exodus imagery, the inauguration of Jesus's ministry via the citation of Isaiah in Luke 4:18–19, one blood doctrine from Acts 17:26, and assorted verses that predict divine justice will prevail. By taking control of the text, speakers assume the Bible's authority for themselves. These texts become the chords of spoken and sung protest, as instantly recognizable as the first chords of a familiar rock song. Any verse can function as synecdoche, reminding hearers of a whole body of texts that support their aims. Every group that claims Scripture invariably develops such a mini canon, naturally raising the stature of some writings.

The immediate effect of this smaller canon is to undermine other material and neutralize competing, racist uses of Scripture. For example, George Timmerman, the segregationist governor of South Carolina, put forth a weak argument from silence in the immediate wake of the Supreme Court decision on *Brown v. Board of Education*, "Nowhere in my Bible does forcing little children in their formative years to mix with other races seem to me to be an application of the Golden Rule."[83] By contrast, the "one blood" verse from Acts 17 implicitly rejected Black inferiority, and had been used since the days of slavery to refute "the curse of Ham," interpretation of Genesis 9. Powery and Sadler remark that in the days of slavery, a "communal hermeneutics of suspicion" inoculated African Americans from taking seriously apparent proslavery statements of Paul (or Deutero-Paul).[84] Similarly, preachers and speakers during the civil rights era simply ignored material not useful to them. As Mitzi Smith says of African American interpretation in general, "the biblical text is not synonymous with God . . . critical engagement with the Scriptures could involve a resistance to and/or a rejection of some biblical texts and yet leave 'my Jesus' intact."[85]

Proof-texting

King and Hamer in particular engage in a practice called "proof-texting," plucking individual verses from all over the Bible to "prove" the truth of their statements and the course of the movement. By design, these verses are out of context. When Fannie Lou Hamer predicts the defeat of their enemies and cites, "Whoso diggeth a pit shall fall therein; and he that rolleth a stone, it will return upon him,"[86] she is unconcerned with its original context. As Scripture it is a touchstone of truth. This method appears throughout rabbinic and patristic literature, as well as in the New Testament. Jesus was a proof-texter, as Mark 7: 1–10 shows. Proof-texting allows its user to borrow the authority of Scripture for one's own experience and to situate oneself within the broad sweep of divine history.

Midrash

Rabbinic interpretation of Scripture is both a general and a technical term that encompasses the multiple creative ways that the ancient rabbis made sense of their lives by linking their reality to the biblical text. Strictly speaking, the term applies to a particular body of works that employ specific categories and methods.[87] Employing wordplay, parables, stories, and a raft of creative methods, the results often range far afield from the supposed "plain meaning" as it weaves together text, interpretation, and experience. African American interpreters shared with this ancient form a grounding in the authority of the biblical text, an imaginative approach that stretched textual boundaries, mutual reinforcement of text and experience, and a performative, oral context.

Looking at a well-known text from the rabbis, *Mishnah Sanhedrin* 4.5 shows an exegetical journey that begins with the question of how to warn witnesses in capital cases, where the death penalty is a possible outcome. It wends its way through different topics and pulls up verses from Genesis, Leviticus, and Proverbs, transmitting sayings, expounding on rabbinic values of the dignity of every individual life, the equality of all humanity because of shared descent from Adam, a recoiling from polytheism, the need to punish murderers, and God's uniqueness, finally returning to remind the reader of the seriousness of capital cases. Tethering themselves to the biblical text, the rabbis preserve earlier voices, provide a record of a long-running engagement with the text, and hark back to earlier oral performance.

Civil rights thinkers also engaged text in an associative way. Biblical verses were mined from all over the text to create a narrative that addressed their own experiences. The sermons of Hamer and King are similarly layered, preserving biblical interpretations coming out of the community, linking them to their current challenges, encapsulating their values, and preserving in writing many early sayings.

Orality and Performance

In spite of the term "Scriptures" (meaning "writings") and the notion of the Bible as a book, biblical narratives and traditions began as orally transmitted stories, and function within the civil rights movement as oral performance. While many of the speeches are written, their power resides in their performance before communities, church meetings, mass voter registration rallies, or televised broadcasts on the nightly news.

The precise origins of both the biblical materials and the earliest African American biblical interpretations are lost to us in part because of their oral and communal nature, some going back to the days of slavery and Reconstruction. We cannot say who first used Luke's call to prophetic ministry: "the spirit of the Lord is upon me," or Acts assertion that "God hath made of one blood all nations." Like the biblical narratives themselves, the interpretations are rooted in oral traditions, are very old, and cannot be pinned down. The biblical text is nomadic, wandering into different places and times and making itself useful.[88] We see wandering traditions in the Bible itself, in the two creation narratives of Gen. 1 and 2, or more clearly in the story of the defeat of Sisera by Deborah and Yael in Judges 4 and 5, told in two different versions in narrative and poetry. The antiquity of the Bible itself and the antiquity of its uses in enslaved people's narratives, spirituals, and self-understanding impart an idea that this movement is playing out on a grand scale.

Authority of Experience

Finally, the intimate relationship between the experiences of those in the fight for social justice with the biblical text further cements the authority of their own experience. Identifying with people who put their bodies on the line for the right means, these are not mere exegetical exercises. The prophets Jesus, Paul, and Samson suffer persecution and worldly defeats. Hamer and King, both imprisoned for their actions, see themselves in the Apostle Paul, imprisoned and beaten, but rejoicing in his suffering.[89] They live out two narratives simultaneously—the earthly, immediate one and the larger cosmic one where truth wrestles the powers of evil.

Two strands of narrative, the scriptural and the experiential, constantly interpret one another. As with any group that inhabits the text, civil rights activists treated the text as something alive that spoke to their own experience and wrested forth meaning from its words. They took control of the Bible, reversing the situation in the debates over slavery a hundred years before. Proslavery people had material close at hand (though some bizarre interpretations). Abolitionists had more of an uphill battle and resorted to some maneuvers like "the seed growing secretly." But by the mid-twentieth century, the segregationists did not use the Bible effectively or often, resorting more often to a states' rights approach, protesting federal meddling in their "way of life." Predicting the judgment of God and history, no one was certain how it would finally unfold. The title of King's last sermon "Why America May Go to Hell," unwritten and never given, remains an open question.

The civil rights hermeneutic is part of a long and varied reception history of the Bible, from the New Testament and other early literature's appropriation of the Hebrew Bible, through the rabbis, the church fathers, Luther, and on. It continues in contemporary contexts, especially Two-Third's World interpretations, where communities take back texts, overturn received interpretations, and interpret in light of their own experiences.[90]

CHAPTER 5

Contemporary Progressive Movements

MANY REFORM MOVEMENTS today do not use religious themes but argue directly from the principles of human rights, particularly the Universal Declaration of Human Rights, adopted by the UN General Assembly in 1948. The Bible is less the *lingua franca* of American reform, especially as groups want to acknowledge the multiplicity of different religious and nonreligious members of society as they fight on multiple fronts to address human trafficking, prison reform, climate change, food insecurity, racial inequities, immigration justice, and more. Yet the Bible remains a vibrant resource for a surprising number of reformers; the number of biblically inflected initiatives are too numerous to include in one chapter. Here are just a few from Jewish, Protestant, Catholic perspectives.

Just as the four historical movements discussed in earlier chapters were intertwined and drew from each other's wells of thought, contemporary reform movements are deeply embedded with one another. Tarana Burke honed her thought in civil rights and labor movements and her founding of MeToo began focused on the vulnerability of Black and brown girls in particular. The work of Repairers of the Breach addresses a panoply of moral imperatives, including voting rights, poverty, immigration justice, and LGBTQ+ rights. The Jewish group T'ruah also takes on a host of human rights initiatives, including antisemitism and worker justice. Hillary Clinton told us, "human rights are women's rights and women's rights are human rights."[1] The saying could be expanded many times to include every marginalized person's rights. Human rights are immigrants' rights, poor people's rights, incarcerated people's rights, and more.

Many contemporary movements quite consciously draw on the legacies of earlier reformers. Repairers of the Breach invokes mid-twentieth-century civil-rights activists, citing Martin Luther King and using the earlier label "Poor People's Campaign." T'ruah points to Abraham Joshua Heschel's broad-based involvement in multiple struggles, including civil rights, anti-Vietnam, and anti-nuclear movements. These groups are not throwbacks, however, merely imitating earlier groups. No one wants to replicate the male-dominated leadership of the civil rights movement, nor the racism and nativism of some first wave feminists and temperance leaders. Nor can they assume everyone will respond to biblical language. American society includes people of many religions and no religion on equal footing.

Rooting social reform work in religious traditions has explicit benefits, as these groups make clear. Religious affiliation is a hedge against despair. The seeming impossibility of making a difference in eradicating poverty and racism or changing the trajectory of climate change seems so intractable that one is tempted to despair. But the long history of Judaism and Christianity turns up many challenges faced and injustices overcome. Not surprisingly, the Exodus story shows up in the language of both early reformers and contemporary ones. Its story of liberation from seemingly hopeless conditions of injustice shows that God upholds the oppressed. A tongue-tied, reluctant leader, under God's direction, leads the suffering masses to freedom. Furthermore, religious voices have always been part of our national narrative (as the four earlier groups make clear) and progressive religious voices need to be heard. Evangelicals, a varied and frequently stereotyped group, are cited as having an outsize effect on presidential and lower-level politics. Progressive voices need to strive for more influence. Finally, the cherished principle of separation of church and state is not confounded by people speaking from religious conviction. The first line of the First Amendment not only rejects the establishment of a state religion, but also guarantees freedom of religious expression.

MeToo

Activist Tarana Burke started the MeToo movement when she posted the phrase to MySpace in 2006. A survivor of sexual assault as a child, she worked to empower Black and brown girls and to publicize the prevalence of sexual violence in society. Eleven years later, Burke reported that she was initially jarred by the response to actor Alyssa Milano's tweet on October 15, 2017, inviting anyone who had been sexually harassed or assaulted to reply with the words "me too." Thousands responded on social media to #MeToo with their own stories, leading to an unveiling of the prevalence of sexual assault, a raised awareness, and open discussion. Today, most people recognize Burke's significance as the founder of the movement, as well as its evolution because of Milano's tweet and the enormous reaction to it. The work continues on several fronts, with many people at work to make society safer for women and girls.

The #MeToo movement is not a religious one, but Burke's own story is laced with religious language and her own love of the Bible. When she experienced her second sexual attack at age eleven, she prayed and experienced her own power to resist:

> As I felt him [the attacker] struggle to loosen my belt, I knew God was answering my call. He yanked hard, causing him to stumble back and hit my cast [after surgery on her foot]. I screamed at the top of my lungs. I screamed the way I had always wanted to scream in that nasty, dark little room. I screamed for every moment he ever laid a hand on me. I screamed like I was jolted out of a nightmare. I screamed for seven-year-old me [when she was raped], who wouldn't . dare scream.

Her fear evaporated, and her assailant ran away.[2] But because of her vulnerability and fear for herself and her family, she kept silent, her secrets carried "in the vast cemetery I carried in my soul."[3]

The Bible is a companion in her struggles, despite her seeing its uses by others to support slavery, racism, sexism, and other forms of oppression. When she experienced flashbacks of her own experience of sexual assault and was tortured by memories and feelings of failure to help other survivors, she begged God for help, and opened her Bible. She read the story of Ruth, "a symbol of loyalty and devotion," going over it several times. Then flipping through and landing on Psalm 139, she was comforted by the words of v. 1, "You searched me O' Lord, and You know me (NIV)." Finally, she experienced a sense of purpose in all her suffering,

> How different would it all be if I just had a little bit more courage? How could I find it if I didn't know what it looked like? Maybe Heaven [a young survivor] had courage because she had me. Maybe community creates courage? What if courage creates community? Maybe empathy creates courage? How can you express empathy towards others if you can't empathize with yourself? Is the core of healing empathy and courage? ... The questions were coming faster than the flashbacks now, but so were the answers ... I searched around for a blank piece of paper ... I wanted to capture this while it was coming ... I opened the pad and at the top of the page I wrote two words. me too.[4]

Burke suddenly felt called to leave Selma and expand her work, to use her empathy and courage to help girls of color who had suffered sexual exploitation. She considered this a profound knowledge of God's plan for her, causing one salesclerk to observe, "you walk like you got an anointing on you."[5] Burke has continued to found and serve advocacy groups that focus on programs for young women of color. "I'm the kind of Christian that recognizes who Jesus was—and Jesus was the first activist that I knew, and the first organizer that I knew, and the first example of how to be in service to people."[6] In an interview with *The 19th*, Burke reflects on the shift in communal responsibility around gender and sexual violence and its importance as a social-justice issue. She notes the many people who work on many fronts to make the country safer: "there should be many, many courses of action at this point because the problem is just too big... I always use cigarettes as my example. We used to be able to smoke everywhere. It took multiple interventions [communal, legal, educational] for us to be able to shift that."[7]

The #MeToo movement has opened up space to talk about the role of biblical narratives in normalizing or trivializing sexual exploitation of women, a topic explored by Johanna Stiebert in *Rape Myths, the Bible, and #MeToo*. Stiebert reads the Bible in tandem with the narratives coming out of the #MeToo movement, looking at stories of gendered sexual violence. While respecting the differences of time and place in the two sets of texts, she outlines similarities between biblical stories of violation and #MeToo narratives in that they are predominantly (with some exceptions) about men harming women, revealing a significant power differential between the perpetrators and survivors of sexual violence. Biblical stories are different, however, in that they give no voice to the victims of violence, and they appear in texts that have been canonized and revered for centuries.[8] As such, interpreters may go to great lengths to sanitize the biblical stories, to make them seem "not that bad."

Several examples of outright rape appear in the Hebrew Bible, including the rape of Dinah by Shechem in Genesis, who "seized her and lay with her by force," the rape of Tamar by her half-brother Amnon in 2 Samuel, and the gang rape of an unnamed concubine in Judges.[9] The theologizing voice of the narrative clearly disapproves of these actions, not always because of the violation of the women, but because of the trampling of men's rights, or in the case of Amnon, because he commits incest. The laws of Deuteronomy 21:10–14 seem to assume rape allowable, as do the stories of the abduction of young women in Judges 21.

More insidious are the narratives where rape is invisible or submerged in the lack of agency or consent of women. When Sarah is passed off as Abraham's sister in Gen. 12 and 20, the text assumes she is available for sexual possession, "taken into Pharaoh's house," and "the woman you have taken," whom the king just happens to have not yet "approached." When the enslaved Hagar is handed over to Abraham to bear a child for him and is mistreated by Sarah in Gen. 16, is any consent even possible? Is there any redress for her abuse? Stiebert notes that the verb "afflicted" or "mistreated" carries a sense of sexual aggression in the Bible.[10] When David sends for Bathsheba "to get her" and "lays with her" in 2 Sam 11, is there any chance of consent or choice? The text declines to tell us. David's power is assumed, and Nathan's parable denoting David's crime also assumes the sin, and therefore control, are entirely David's. In all these cases, the women are at the mercy of powerful men, and their own agency is not there.

The prophets, for all that they are moral voices in other ways, often use women as ugly metaphors for unfaithful Israel or Jerusalem. The women are often oversexed, exhibitionist, and deserving the punishment meted out by their husbands and God. The "wife of whoredom" of Hosea suffers physical abuse in chapter 2 before she is returned to her husband, just as Israel suffers before being reconciled with God. Jerusalem is depicted as a wanton woman, showing her beauty to the world in Isaiah 3:16–23, who will be shamed and impoverished. Ezekiel 16 similarly depicts the nation as a whoring wife who suffers her husband's (God's) fury and abuse before being restored. Such stories help sustain a "rape culture" in our own society, according to Stiebert, where sexual violence becomes normalized, and victims are not heard. Because of the Bible's authority, they exert an influence that becomes part of a wider community and its discourses.[11] Sacred texts are not always safe spaces.[12] Confronting, identifying, and resisting damaging texts, however, can be a step toward self-empowerment and healing.[13]

Pastor and survivor Ruth Everhart engages in empowering interpretation in confronting her own experiences within her Presbyterian church as she calls on people of faith to embrace the reckoning of the #MeToo movement. She calls out the Bible's ideologies and lacunae that shore up a patriarchy that winks at sexual assault against women.

Inspired by #MeToo, Everhart also culls the biblical texts for models and narratives to empower survivors and communities to stand up to sexual violence. She is unsparing in calling her own Presbyterian church to account for its failures in accountability: victim-blaming, protection of abusers in the name of healing, and calls to "move on," all a form of "cheap grace."[14]

Everhart alternates stories of her own and others' experiences of sexual assault and inadequate institutional response with biblical stories that provide insight and models of resistance to injustice. She recounts her own sexual harassment by a senior pastor and the church's rush to minimize her experience and protect the perpetrator. As counter to the devaluing of her suffering, Everhart looks to the stories of Jesus's valuing of women's bodies and seeing them as daughters, as he heals the woman with chronic gynecological bleeding (whom he calls "daughter") and Jairus's daughter.[15] In another case, when a youth group leader was discovered to have abused a young boy, the initial response was to keep quiet and deal with it as a unique case, eroding the health of the community. Everhart understands this instance through Paul's metaphor of the body of Christ in 1 Corinthians, where he shows that the church is a living body, a body she suggests with an immune system to protect it. The secrecy and inaction had allowed the illness to fester in the body of the church.[16] When the name of the abuser was finally revealed two years later, other victims came forward, victims who might have been spared had the church responded openly.

Rape culture and purity culture provide the backdrop for Everhart's interpretation of the David and Bathsheba story.[17] The former teaches that a woman who "loses" her virginity, including by way of rape, is less valuable or damaged goods. But women somehow become responsible for men's actions by being seductive. The latter idea says that men rape because they can, but women open themselves up to it by being attractive. The two ideas, she argues, support one another, "and both labels, saint and slut, assume a central tenet of both purity culture and rape culture: that women are somehow responsible for the male gaze."[18] Everhart mentions some interpretations of the story she heard growing up, that Bathsheba was complicit because of her beauty and her bathing on her roof.[19] But the text tells us nothing of Bathsheba's motives or knowledge of anyone's presence. Her only act of volition is to inform the palace when she finds herself pregnant.

The text clearly finds David responsible, as the prophet Nathan accuses him alone. The parable of the rich man stealing and slaughtering the poor man's one ewe lamb shows David alone is guilty of murder, deceit, and theft. While the narrative assumes the woman "belongs" to her husband and David is trampling *his* rights, a less-than-acceptable idea to us, it does not wholly endorse purity culture and rape culture, "By naming David's sin as theft, he doesn't name it as a sexual sin, the paradigm commonly applied to Bathsheba's story."[20] Indeed, as sexual predator David steals from Uriah by taking his wife, and from Bathsheba, not only her autonomy, but in the end her husband and baby. David at least is called to account, admits his guilt, and is punished. Such is not always the case with today's predators.[21] The Bible is complicit in injecting stories of sexual violence into our Western cultural narrative and giving them staying power. Yet it contains liberating tropes that can be used to resist the injustice of sexual violence and restore a sense of agency to survivors.

T'ruah, Dayenu, and Jewish Advocacy

A plethora of Jewish groups address contemporary social concerns—immigrants' rights, hunger and poverty, climate change, LGBTQ+ inclusion, racism, antisemitism, and more. Nearly every synagogue includes some kind of social action advocacy or aid group. While many of today's initiatives have a general sense of performing Jewish values, often invoking the term "Tikkun Olam," repair of the world, or citing "Justice, justice you shall pursue,"[22] several groups ground themselves more deeply in biblical law and narrative, engaging in interpretation of specific verses and consulting rabbinic and other later Jewish commentators. The ancient rabbis in particular concerned themselves with the nitty-gritty of daily life, including the treatment of their neighbors who fell into poverty, the use of scarce resources, and dealing with hostile or indifferent authorities.

Abraham Joshua Heschel (1907–1972) provided a prime model for today's activists, bringing protest and advocacy into the Jewish mainstream. Descended from a Hasidic dynasty of rabbis, he also studied philosophy and art history in Berlin, and suffered the loss of most of his family in the Holocaust. He fused intellectualism, deep commitment to traditional Judaism, and the mandate to involve oneself in the pressing moral issues of the day. Many know him from the famous photograph of him locked arm in arm with Martin Luther King and others marching for civil rights from Selma to Montgomery in March of 1965, of which Heschel famously said, "I felt my feet were praying." Like King, Heschel was frustrated with liberal incrementalist approaches to racism and declared "racism is Satanism, unmitigated evil."[23] Yet Heschel involved himself in multiple movements: joining a group of rabbis marching in Washington in 1943 to try to force the US government to do more for Jews trapped in Europe, protesting the treatment of Soviet Jewry, working to further Jewish-Catholic relations and help bring forth *Nostra Aetate*, and opposing the war in Vietnam, even asking Henry Kissinger point blank how he, as a good Jew, could prosecute the war. He responded to the "immense silent agony in the world."[24]

T'ruah is the name of one of the notes sounded on the shofar at Rosh ha Shanah, the act of calling Israel back to God. Fusing the Torah's respect for human dignity and equality, the ideals of democracy, and human rights, the group by that name was founded in 2002 when it separated from Rabbis for Human Rights-North America. It trains and joins together the voices of over 2,300 rabbis and cantors to address a spectrum of human rights issues, including human trafficking, immigration rights, mass incarceration and solitary confinement, and mistreatment of Palestinians in the occupied territories. They have mounted public protests against policies like the Muslim ban or the separation of families of asylum seekers and joined with the Immokalee Workers in South Florida to stop forced labor and low wages. The group protested to cut off funding from US nonprofits that filtered down to violent nationalist groups in Israel. Affirming a two sovereign state solution of Israel and Palestine, they fought home demolitions and annexation of Palestinian lands.

Rabbi Jill Jacobs, the founder of T'ruah, studied for the rabbinate at the Jewish Theological Seminary, the same institution where Heschel taught decades earlier. Like Heschel, she fuses the study of sacred texts with social justice activism. She argues that the laws and narratives of the Bible inform one another, and that law, the traditional focus of rabbinic studies, reveals the values and vision of an ideal society. One of her signal texts is Deuteronomy 15:4–11, which yields a rich set of values for economic and social justice.

> There shall be no needy among you—since your God Adonai will bless you in the land that your God Adonai is giving you as a hereditary portion—if only you heed your God Adonai and take care to keep all this Instruction that I enjoin upon you this day. For your God Adonai will bless you as promised; you will extend loans to many nations, but require none yourself; you will dominate many nations, but they will not dominate you. If, however, there is a needy person among you, one of your kin [*achika*, your brother] in any of your settlements in the land that your God Adonai is giving you, do not harden your heart and shut your hand against your needy kin. Rather, you must open your hand and lend whatever is sufficient to meet the need. Beware lest you harbor the base thought, "The seventh year, the year of the remission [sabbatical], is approaching," so that you are mean and give nothing to your needy kin—who will cry out to Adonai against you and you will incur guilt. Give readily and have no regrets when you do so, for in return your God Adonai will bless you in all your efforts and in all your undertakings. For there will never cease to be needy ones in your land, which is why I command you: open your hand to the poor and the needy kin in your land (The Contemporary Torah, JPS, 2006).

The passage rests on the principle of the dignity of the poor person. She notes the implication of the Hebrew word *achika*, "your brother," for one of the family. People living in comfort are tempted to see the poor as different from themselves, perhaps even deserving their situation because of their own decisions or habits, an approach that shields the fortunate from the realization that they too could become poor. This text insists on every human's dignity as made in the image of God, a member of the community whose fate is intertwined with every other community member. Rabbinic material too tends to treat poverty as temporary, a state that a person falls into because of circumstances, not something that defines their essence.

Jacobs notes the seeming contradiction of v. 4, "there shall be no needy among you," and v. 11, "for there will never cease to be needy ones in your land," reconciling it by way of the medieval Spanish commentator Ramban (Rabbi Moshe ben Nachman). The first verse anticipates a perfected world when Israel obeys the commandments perfectly, while the second verse recognizes that such perfection is not the state of the world as we know it. Jacobs reflects on the apparent tension today between short-term anti-poverty measures like soup kitchens or homeless shelters versus working for systemic change so that such programs will not be necessary. It is a false choice, according to the text, as she explains, "The Deuteronomic response to this debate is a refusal to take sides, or better, an insistence on both."[25] People need hot meals today and long-term economic and food security. The *sh'mitah*, or sabbatical year in which all debts are canceled, might tempt the wealthier members of a community to stop lending to the poorer members as the year approaches. The text forbids this pulling back. The routine cancelation of debts, Jacobs argues, temporarily narrows the gap between rich and poor, and may help the richer to adopt less cautious attitudes toward lending. They may realize that this "starting over" and wiping out debts does not threaten their lives, and may improve them.[26]

Jacobs gleans many more insights than can be mentioned here. From study and interpretation of this one passage, guided by rabbinic codes and commentaries, she articulates seven principles of Jewish economic law, the bedrock of Jewish social justice work. They appear here slightly abridged:

1. The world and everything in it belongs to God; human beings come upon wealth only by chance and do not necessarily "deserve" their wealth or possessions.
2. The fates of the wealthy and poor are inextricably linked.
3. Corrective measures are necessary to prevent some people from becoming exceedingly rich at the expense of others.
4. Even the poorest member of society possesses inherent dignity; each member of the community is responsible for preserving the dignity of others.
5. The responsibility for poverty relief is an obligation, not a choice.
6. Strategies for poverty relief must balance short-term and long-term needs.
7. The eradication of poverty is an essential part of bringing about a perfected world, and each person has an obligation to work toward the creation of that world.[27]

The idea of being commanded to uphold human dignity and show communal responsibility informs T'ruah's many programs to change public policy. The group also stresses the importance of the local, taking care of one's own workplace, synagogue, city, and state. Similarly, the quest to humanize one's own immediate place undergirds Abraham Unger's *A Jewish Public Theology*. Unger looks to biblical and rabbinic values to create a Jewish theology that informs policies for towns and cities. In his chapter, "Cities That Believe," he argues for programs that recognize the sanctity of the individual, the socializing role of the family, and the public justice role of the city, noting the Talmudic principle, "the poor of your own city come before the poor of another city" (B. Meṣ. 71a). Programs that allow parents to be home to help children with homework or initiatives that resist gentrification put human values over corporate ones. Prioritizing local needs, seeing the building of community as a sacred task, and exercising stewardship allow individuals to create and thrive, seeing the person "not simply as an economic contestant, but a creature uniquely endowed with a piece of Divinity."[28]

Dayenu

Rabbi Jennie Rosenn founded Dayenu in 2020 to respond to the climate crisis with "spiritual audacity and bold political action."[29] Its name comes from a song sung at the Passover seder, which shows gratitude for God's many gifts and salvation with the word *dayenu*, "it would have been enough." But for this group the name also means "we have had enough"—of degradation of the planet and delay in finding solutions, but also "we have enough—we have what we need to transform our world." The group attracts people in different stages of life and diverse parts of the Jewish community. It also emphasizes local organizing, "dayenu circles" for action at the grassroots level. "Spiritual audacity" echoes the words of Abraham Joshua Heschel on the prophets, who spoke of "moral grandeur and spiritual audacity."[30]

A distinguishing feature of this group is its attention to the psychological needs of those who work for justice, helping to develop "spiritual courage" to stave off fatalism or feelings of powerlessness. Rosenn asks, "how can our souls and psyches bear such a painful possibility?" People need the support of a deep and spiritually rooted movement. A pillar of their work is its grounding in Jewish values, wisdom, and tradition. Torah study on sources related to the environment is part of training and organizing. Rosenn in her talk "Speak Torah to Power" notes that the climate crisis embodies nearly all other crises, economic, racial, and social, and is the ultimate social justice issue. She notes the multiple biblically rooted Jewish values that fire the movement, *shomrei adamah* (guarding the earth), *bacharta chaim* (choosing life), *shomer ger, yatom, valmanah* (protecting the stranger, orphan, and widow, i.e., the vulnerable).[31]

On December 15, 2022, Dayenu issued a major report to encourage the Jewish community to withdraw investments from fossil fuel industries, "'With All Our Might': How the Jewish Community Can Invest in a Just Livable Future."[32] In Deuteronomy 6:5, we are commanded to "love the Lord your God with your whole soul, with your whole heart, and with your whole might." The report notes that "might" is interpreted by some ancient rabbis to mean money or possessions. The report identifies the total amount of Jewish institutional investments and the percentage that supports fossil fuel industries. It calls on the four Jewish denominations, Jewish federations, and foundations to screen out such industries from their investments and to move their money to green energy initiatives.

Repairers of the Breach/Poor Peoples' Campaign

The movement Repairers of the Breach (ROTB), launched in 2015 by Rev. Dr. William J. Barber II, employs the language of moral regeneration to address a spectrum of social justice crises. Its name draws on Isaiah 58:12, "your ancient ruins shall be rebuilt; you shall raise up the foundations of many generations; you shall be called the repairer of the breach, the restorer of streets to live in (NRSVue)." Isaiah 58 as a whole depicts a God disgusted with outward piety and performance of religious ritual by a people who neglect the poor and suffering around them, but promises a renewal when they turn to caring for others. Consciously linking itself to Martin Luther King, ROTB calls for a Third Reconstruction to follow the nineteenth-century rebuilding after the civil war and the twentieth-century civil rights movement—this reconstruction enclosing multiple issues and welcoming diverse groups, what its members often call a "moral fusion" movement.[33]

The principles articulated in the 2016 document "Higher Ground Moral Declaration: A Call to Action for a Moral Agenda" are prefaced by King's call for "a revolution in values" from his 1967 speech at Riverside Church, followed by citation of Jewish, Muslim, and Christian scriptures, Isaiah 58:9b–12, Qu'ran Sura 9:71, and Luke 4:18–19. Listing its aims as "the deepest public concerns of our faith," it includes treatment of the poor and marginalized, pro-labor, anti-poverty, and anti-racist policies, equality in education, healthcare for all, fairness in the criminal justice system, voting rights, women's rights, LGBTQ+ rights, labor rights, religious freedom, immigrant's rights, and equal protection under the law. A section entitled "Moral Grounding in Scripture and Our Founding Creed" cites Micah 6:8 and Proverbs 31:9, along with excerpts from the Declaration of Independence and the Constitution.[34] Like King, the movement draws on religious scripture, but also treats the founding documents as a form of sacred text for civic society.

The Poor People's Campaign (PPC), coanchored by ROTB and the Kairos Center for Religious Rights and Social Justice, sees itself as the continuation of the 1968 movement of the same name, the brainchild of Marion Wright and King (who was assassinated a month before the protest). Today's campaign amplifies the idea of the poor and marginalized as leaders in the movement to restore the nation. PPC retains its religious moorings but stresses the multi-faith, multicultural nature of its constituents. Barber calls for the joining of many hands: "hands that once picked cotton, Latino, progressive whites, farm laborers, Asian, Native American, poor, wealthy with a conscience, gay, straight, trans, Christian, Jewish, Muslim, Hindu, Buddhist. When we all get together we are an instrument of redemption. And when we join hands we can revive and make sure that the power of life, liberty, and happiness and equal protection under the law is never taken away from anybody."[35]

Like Jewish advocacy groups, ROTB and PPC look to Deuteronomy's laws of economic distribution, cancelation of debt, the manumission of slaves, and communal support for the poor and vulnerable. Bible scholar and minister Rick Lowery expands this to identify "the moral heart of the Torah" embedded in all five books, citing the love for the immigrant, the Exodus story, and the implications of the Sabbath in Genesis 2 and in the ten commandments.[36] "There is a double significance to sabbath. First it underlines the broader significance of the creation narrative that God creates a world of abundance, where there is enough for everyone to survive and thrive. We get seven days of wealth for six days of work. This abundance frees us to share, to live lives of generosity, unconstrained by fear and obsessive acquisition. Second, it completes the radical proposal a few verses earlier in the story that all human beings are created 'as the image of God in the world.'"[37]

Similarly, Liz Theoharis, a Presbyterian minister and cochair of the PPC, zeroes in on Deuteronomy 15:11 in her book, *We Cry Justice*, "When Jesus says, 'the poor you will always have with you,' he is quoting Deuteronomy 15, which says there will be no poor person among you if you follow God's commandments to forgive debts, to release slaves, pay fair wages, and lend without worrying about being repaid."[38] In the same volume, educator Solita Alexander Riley looks at the cancelation of debt in Deuteronomy 15 as a structural safeguard against excessive debt, describing how today's economic practices result in families crushed by debt, the opposite of "God's economy." She combines the verse with 2 Corinthians 6, "now is the time," to mean the time to create a world that reflects God's economy where everyone flourishes. A prayer attached to the article addresses God, "you suggest laws to create an economy in which everyone thrives."[39] Behind these laws is an assumption, also mentioned by Jacobs in regard to Jewish interpretation, that poverty should be understood as a temporary state of misfortune remedied by communal safeguards, not a permanent or essential state that defines a person. A speaker for the PPC, identified as Claire in Flint, Michigan, describes the monumental shift today, "At one time, poverty was a temporary condition. You were on a downslope for a minute, but you could bounce back up. We can't bounce back up today. It's permanent. We're not going back to the factory and build cars and trucks like we once did."[40]

The New Testament carries its own directives to care for the poor, most fundamentally by understanding Jesus as not only a poor man but a leader of a moral movement made up of the poor and rejected. The preponderance of misfits and outsiders as God's agents in the Scriptures, professes Barber in a sermon at the National Cathedral in Washington in 2018, means "God uses the rejected to lead the moral revival of nations."[41] Theoharis reminds us that Jesus's ministry, as described by Luke, begins with his mission, harking back to the prophet Isaiah's anointing, to bring good news to the poor, release of captives, sight to the blind, freedom for the oppressed.[42] Passages Like Matthew 25, with its parables about handling resources, the Sermon on the Mount, and sayings about the birds of the air and the lilies of the field show Jesus as a teacher, embedded in the experience of poverty, but reassuring his flock of God's care.[43] Theoharis notes the adopting of a simple life style and rejection of the value of wealth situated his followers in the Kingdom of God, in direct opposition to the Roman empire and the grossly inequitable distribution of wealth in first-century society. Early Christ followers appropriated liberatory themes from the Hebrew Bible and presented a model that valued labor and distributed it fairly. Laborers appear throughout the New Testament—fishers, tentmakers, dyers of cloth, carpenters—"it affirms the dignity and worth of people who have to work to survive. It affirms that the intention in the Kingdom of God is to have community flourishing and prosperity for all, from the bottom up."[44] She notes examples like Paul's collection for the poor,[45] the Feeding of the 5000 [and 4000], and the ideal of holding all good in common in Acts 2 and 4 to indicate an ethos that valued communal survival and support over self-interest and accumulation of wealth. One could add the many themes that decry wealth as inimical to the kingdom of God—the rich young man, woes against the rich, and the rich man and Lazarus.[46]

Biblical rootedness provides sustenance and hope in the frequently disheartening fight for justice. Theoharis's edited work *We Cry Justice*, contains fifty-three chapters by different activists, clergy, educators, many who wear multiple hats. Suggested for weekly contemplation, each chapter juxtaposes a contemporary example of a social inequity with an explication of a Bible reading applied to that problem, ending with a prayer. The prophets, as always, continue to guide leaders and activists. Activist Stephen Pavey's entry puts remarks by James Baldwin in tandem with the similarly acerbic eighth century BCE prophet Amos. Baldwin says "people have deluded themselves for so long that they really don't think I'm [a Black man] human. . . . And this means that they have become in themselves moral monsters."[47] Pavey cites Amos's denunciation of the wealthy for their hypocrisy, performing religious ritual while blind to the suffering of the powerless and impoverished around them. Amos predicts the end of the northern kingdom in Amos 5:16, "there will be wailing in the streets." Pavey compares it to the wailing of Callie Greer, a PPC organizer, who lost two children, one to gun violence, and one because she lacked insurance to get adequate medical treatment for breast cancer, "You must let me wail for the children I've lost to poverty and will never get back, wail for all the children we mothers have lost. I won't waste my pain. I hope I make you feel uncomfortable. I hope I make you feel angry. I'm wailing because my babies are no more."[48] Another prophetic image springs to mind: Rachel weeping for her children because they are no more.[49]

King's "divine dissatisfaction,"[50] which typified the prophets' view of distribution of material benefits, also applies to real estate and housing. Charon Hribar, a director at the Kairos Center and codirector at the Poor People's Campaign, looks at Isaiah 10:1–2, "Woe to you who pass unjust laws," applying it to laws that encourage landlords to leave properties vacant and blight neighborhoods, while promoting speculation in neighborhoods undergoing gentrification.[51] She cites statistics that show New York City's vacant properties could house the homeless many times over if it weren't more profitable to leave properties empty. Similarly, Aaron Scott looks at the woes aimed at "those who join house to house, who add field to field, until there is no room," in Isaiah 5:8–10 to decry the destruction of homeless encampments in Aberdeen, Washington. Like the prophet, Scott underlines the hypocrisy involved. While public works statements cloak their actions in words like "eyesore" or "public nuisance," homeless watch their meager shelter of tents and shacks razed by bulldozers.[52]

Like other groups, ROTB and PPC draw on the tropes of the Exodus narrative, as the very term "liberation" and the focus of concern for whole groups of people carries the tone of God's rescue of the oppressed from Egyptian servitude under a tyrannical Pharaoh. Daniel Jones, an educator and organizer, notes King's well-known remark about one of Pharaoh's strategies, to keep the slaves fighting among themselves. To combat similar tyrants today, Jones looks to the term "mixed multitude" (*erev rav*) that came out of Egypt, noting that the term "erev" appears in Leviticus to mean threads in woven cloth. He stresses the strength in diversity as multiple groups fighting for justice pool their power and anger. "Our fusion is God's instrument of liberation . . . 'the mighty hand and outstretched arm' of God emerge from this unity. And it will deliver us from bondage again today."[53] Another message from the Exodus story is that there are enough resources for everyone as long as certain groups do not hoard them. Jones looks at the story of manna sent from heaven to show God created food for everyone to "gather what they need," but not to take more or hoard it. Manna hoarded becomes rotten. Today's suffering comes not from lack of resources but the hoarding of those resources by elites.[54]

Shareholder Activism
Promoting Corporate Responsibility

Public protest against institutions, government, and corporations is a time-honored method for people of conscience to try to change society. Yet even the sincerest activist could hardly avoid participating in injustices—by attending a university with dubious investments, by wearing clothes made by child labor abroad, or by using products whose production harmed the environment. Living a life that synchronized with one's personal values means looking at the power of business in our lives. Shareholder advocacy arose to call corporations to account by becoming shareholders in order to introduce shareholder resolutions at annual meetings and create dialogue with them on moral matters.

Few individuals had the resources to buy up many shares, but churches and religious orders had significant pension funds and other monies to invest. In 1971, after a federal appeals court ruled that socially responsible investment actions were admissible, Paul Neuhauser, an Episcopalian disturbed by apartheid, drafted the first religious share-holder proposal, asking General Motors (GM) to stop doing business in South Africa until apartheid was dismantled. The presiding bishop of the Episcopal church John Hines, along with others, showed up at the GM meeting to present the proposal. From these activities emerged The

Sullivan Principles, workplace ethics for companies doing business in South Africa (no separate restrooms or drinking fountains for Blacks, equal pay for equal work, and more). Eventually all US companies doing business in South Africa signed on to these principles.[55] Another initiative held open hearings on the environmental and human impact of opening copper mines in Puerto Rico. These actions of a group of Protestant denominations led to the formation of the Interfaith Center on Corporate Responsibility (ICCR), an advocacy organization that today has hundreds of faith-based groups as members, whose biggest single category today are Catholic organizations, including many religious orders. Associate and affiliate members who do not have a religious orientation may also be members, but at a different level of participation and benefits. Broad areas of action include worker justice, corporate governance, health care, human rights, climate change, responsible finance, and investor action on the Covid crisis. Within these areas are many specific programs, for example, responsible lending, reducing gun violence, and stopping human trafficking.

As Neuhauser put it, the impetus for shareholder actions is the "stewardship of your assets . . . it's God's property so I've got to treat it in a certain way."[56] The notion of assets matching investors' values led to faith-based investment services. These exist to match a spectrum of religious views. Socially responsible investing (SRI) filters out objectionable elements (for example, investing in tobacco, alcohol, or, for some, abortifacients) and supporting companies that reflect positive ideals (for example, protecting the environment or workers' rights). An early example, formed by Catholic congregations, was Tri-State Coalition for Responsible Investment (Tri-CRI), now called Investor Advocates for Social Justice (IASJ), which is still primarily made up of Catholic orders, though it is officially nondenominational.

An early attempt to influence corporate behavior came from the Adrian Dominican Sisters, who took up shareholder investing in 1974, forming their Portfolio Advisory Board to consider where they invested their group monies in their pension funds, to "evaluate its investments in relation to Gospel principles and to create a way to work for change through justice in the business practices of corporations in which the Adrian Dominicans invest."[57] Their first effort, with Gulf and Western (no longer in existence), called for awareness and reform of labor conditions in the company's sugar cane harvesting in the Dominican Republic. Sister Annette Sinagra and others gathered evidence of what she calls "abominable" working conditions especially for Haitians, who worked for low wages, were forced to meet arbitrary quotas, and had to buy goods from company stores, all while enduring violence and intimidation from supervisors on horseback. She helped document these conditions, leading to a report copublished with ICCR that led to minimal reform. In the 1980s, the sisters divested funds and joined boycotts of Shell and Coca-Cola over their presence in South Africa under apartheid. They have launched many actions in their forty-year history to influence companies in the areas of human trafficking, to agitate for workers' rights, to promote environmental responsibility, and more. In a notable success, they joined with the Coalition of Immokalee Workers (CIW) and the AFL-CIO to convince McDonalds to adopt fair labor practices and to raise their payment of Florida tomato pickers, many of whom came from Haiti, Mexico, and Central America and had been trapped in situations of virtual enslavement. Sinagra notes that her work as a corporate responsibility analyst "has opened my eyes" to the reality of slavery in the United States, noting that "slavery also exists in the hotels in our country, in the restaurants, not just in the fields."[58] The other side of the Adrian Dominican Sisters work is community investing, offering loans to small, community-based businesses and to community development of financial institutions that administer loans to local businesses. They have discovered that it not only leads to stronger communities but it is also good business. Since 1978, the sisters have proffered nearly 500 loans—over 98% have been paid back in full.

The late Sister Patricia Daly was a regular participant at Exxon annual meetings, in 2007 appearing for the tenth year to query what the company was doing to address its impact on global warming. Her order, the Dominicans of Caldwell, New Jersey, owned 300 shares of the company, giving them the right to present shareholder resolutions.

Father Michael Crosby, a Capuchin Franciscan, had filed the first share-holder resolution to address climate change in 1997 and he and Daly formed Campaign ExxonMobil to demand accountability from the company on its role in the climate crisis. Daly and others joined in the effort to reduce greenhouse gas emissions. Her resolution in 2007 garnered 31 percent of the votes.[59] On January 18, 2022, ExxonMobil announced its goal of achieving net zero greenhouse emissions by 2050. Daly also was part of an initiative to ask General Electric to clean up polychlorinated biphenyls (PCBs) from the Hudson River, as well as other initiatives to fight climate change and human trafficking. She, like many, claim to not overtly "play the God card," but are propelled by their own religious values, and their very stature as representatives of religious orders forces a consideration of religious and ethical values: "preaching truth is what we are all about."[60]

Catholic activism for worker rights, service to and advocacy to the poor and the immigrant, peace activism, anti-nuclear activities, and protest against authoritarian governments have a deep history, one that has often included civil disobedience. One need only think of Dorothy Day, Fathers Daniel and Patrick Berrigan, Sister Elizabeth McAlister, and Cesar Chavez, names known to most Americans. Catholic share-holder activists have taken a very different path to social change but are inspired by the same Catholic Social Teaching with its scriptural and ecclesiastical roots. One can hardly imagine Dorothy Day, the cofounder of the Catholic Worker movement, who regularly engaged in acts of civil disobedience, at a shareholder's meeting. Yet it is fair to say she would have agreed with the aims of calling for corporate respon-sibility on behalf of the vulnerable.

All the faith-based groups mentioned in this chapter filter their understanding of the biblical text through their traditions of textual interpretation and histories of preaching and ministry. Catholic social teaching has its own emphases that quite deliberately balance biblical sources and church tradition.[61] Catholic social justice activ-ists will often cite Scripture first, then the traditions of their founding saint if they belong to an order, and/or papal encyclicals, particularly

Rerum Novarum (1891), Pope Leo XIII's encyclical on the rights of labor and addressing the situation of the working classes and poor in the Gilded Age; *Caritas in Veritate* (2009), Pope Benedict XVI's teaching on the economic implications and abuses in a global economy; and *Laudato Si* (2015), Pope Francis's pronouncement on the climate crisis resulting from overdevelopment. All three encyclicals lament the effects of runaway capitalism, unrestrained by ethics.

Séamus Finn, a priest of the Oblates of Mary Immaculate and former chair of the board of ICCR, explains Catholic social teaching as an interplay of biblical teaching, church tradition, and the continuing presence of the Holy Spirit in the people of the church. Following the US Council of Catholic Bishops pastoral letter, "Economic Justice for All," published in 1986, he cites a raft of biblical resources,[62] beginning with the overarching creation theology of the Hebrew Bible that sees the world as good and in need of human care.[63] Like the other groups in this chapter, he cites the covenant theology that binds the people of Israel to God by commandments to care for the land and for one another, especially the poor and marginalized, by way of the sabbatical year and the Jubilee year, which allows the land to rest and mitigates the effects of poverty.[64] The prophets call the whole nation back to the covenant, in particular by way of the commands to social and economic justice. Jesus affirms the command to love of God and neighbor. He calls others to follow him by offering service to others, as Catholic teaching underlines the now familiar verse from Isaiah that Luke invokes as Jesus inaugurates his ministry, that Jesus himself is the prophet anointed by God to bring good news to the poor, proclaim release of the captives, recovery of sight to the blind, and freedom for the oppressed. In the last judgment, Jesus reminds his followers they will be judged according to whether they fed the hungry and thirsty, visited the sick and imprisoned because "Truly I tell you, just as you did it to one of the least of these brothers and sisters of mine, you did it to me."[65] These and many other biblical sources are the first leg of the tripod that forms Catholic social teaching and guides these activists in their interactions with business and industry.

CONCLUSION

THE BIBLE IS a vast landscape. Many Americans have lived in that landscape, fusing it with America's own. This was especially true of the groups examined here, who undertook the tasks of reimagining our society and leading it toward its professed ideals. For today's readers, and especially for those who work for a better future for our descendants, these activists can be a resource. No one should imitate them blindly, neither repeating the moral myopia that afflicted certain players in matters of sexism, nativism, and antisemitism, nor in assuming an exclusively Christian audience in America. But reclaiming the religious roots of some progressive movements can produce depth, understanding, and spiritual stamina and counter the image that the Bible in the public square was always a weapon used to ward off social change. Themes within Scripture lay close at hand for reformers—especially God's prejudice on behalf of the downtrodden and disdain for the powerful, which plays out in the Exodus story, echoes through the prophets, grounds the Beatitudes, and appears in the poetry of Mary's Magnificat.

Hope is the underlying plank of reform. For some reformers such hope is couched in religious terms. The contemporary movement for corporate responsibility, for example, began with the simple idea that the earth belonged to God and humanity was its steward. Paul Neuhauser, one of the founders of the ICCR, expressed the idea that everything is God's property and everyone had to treat it as such. A similar idea emerges from the passage in Deuteronomy 15, the idea of God's economy, one in which no one is allowed to remain poor. Even the more apocalyptic thinkers who predict destruction of enemies nevertheless assume a God in control of the world who acts on behalf of justice.

Anyone may become a prophet. Anyone who rejects helplessness and steps up to condemn hypocrisy calls the nation back to its professed values. A repairer of society in our time stands in a long line of individuals and groups who have met unjust power with the power of truth. Looking at the people in this book shows they looked even further back for the confirmation of their message. Douglass and King frequently identified with the prophets Isaiah and Amos, who spoke for the marginalized. Stewart and Hamer identified with the "heroic Paul" of the letters and Acts as a warrior battling principalities and powers, forces of evil that seemed invincible but were destined for defeat.

Linking oneself to a long tradition of others who have struggled against intractable odds staves off despair. Imagining the intractability of the institution of enslavement or the centuries-long subordination of women must have seemed overwhelming to earlier thinkers. But to find their convictions echoed in biblical texts meant they were not alone. A reluctant, ill-prepared Moses was able to lead the people out of Egypt with God as the rescuer of Israel. A brother named Joseph was carried away to Egypt and enslaved, but because God was with him, he was reunited with his brothers and they were saved from famine, preserving the people of Israel. Israel survived the trauma of exile and the crisis of the Temple's destruction. Followers of Jesus survived the trauma of their founder's death and the hostility of the Roman empire. No wonder that when Fannie Lou Hamer escaped death because of her absence the night white supremacists fired into her bedroom, she declared, "don't you see what God can do?" Today's crises too may be overcome.

Seeking out tropes of liberation and examples of agency in religious texts and in earlier reformers has another effect: it drives out fear. Clark, Hamer, and King quite openly said they were not afraid because they felt in some ways God accompanied them on their perilous journey. Angelina Grimké stood her ground and finished her antislavery speech in Philadelphia as hostile crowds shouted and broke windows.

These thinkers also taught everyone not to be afraid to use their own experience as an authority. All the reformers here (save the part of the women's movement that gave up on the Bible) at some points fused their own struggle with the larger narrative of biblical history and heroic battles against evil. One need not share all the religious convictions of earlier reformers to see one's own life and striving for justice as part of a narrative of grandeur, a forward thrust toward a more equitable society. Looking to their successes against seemingly intractable odds is a hedge against one's own despair.

Despite their attachment to the narratives and themes of the text, all the reform-minded thinkers reflected some kind of critical approach to the Bible. Literalist interpretation would not work for any of these groups, as they argued a certain distance in time and place from the narratives. Early feminist critics cited the imprint of later culture on patriarchal interpretation. Abolitionists argued that slavery in the patriarchal period was not akin to the nineteenth-century American situation. Similarly, temperance writers claimed words for wine in antiquity meant something different than wine of their own time. Some writers, like Frances Willard and Elizabeth Cady Stanton, make explicit their awareness of and acceptance of the insights of historical critical scholarship coming out of Europe in the nineteenth century. When feasible, interpreters turned scholarly methods to their own uses.

For progressives today, earlier reformers provided abundant kinds of religious resources, many previously untapped. Reformers today may draw on legacies of earlier activists, not only the better-known biblically infused rhetors like Frederick Douglass, Abraham Joshua Heschel, and Martin Luther King, but also Maria Stewart, Septima Clark, and Fannie Lou Hamer. Stewart, in her short, but dramatic career as the first American woman platform speaker, took on the prophetic mantle and delivered a broadside against society for its maintenance of the enslavement of her people. Wielding the dramatic style of the jeremiad, she was active before better-known figures like Sojourner Truth and Frederick Douglass. Septima Clark devoted her long lifetime to teaching literacy and voting rights to African Americans, and preceded and accompanied the more dramatic and better-known male preachers of the movement. She illustrated the quotidian work of teaching and organizing, often the purview of unsung women activists, that allowed the civil rights movement to flourish. Fannie Lou Hamer, despite lacking the educational advantage of many of the male preachers, became a powerful, memorable preacher who placed the struggle of their own time on the larger canvas of the cosmic battle between God and Satan, good and evil, through the ages.

The Bible, like any religious text, is not innocent, and readers should not close their eyes to its inherent patriarchy and encouragement of violence toward other peoples, nor the ways it has been wielded to amplify patriarchy, racism, and colonialism in later eras. Contemporary interpreters inspired by the #MeToo movement have shown how biblical texts have been complicit in promoting misogyny and undermining women's agency in our culture. Some feminist interpreters, then and now, have indulged in variations of antisemitism, from blaming the Jewishness of Paul for anti-women attitudes in Christianity to relegating Jews and Judaism to a more primitive stage in humanity's development. It took someone of Frances Harper's wisdom to call out the prejudices of the early women's movement. In her speech to the National Women's Rights convention in 1866 entitled "We Are All Bound Up Together," she showed the interlocking nature of sexism, racism, classism, and suppression of free speech, asking for vigilance on all fronts.

Reclaiming the voices of religious progressives upholds the delicate balance of the First Amendment. The establishment clause meant government could not dictate religious belief or affiliation, while the free expression clause protects everyone's right to practice their own religion no matter which religion they claim. The religious reformers offer a history that unfolded in tandem with legal and legislative gains. Some, like certain abolitionists, questioned the essential morality of the Constitution viewed against the backdrop of a higher code of ethics. More often, they tried to rely on both sets of documents. King, in his public speeches, cited the Declaration of Independence in the same way he cited Scripture; both were documents whose value everyone agreed upon, but most failed to live up to.[1]

For most Americans today, reading the Bible is not a daily event. A number of surveys have demonstrated that readership of the Bible is low. Yet the surveys also show that Americans have a high view of it, more than half saying America would be worse off without the Bible.[2] A surprising number view it as the word of God, either inerrant or divinely inspired, even if they never read it.[3] Looking at these reformers can help illuminate this particular prejudice Americans have for the old book, one not shared by many other nations, including those professing a state religion. Those who grow up in the United States absorb biblical material by osmosis, from literature, history, and political discourse. In popular culture, Bible references seep into music, TV shows, video games, gaming platforms, TikTok, and more.[4] In crafting lives of meaning, people have always had choices, including whether or not to use religious texts at all, and in how to use them, whether as a wellspring of wisdom, a cultural touchstone, or a weapon against others.

For students of American history, reclaiming the role of religion and biblical interpretation in social change presents a fuller, more honest view of the development of the nation. It acted alongside and combined with other drivers of change—politics, economics, science and technology, and law—to motivate, justify, rationalize, and encourage. Considering most of America's great debates, the ones in this book as well as evolution versus creationism, LGBTQ+ rights, abortion, prayer in schools, and more, one will find religious arguments propelling controversy, and biblical texts frequently invoked by both sides.

For everyone who reads this book, it should be clear that no one owns the Bible nor can say what it *really* means. This includes anyone who engages in reductionism—painting with a broad brush that "it teaches slavery" or "it oppresses women." If it was used by Southern ministers and planters to endorse slavery, so too did abolitionists carefully outline the fundamental sinfulness of the institution. If

it was combined with Victorian ideas to argue against women's full
equality, so too did early women's rights advocates show its prefer-
ence for the idea that men and women were both created in God's
image and enjoyed full equality. The Bible has no agency of its own
but comes to life as interpreters extract meaning through interpretation. Those who seek to create a more just society are some of the
many interpreters who have found themselves and their struggles
in its pages.

NOTES

INTRODUCTION

1. https://tinyurl.com/4ytrt4sa. Jesus cites a part of Lev 19:18 here.
2. Emma Green, "A Pastor's Case for the Morality of Abortion," *The Atlantic,* May 26, 2019, https://tinyurl.com/rre6v449; Leslie Ann Scanlon, "A Q and A with minister and professor Rebecca Todd Peters," *The Presbyterian Outlook* Dec. 3, 2021, updated Feb. 13, 2022, n.p. https://tinyurl.com/yveaja6b /; https://tinyurl.com/mr3nf5ex; https://tinyurl.com/4xau24rs; https://tinyurl.com/4mra76az; https://tinyurl.com/nfwzp4nt.
3. The word "progressive" has never been perfectly defined, and debate over who gets to call themselves progressive engages some politicians, including Hillary Clinton and Bernie Sanders in the Democratic primary for the 2016 presidential election, Tara McKelvey, "What Does It Mean to Be a Progressive in the US?" Feb. 5, 2016, https://tinyurl.com/36ushz5jR.
4. Rather than produce an apologetic for the Bible, we are underscoring its frequently unrecognized utility for progressives. See Jill Hicks-Keeton, *Good Book: How White Evangelicals Save the Bible to Save Themselves* (Minneapolis: Fortress, 2023).
5. A Pew Research study in 2019 on Americans' knowledge of religion showed that overall Americans scored 4.2 out of 7 very basic questions on the Bible. Even evangelicals and Mormons, the most knowledgeable groups, scored far below 100% on all questions. See "What Americans Know About Religion," Pew Research Center, July 23, 2019, https://tinyurl.com/3tvs8a8u. See also https://tinyurl.com/2rcjf6z8.
6. Exod 21:16, Deut 24:7, and 1 Tim 1:9–10 in the New Testament. Much is also made of the horror of Joseph's being sold into slavery and exile to Egypt.
7. Deut 23:15.

8. I can hardly begin to enumerate all the scholars who have contributed to the subject of America's relationship to the Bible, except to mention a few: Mark Noll, Lincoln Mullen, Candida Moss, Jill Hicks-Keeton, and Cavan Concannon.

9. Lincoln A. Mullen, "Bible-filled pages: Newspaper pages that were primarily Bible quotations," *America's Public Bible: A Commentary*, (Stanford University Press, 2023): https://americaspublicbible.org/.

CHAPTER 1

1. Henry Watson, *Narrative of Henry Watson. A Fugitive Slave* (Boston: Bela Marsh, 1848), 39, https://tinyurl.com/4n4apxv2.

2. Frederick Douglass, *Narrative of the Life of Frederick Douglass, an American Slave, Written by Himself* in *Slave Narratives*, eds. William L. Andrews and Henry Louis Gates, *Literary Classics of the United States* (1845; repr., New York: Literary Classics of America, 2000), 334.

3. Valerie Cooper calls the Bible a "Rosetta stone," an essential decoder of experience for African Americans, Valerie Cooper, *Word, Like Fire: Maria Stewart, The Bible, and the Rights of African Americans* (Charlottesville: University of Virginia, 2011), 8. See also the work of Vincent Wimbush, whose work on the Bible and social location has created a sub-field within biblical studies.

4. For the use of the Bible to defend slavery and antislavery response, see Mark Noll, *The Civil War as a Theological Crisis* (Chapel Hill: University of North Carolina, 2006), 31–50.

5. Manisha Sinha, *The Slave's Cause* (New Haven: Yale University Press, 2016), 266.

6. Catherine Brekus, *Strangers and Pilgrims: Female Preaching in America 1740–1845* (Chapel Hill: University of North Carolina Press, 1998).

7. Marilyn Richardson, *Maria W. Stewart, America's First Black Woman Political Writer: Essays and Speeches* (Bloomington: Indiana University Press, 1987), 14–15.

8. Sinha, *Slave's Cause*, 205, 267–69.

9. See Kristin Waters, "Crying Out for Liberty: Maria W. Stewart and David Walker's Black Revolutionary Liberalism," *Philosophia Africana* 15 (2013), 35–60.

10. Emerson Powery and Rodney Sadler, Jr., *The Genesis of Liberation* (Louisville: Westminster John Knox, 2016), 1–10.

11. Cooper, *Word, Like Fire*, 96.

12. Stewart, "Lecture Delivered at Franklin Hall," in Richardson, *Maria Stewart*, 45.

13. Neh 1:3; 2:17; 4:4; 5:9; 6:13.

14. Ps 44:14; 79:4.

15. Ex 15:20; Judg 4:4; 2 Kings 22:14; 2 Chron 34:22; Neh 6:14; Luke 2:36; Acts 1:14; 2:17; 21:9.

16. The Grimké sisters were criticized for speaking to "crowded, promiscuous" [mixed gender] assemblies and clergy in the audience opposed them, as Elizabeth Cady Stanton notes, *History of Woman Suffrage*, 6 vols. (Rochester, NY: Susan B. Anthony, 1889) vol. 1, 53. In her farewell address, Stewart refers to attacks upon her, enduring "fiery darts of the devil," and defends her right to speak as a woman.

17. Stewart, "Farewell Address to Her Friends in the City of Boston," in Richardson, *Maria Stewart*, 68–70.

18. 1 Cor 7:21–24; Eph 6:5; Col 3:22; 1 Cor 14:34.

19. Here she paraphrases Rom 15:29.

20. Luke 2:49.

21. Stewart, "Farewell Address to Her Friends in the City of Boston," in Richardson, *Maria Stewart*, 67.

22. For a discussion of Jeremiah that draws on trauma theory and studies of responses to disaster, see Kathleen O'Connor, *Jeremiah. Pain and Promise* (Minneapolis: Fortress Press, 2011).

23. Jer 2:29, 34, 35.

24. Sacvan Bercovitch describes a peculiarly American version of the jeremiad in his well-known book from 1978, where he describes the Puritan adaptation of the prophetic critique to a worldly mission, making America the "new Israel," settling and populating the "wilderness," and creating a theocratic state, *The American Jeremiad* (Madison: University of Wisconsin, 1978). These assumptions of chosenness, he argues, undergird a social and cultural ethic of American exceptionalism. See also Perry Miller, *Errand into the Wilderness* (Cambridge, MA: Harvard University Press, 1956), which recalls Samuel Danforth's 1670 sermon of the same name, affirming New England's role to create a theocracy and further Christian mission.

25. David Howard-Pitney traces the pedigree of the African American jeremiad tradition that characteristically addresses *two* American chosen peoples—Black and white, *The African American Jeremiad* (1990; repr., Philadelphia: Temple University Press, 2005).

26. Stewart, "Religion and the Pure Principles of Morality," in Richardson, *Maria Stewart*, 34–35.

27. Stewart, "Address Delivered to the African Masonic Hall" (1833) in Richardson, *Maria Stewart*, 57–58.

28. Stewart, "Religion and Pure Principles," in Richardson, *Maria Stewart*, 39.

29. Stewart, "Religion and Pure Principles," "An Address Before the Afric-American Female Intelligence Society," and "Address Delivered to the African Masonic Hall, in Richardson, *Maria Stewart*, 33, 55, 58.

30. Stewart, "Religion and Pure Principles," in Richardson, *Maria Stewart*, 39–40.

31. Lisa Bowens, *African American Readings of Paul* (Grand Rapids: Eerdmans, 2020), 139.

32. Rom 8:38–39 in Stewart, "Farewell Address to Her Friends in the City of Boston," in Richardson, *Maria Stewart*, 66.

33. Bowens, *African American Readings of Paul*, 137.

34. Stewart, "Religion and Pure Principles," in Richardson, *Maria Stewart*, 35.

35. She uses familiar images from Jer 29:18 and Isa 58:5, Stewart, "Religion and Pure Principles," in Richardson, *Maria Stewart*, 37.

36. Stewart, "Lecture Delivered at Franklin Hall," in Richardson, *Maria Stewart*, 49.

37. Stewart, "Address Delivered to the African Masonic Hall," in Richardson, *Maria Stewart*, 57–58.

38. Stewart, "Religion and Pure Principles," in Richardson, *Maria Stewart*, 37–38.

39. Bowens, *African American Readings of Paul*, 129–30, 134.

40. Bowens, *African American Readings of Paul*, 142.

41. Powery and Sadler, *Genesis of Liberation*, 17.

42. Stewart, "Address Delivered to the African Masonic Hall," in Richardson, *Maria Stewart*, 58

43. Kerri Greenidge shows that while the Grimkés and Weld were heroes of the abolition movement for many, their participation was relatively brief. By 1843, they were somewhat disillusioned and concentrating on raising their family and running their farm in Belleville, NJ, *The Grimkes. The Legacy of Slavery in an American Family* (New York: Liveright, 2023), 95–101.

44. Weld-Grimké Letters II 536–39 in *The Grimké Sisters of South Carolina*, ed. Gerda Lerner (Boston: Houghton Mifflin, 1967), 218.

45. Lisa Vetter addresses contemporary criticism of Grimké for sentimentality, arguing for the legitimacy of her approach as in line with the ideas of Adam Smith, and noting a degree of intersectionality in

her arguments for women's rights. See Vetter, *The Political Thought of America's Founding Feminists* (New York: New York University Press, 2017), 101–23.

46. Angelina Grimké, *An Appeal to the Christian Women of the South*, https://tinyurl.com/bdd2vnhx. Multiple editions of this work are available online, I have chosen one of the few that includes pagination.
47. Gen 15:2; 17:9–14; 18:1–15.
48. Grimké, *Appeal*, 4.
49. Grimké, *Appeal*, 6–7, relying on Deut 20:14; Lev 35:44.
50. All of these laws appear in Exodus 21. Grimké, *Appeal*, 7–8.
51. Lev 25:10. Grimké, *Appeal*, 10.
52. Eph 6:9; Col 4:1; Titus 1:7; 1 Tim 1:10.
53. Acts 10:34; Matt 7:12; Lev 19:18; Matt 22:35–40.
54. Gen 1:26–28; Ps 8:6–8; renewed after the Flood in Gen 9:1-7.
55. Grimké, *Appeal*, 3.
56. This unfortunate example based on Acts 2:22–23 follows the standard view of the time of Jewish complicity in Jesus's death.
57. Ex 21:16; Deut 24:7; Ex 21:26, Angelina Grimké Weld in Theodore Dwight Weld, Sarah Moore Grimké, and Angelina Grimké Weld, *American Slavery As It Is* (New York: Anti-Slavery Society, 1839), 54. https://www.google.com/books/edition/American_Slavery_as_it_is/
58. Deut 23:15.
59. I Cor 7:21.
60. Grimké, *Appeal*, 21.
61. Grimké, *Appeal*, 26.
62. I Cor 1:28, which she alters slightly.
63. Ex 19:16; 2 Sam 1:20 Isa 40:3; Mark: 1:3; John 1:23; Isa 58:6; Jer 22:3: Luke 4:18.
64. Angelina Grimké, "Speech at Pennsylvania Hall, https://tinyurl.com/yvs73h86.
65. Grimké, *Appeal*, 30.
66. See Jacqueline Bacon, who argues that white women abolitionists' "essentialist sympathy with enslaved people does not challenge the white power structure," *The Humblest May Stand Forth: Rhetoric, Empowerment, and Abolition* (Columbia: University of South Carolina, 2002), 124.
67. Greenidge's work does much to dismantle any hagiographic picture of the Grimké sisters and Weld. The sisters are often culpable by omission, for example, by failing to acknowledge or involve themselves in the violence against Black residents of Philadelphia and their property in

1834, despite living near the events, *Grimkés*, 3–11. They were guilty of emotional cruelty toward their mixed-race nephews whom they groomed to enter polite society, *Grimkés*, 209–11. Greenidge shows that the enduring effects of slavery and racism implicate several generations of the family.

68. Theodore Dwight Weld, *The Bible Against Slavery, or, An Inquiry into the Genius of the Mosaic System, and the Teachings of the Old Testament on the Subject of Human Rights* (1864; repr., Detroit: Negro History Press, 1970).

69. Weld, *Bible Against Slavery*, 94.

70. Weld, *Bible Against Slavery*, 20

71. Weld, *Bible Against Slavery*, 18–19.

72. Weld, *Bible Against Slavery*, 26–27.

73. Weld, *Bible Against Slavery*, 21–22.

74. Weld, *Bible Against Slavery*, 49.

75. Weld, *Bible Against Slavery*, 95.

76. David Blight, *Frederick Douglass. Prophet of Freedom* (New York: Simon and Schuster, 2018), 38; Frederick Douglass, *Narrative of the Life of Frederick Douglass, An American Slave* (Boston: Anti-Slavery Office, 1845), 32–34, https://docsouth.unc.edu/neh/douglass/douglass.html.

77. Richard Newton, "The African American Bible: Bound in a Christian Nation," *Journal of Biblical Literature* 136 (2017), 222.

78. Frederick Douglass, "What to the Slave is the Fourth of July," *Frederick Douglass Papers*, ser. 1, vol. 2: 368. https://tinyurl.com/2p994knd.

79. John 8:44.

80. See, for example, Adele Reinhartz, "John and Anti-Judaism," in *The Jewish Annotated New Testament*, 2nd ed (New York: Oxford University Press, 2017), 172–73.

81. Amos 5:21–24; Isa 58:6–11.

82. Lev 19:18; Mark 12:31; Matt 22:39; Gen 4:9.

83. Acts 17:26; 10:34.

84. Amos 2:7; 8:4.

85. Isa 1:13–14.

86. Isa 59:1.

87. Frederick Douglass, *My Bondage and My Freedom*, ed. Henry Louis Gates (1855; repr., New York: Literary Classics of the United States, 1994), 298–300.

88. Douglass, *My Bondage and My Freedom*, 293.

89. Douglass, *My Bondage and My Freedom*, 252.

90. Douglass, *My Bondage and My Freedom*, 257.

91. Douglass, *My Bondage and My Freedom*, 306.
92. Douglass, *My Bondage and My Freedom*, 301–2.
93. Douglass, *My Bondage and My Freedom*, 245.
94. Gen 28:10–17; Dan 7:13–14.
95. Douglass, *My Bondage and My Freedom*, 245.
96. Frederick Douglass, "The Lessons of the Hour," Jan. 9, 1894, State Historical Society of Iowa. https://tinyurl.com/apxtmhdp.
97. Douglass, "The Fall of Richmond," *The Frederick Douglass Papers*, ed. John W. Blassingame and John R. McKivigan (New Haven: Yale University Press, 1991) ser. 1, vol. 4: 69–74.
98. Luke 16:19. Douglass, "The Fall of Richmond," 73–74.
99. Luke 16:31.
100. Theodore Parker published an extended discussion of David Friedrich Strauss's *Das Leben Jesu* in 1840 in *The Christian Examiner*, quoting the work at length. Strauss's work was part of the first Quest for the Historical Jesus, which attempted to separate fact from fiction in New Testament narratives. Three years later Parker published an English translation of Wilhelm de Wette's *Beiträge zur Einleitung das Alte Testament*, two volumes of early source criticism, identifying different authors and time periods for portions of the Hebrew Bible.
101. J. Albert Harrill, "The Use of the New Testament in the American Slave Controversy," *Religion and American Culture* 10 (2000), 158.
102. Mark A. Noll, *America's God. From Jonathan Edwards to Abraham Lincoln* (New York: Oxford University Press, 2002), 17.
103. Mark Noll, *The Civil War as a Theological Crisis* (Chapel Hill: University of North Carolina, 2006), 64.
104. Henry Bibb, *Narrative of the Life and Adventures of Henry Bibb, an American Slave, Written by Himself* in *Slave Narratives*, eds. William L. Andrews and Henry Louis Gates with an introduction by Lucius C. Whitlock (1849; repr., New York: Literary Classics of America, 2000), 501.
105. Bibb, *Narrative of the Life and Adventures of Henry Bibb*, 562.
106. Sojourner Truth, *Narrative of Sojourner Truth, A Northern Slave* in *Slave Narratives*, eds. William L. Andrews and Henry Louis Gates (1850; repr., New York: Literary Classics of American, 2000), 611.
107. Truth, *Narrative of Sojourner Truth*, 597
108. Truth, *Narrative of Sojourner Truth*, 647.
109. Harriet Jacobs, *Incidents in the Life of a Slave Girl, Written by Herself* in *Slave Narratives*, eds. William L. Andrews and Henry Louis Gates (1861; repr., New York: Literary Classics of American, 2000), 814.

110. William Wells Brown recalls a seller at an auction block recommending a slave as "a good and obedient servant, she has got religion," *A Narrative of William W. Brown, Fugitive Slave, Written by Himself* in *Slave Narratives*, eds. William L. Andrews and Henry Louis Gates (1847; repr. New York: Literary Classics of American, 2000), 410. Harriet Jacobs reports that after Nat Turner's rebellion "slaveholders came to the conclusion that it would be well to give the enslaved people enough of religious instruction to keep them from murdering their masters."

111. Bibb, *Narrative of the Life and Adventures of Henry Bibb*, 445.

112. Theodore Parker, "A Sermon on Slavery," in *Forerunners of Black Power*, ed. Ernest G. Bormann (January 31, 1841, and June 4, 1843; repr., Englewood Cliffs, NJ: Prentice-Hall, 1971), 204.

113. Gen 8:21b.

114. Rom 5–7.

115. Ex 21:16.

116. William Lloyd Garrision, *No Compromise with the Evil of Slavery* (1854), https://www.blackpast.org/african-american-history/1854-william-lloyd-garrison-no-compromise-evil-slavery/.

117. George Bourne, *The Book and Slavery Irreconciliable* in *George Bourne and the Book and Slavery Irreconciliable*, eds. John W. Christie and Dwight L. Dumond (1816; repr.,Wilmington: Historical Society of Delaware, 1969).

118. Grimké Weld, Weld, and Grimké, *American Slavery As It Is*, 52.

119. Henry Highland Garnet, "An Address to the Enslaved people of the United States of America," https://tinyurl.com/yt5yun95.

120. Theodore Parker, *A Sermon of Slavery* (Boston: Thurston and Tory, 1843), 16, https://tinyurl.com/cymtsm33.

121. Sinha, *Slave's Cause*, 178–80.

122. Douglass, "Love of God, Love of Man, Love of Country," in *The Frederick Douglass Papers*, eds. John Blassingame et al. (New Haven: Yale University Press, 1991), ser. 1 vol. 2: 96.

123. Jacobs, "Incidents in the Life," in *Slave Narratives*, 774.

124. Sarah Remond, "Speech by Sarah Remond," in *Black Abolitionist Papers*, eds. C. Peter Ripley et al. (Chapel Hill: University of North Carolina, 1985–2015), vol. 1: 23.

125. John Brown, "Speech by John Brown," in *Black Abolitionist Papers*, vol. 1: 264.

126. Herbert Robinson Marbury, *Pillars of Cloud and Fire: the Politics of Exodus in African American Biblical Interpretation* (New York: New York University Press, 2015).

127. David Walker, *Appeal to the Coloured Citizens of the World* (Boston: David Walker, 1829), 6, https://docsouth.unc.edu/nc/walker/walker.html.

128. David Walker, *Appeal*, 45.

129. Douglass, "We Are Not Yet Quite Free: An Address Delivered at Medina, NY on 3 August 1869," in *The Frederick Douglass Papers*, eds. John Blassingame et al. (New Haven: Yale University Press, 1991), ser. 1, vol. 4: 230.

130. Douglass, "Parties Were Made for Men, Not Men for Parties: An Address Delivered at Louisville on 25 September, 1883," in *The Frederick Douglass Papers,* eds. John Blassingame et al. (New Haven: Yale University Press, 1991), ser. 1, vol. 5: 101.

131. Douglass, "William the Silent: An Address Delivered at Cincinnati on 8 February, 1868," in *The Frederick Douglass Papers* ser. 1, vol. 4: 187.

132. Wongi Park lays out the history of interpretation of this narrative using critical race theory, "The Blessing of Whiteness: Reading Gen 9:18–29 in the Antebellum South," *Religions* 12 (11) (2021): 928, https://doi.org/10.3390/rel12110928.

133. For a discussion of the natures of the Yahwist and Priestly strata, and the general state of the theories of composition called The Documentary Hypothesis, see Joel P. Baden, *The Composition of the Pentateuch. Renewing the Documentary Hypothesis* (New Haven: Yale University Press, 2012).

134. "Inevitably, these genealogies are fictional," notes John J. Collins, "but they served to bring a sense of order to the diversity of human society, and also helped to keep the biblical focus on the story of Israel in perspective," *Introduction to the Hebrew Bible* (Minneapolis: Fortress, 2004), 81.

135. Gen 4:15.

136. Anonymous, *African Servitude* in *The Bible and American Culture*, eds. Claudia Setzer and David Shefferman (London: Routledge, 2011), 101, *Sabin Americana Digital Collection*.

137. Powery and Sadler, *Genesis of Liberation*, 94.

138. Noll notes "the acceptance of black racial inferiority that supplied the missing term to many of the arguments that defended American slavery by appeal to Scripture," *Theological Crisis*, 56.

139. Noll, *Theological Crisis*, 54–56.

140. Frederick Douglass, *Narrative of the Life of Frederick Douglass,* in *Slave Narratives*, eds. Andrews and Gates, 283–84.

141. Noll, *Theological Crisis,* 54–64.

142. Targum Onkelos, Targum Jonathan on Gen 12:5.
143. See Kenneth Cleaver, "An Examination of Albert Barnes' Handling of the Bible in the Debate of Slavery in the Mid-Nineteenth Century," PhD diss., Trinity Evangelical Divinity School, 25–33.
144. Albert Barnes, *An Inquiry into the Scriptural Views of Slavery* (Philadelphia: Perkins and Purvis, 1846), https://archive.org/details/inquiryintoscrip1846barn/page/70/mode/2.
145. Barnes, *Inquiry*, 109–10.
146. Barnes, *Inquiry*, 68.
147. Barnes, *Inquiry*, 70.
148. Barnes, *Inquiry*, 110.
149. Gen 17:12–13.
150. Deut 32:6.
151. Barnes, *Inquiry*, 76.
152. Powery and Sadler, *Genesis of Liberation*, 16–17.
153. Frank Lothar Hossfeld and Erich Zenger, *Psalms 2: A Commentary on Psalms 51–100* (Minneapolis: Fortress, 2005), 160–67.
154. Truth, *Narrative of Sojourner Truth*, in *Slave Narratives*, eds. Andrews and Gates, 646.
155. C. Peter Ripley, ed., *Black Abolitionist Papers* (Chapel Hill: University of North Carolina, Press, 1985), vol. 1: 515–16.
156. 1 Cor 7:21; Eph 6:5–8; Col 3:22–24; Phil 12–14.
157. Barnes, *Inquiry*, 111.
158. Jacobs, *Incidents in the Life,* in *Slave Narratives*, eds. Andrews and Gates, 814.
159. Howard Thurman, *Jesus and the Disinherited* (1949; repr., Boston: Beacon, 1976), 30–31.
160. Allen Dwight Callahan, *The Talking Book* (New Haven: Yale University Press, 2006), 30. Lisa Bowens' work, *African American Readings of Paul*, cited throughout this book, shows that African Americans resisted such interpretations, and used Paul as a model of courage and endurance under suffering.
161. James Gillespie Birney, *The Sinfulness of Slaveholding in All Circumstances Tested by Reason and Scripture* (Detroit: Charles Willcox, 1846), 28–31. https://tinyurl.com/43x4pr4f n.
162. 1 Cor 7:21.
163. Probably based on 1 Tim 1:10, Bourne, *Book and Slavery*, 178–79.
164. Barnes, *Church and Slavery*, 42.
165. For a discussion of these strategies, see Harrill, "Use of the New Testament in the American Slave Controversy," *Religion and American*

Culture 10 (2000), 149–86, and J. Albert Harrill, *Enslaved People in the New Testament. Literary, Social, and Moral Dimensions* (Minneapolis: Fortress, 2005), 166–77.

166. Birney, *Sinfulness of Slaveholding*, 16–17.
167. Abraham Smith, "Paul and African American Biblical Interpretation," in *True to Our Native Land. An African American New Testament Commentary*, eds. Brian Blount, Cain Hope Felder, Clarice J. Martin, and Emerson B. Powery (Minneapolis: Fortress, 2007), 37.
168. Bowens, *African American Readings of Paul*, 141–42.
169. See Blight, *Frederick Douglass*, 672–79.
170. Bowens, *African American Readings of Paul*, 284–90, quotation on p. 288.
171. Douglass, "Oration Delivered at Corinthian Hall," by Frederick Douglass, July 5, 1852, https://tinyurl.com/2p994knd.
172. Bourne, *Book and Slavery*, 162.
173. Birney, *Sinfulness of Slaveholding*, 3.
174. Birney, *Sinfulness of Slaveholding*, 8.
175. Birney, *Sinfulness of Slaveholding*, 8.
176. Thornton Stringfellow, *Scriptural and Statistical Views in Favor of Slavery* (Chapel Hill: University of North Carolina, 1856), 34–35, *Documenting the American South.* https://docsouth.unc.edu/church/string/string.html.
177. Henry Watson, *The Narrative of Henry Watson, A Fugitive Slave* (Boston: Bela Marsh, 1848), 29.
178. Benjamin Banneker, "Benjamin Banneker's Letter to Thomas Jefferson," https://tinyurl.com/2p8j6ey7/.
179. William Lloyd Garrison, *An Address Delivered in Marlboro Chapel, Boston, July 4, 1838* (Boston: Isaac Knapp, 1838) 9, https://tinyurl.com/bdxerv4a.
180. Today's scholars generally understand these remarks as part of the competition and hostility between different groups in first-century Judaism, including believers in Jesus, who differed on matters of practice and belief. An extensive literature discusses both the parting of the ways, or the lack of it, as well as the problem of apparent or real anti-Judaism in the New Testament. See Amy-Jill Levine, "Bearing False Witness: Common Errors Made About Early Judaism," in *The Jewish Annotated New Testament,* 2nd ed. (New York: Oxford University Press, 2017), 759–62. For an up-to-date article on the Pharisees, see Joshua Garroway, "Pharisees," http://www.bibleodyssey.org/people/main-articles/pharisees.aspx.

181. Wendell Phillips, "The Philosophy of the Abolition Movement," [1853] in Bormann, *Forerunners*, 127.

182. Douglass, "The Pro-Slavery Mob and the Pro-Slavery Ministry." in *Douglass' Monthly* 3 (March, 1861), 417–18. Cited in Noll, *Theological Crisis*, 66.

183. See Terence Keel, *Divine Variations. How Christian Thought Became Racial Science* (Stanford: Stanford University Press, 2018).

184. Powery and Sadler, *Genesis of Liberation*, 100.

185. Powery and Sadler, *Genesis of Liberation*, 92–94.

186. Powery and Sadler, *Genesis of Liberation*, 92–94.

187. William and Ellen Craft, *Running a Thousand Miles for Freedom* in *Slave Narratives*, eds. Andrews and Gates, 679.

188. Harrill, "Use of the New Testament in the American Slave Controversy," 159.

189. Susan B. Anthony, "The No Union with Slaveholders Campaign," https://tinyurl.com/ydsh38nj.

190. Frederick Douglass, "Love of God, Love of Man, Love of Country," *Frederick Douglass Papers*, Blassingame and McKivigan, ser. 1, vol. 2. Similar views are expressed in "The Right to Criticize American Institutions," where he goes after the Church and Constitution and country "which is in favour of supporting and perpetuating this monstrous system of injustice and blood," Philip S. Foner, adapted and abridged by Yuval Taylor, *Frederick Douglass: Selected Speeches and Writings* (1950; repr., Chicago: Lawrence Hill Books, 1999), 78.

191. Douglass, "Oration in Corinthian Hall," https://tinyurl.com/zt5v73nj.

192. William Wells Brown, *Narrative of William W. Brown Fugitive Slave,* in *Slave Narratives*, eds. Andrews and Gates, 404.

193. Brown, *Black Abolitionist Papers,* 5:145.

194. Brown, *Black Abolitionist Papers*, 3:245.

195. *New York Tribune*, February 8, 1856.

196. Noll argues that the theological crisis over slavery that led to the Civil War ultimately led Americans to repent of basing public policy on interpretations of scripture and adopt a more secular public outlook, *Theological Crisis*, 160–61.

CHAPTER 2

1. Sarah Grimké, *Sarah Grimké: Letters on the Equality of the Sexes and Other Essays*, ed. Elizabeth Ann Bartlett (New Haven: Yale University Press, 1988), 35. Ginsburg, in a court of law, left out the reference to God.

2. Lucy Stone and Antionette Brown Blackwell, "Soul Mates: Letters between Lucy Stone (1818–93) and Antoinette Brown Blackwell (1825–1921)," https://tinyurl.com/3n9p8zux.

3. *National Anti-Slavery Standard*, June 13, 1865.

4. Faye Dudden, *Fighting Chance. The Struggle Over Woman Suffrage and Black Suffrage in Reconstruction America* (New York: Oxford University Press, 2011).

5. Aileen Kraditor, Faye Dudden, and others have identified the race and class bias of Stanton and others in the women's movement. Nativism and racism surfaced in both the women's rights and temperance movements. Witness Olympia Brown complaining about the United States accepting "all the riff-raff of Europe," Kathi Kern, *Mrs. Stanton's Bible* (Ithaca: Cornell University Press, 2001), 114.

6. "Proceedings of the National Association of Colored Men Held in the City of Syracuse, October 4, 5, 6, and 7, with the Bill of Wrongs and Rights, and the Address to the American People," in *Minutes of the Proceedings of the National Negro Conventions, 1830–1864*, ed. Howard Holman Bell (New York: Arno Press, 1969), 9. See Laura Free, *Suffrage Reconstructed* (Ithaca: Cornell University Press, 2015), 33–41.

7. Elizabeth Frost and Kathryn Cullen-Dupont, *Women's Suffrage in America* (New York: Facts on File, 1992), 3, 166, 208.

8. Elizabeth Cady Stanton, "Temperance and Women's Rights," June 1, 1853, emersonkent.com/speeches/temperance and women's rights.htm.

9. Elizabeth Cady Stanton, *Elizabeth Cady Stanton As Revealed in her Letters, Diaries, and Reminiscences*, eds. Theodore Stanton and Harriet Stanton Blatch (New York: Arno Press and the *New York Times*, 1969), vol. 2: 52–53.

10. Matilda Joslyn Gage, *Woman, Church, and State* (1893; repr., New York: Arno Press, 1972), 469.

11. Gen 2:21–23; 3:16.

12. Gen 2:20.

13. Dr. H. K. Root, "Woman's Rights Convention, Broadway Tabernacle, New York City, September 7, 1853," in *History of Woman Suffrage*, eds. Elizabeth Cady Stanton, Susan B. Anthony, Matilda Joslyn Gage, and Ida Husted Harper (Rochester: Charles Mann Press, 1881–1922), 1:560.

14. Weld, *Bible Against Slavery*, 12–13.

15. Grimké, *Sarah Grimké: Letters*, 32.

16. Grimké, *Sarah Grimké: Letters*, 40. See also Letters 1, 4, 7, 8, 14, and 15; "The Condition of Women," 126–33.

17. Grimké, *Sarah Grimké: Letters*, 32.
18. Grimké, *Sarah Grimké: Letters*, 33.
19. Alice Stone Blackwell, *Lucy Stone. Pioneer of Woman's Rights* (1930; repr., Charlottesville: University of Virginia, 2001), 92–93.
20. Amanda Kerr, *Lucy Stone: Speaking Out for Equality* (New Brunswick: Rutgers University Press, 1992), 20.
21. SojournerTruth, "Women's Rights Convention. Sojourner Truth," in *Anti-Slavery Bugle*, June 21, 1851, 4, https://tinyurl.com/32tjz4kp/.
22. Frances Willard, *Woman in the Pulpit*, published as *The Defense of Women's Rights to Ordination in the Methodist Episcopal Church*, ed. Carolyn DeSwarte Gifford (1888; repr., New York: Garland, 1987), 20.
23. Willard, *Woman in the Pulpit*, 37.
24. Willard, *Woman in the Pulpit*, 33.
25. Willard, *Woman in the Pulpit*, 37.
26. Willard, *Woman in the Pulpit*, 21.
27. Willard, *Woman in the Pulpit*, 80.
28. Grimké, *Sarah Grimké: Letters*, 87.
29. Judg 5:7.
30. Julia McNair Wright, *Saints and Sinners of the Bible*, in *Women of War, Women of Woe. Joshua and Judges through the Eyes of Nineteenth-Century Female Biblical Interpreters*, eds. Marion Ann Taylor and Christiana De Groot (Grand Rapids: Eerdmans, 2016), 98.
31. Sarah Hale, *Woman's Record; or, Sketches of All Distinguished Women, from the Creation to A.D. 1854* in *Women in the Story of Jesus. The Gospels through the Eyes of Nineteenth-Century Female Biblical Interpreters*, eds. Marion Ann Taylor and Heather E. Weir (New York: Harper and Brothers, 1855, 71–72; repr., Grand Rapids: Eerdmans, 2016), 127.
32. Phoebe Palmer, preface in *The Promise of the Father* (Boston: Henry V. Degen, 1859; repr., Sun City West: Holiness Data Ministry, 1993–2005), 2, http://wesley.nnu.edu/wesleyctr/books/2401-2500/HDM2485.pdf.
33. Taylor and Weir, *Women in the Story of Jesus*, 149–50.
34. Elisabeth Schüssler Fiorenza inaugurated feminist New Testament scholarship with *In Memory of Her*, exploring women's discipleship and later attempts to minimize women's role in the early Jesus movement. She coins the term "discipleship of equals" to consider the immediate circle of Jesus's associates as an egalitarian group of men and women. Many scholars followed suit, and women's discipleship around Jesus is something of a given in New Testament circles today.
35. Acts 1:13–14.

36. Willard, *Woman in the Pulpit*, 40–44.
37. Willard, *Woman in the Pulpit*, 34.
38. Willard, *Woman in the Pulpit*, 45.
39. Willard, *Woman in the Pulpit*, 46–49.
40. Elizabeth Cady Stanton et al., *The Woman's Bible* (1895–1898; repr., Mineola, NY: Dover Publications, 2002), 86.
41. Stanton, *Woman's Bible*, 92.
42. Stanton, *Woman's Bible*, 152.
43. William Still, *Still's Underground Railroad Records,* rev. ed. (Philadelphia: William Still, 1886), 768, https://tinyurl.com/e6f42fs3.
44. Frances Smith Foster, ed., *A Brighter Coming Day: A Frances Ellen Watkins Harper Reader* (New York: The Feminist Press at City College of New York, 1990), 58.
45. 2 Sam 21:8–14.
46. Smith, *Brighter Coming Day*, 86.
47. See "Ruth and Naomi," in *Brighter Coming Day*, ed. Smith, 87.
48. See "Moses: A Story of the Nile," in *Brighter Coming Day*, ed. Smith, 138–43.
49. Esther 1:11.
50. Smith, *Brighter Coming Day*, 181–83.
51. Rosalyn Terborg-Penn shows that some later scholarship continued to promote the dual myths that Black women were not involved in suffrage and Black men opposed it. Her own research uncovers multiple Black women suffragists but none of supposed Black male diatribes against feminism, *African American Women in the Struggle for the Vote, 1850–1920* (Bloomington: Indiana University Press, 1998), 3–7.
52. Kathryn Kish Sklar, *Women's Rights Emerges Within the Antislavery Movement, 1830–1870,* 2nd ed., (Boston: Bedford/St. Martins, 2019), 191–94.
53. Several books explore the importance of the interlocking issues of women's rights with abolitionism and social reform, illustrating the signal role of Black women. See Martha S. Jones, *All Bound Up Together: The Woman Question in African American Public Culture* (Chapel Hill: University of North Carolina, 2007).
54. Sklar, *Women's Rights Within Antislavery*, 194.
55. Annual Meeting of the American Equal Rights Association, *The Revolution* 27 (1869), 247.
56. C. C. O'Brien, "'The White Women All Go For Sex,': Frances Harper on Suffrage, Citizenship, and the Reconstruction South," *African*

American Review 43 (2009), 605–20. A similar point is made by Jones, *All Bound Up Together*, 10.

57. Stanton, *Woman's Bible*, 2.213–14.
58. Stanton, *Woman's Bible*, 1.37.
59. Stanton, *Woman's Bible*, 1.14.
60. Stanton, *Woman's Bible*, 1.52.
61. Stanton, *Woman's Bible*, 1.57.
62. Stanton, *Woman's Bible*, 1.40.
63. Stanton, *Woman's Bible*, 2.153–54.
64. Stanton, *Woman's Bible*, 1.21.
65. Stanton, *Woman's Bible*, 1.18.
66. Elizabeth Cady Stanton, *Eighty Years and More* (1898; repr., Charleston, SC: BiblioBazaar, 2006), 289.
67. Kern, *Mrs. Stanton's Bible*, 180.
68. Matilda Joslyn Gage, *Woman, Church, and State* (1893; repr., New York: Arno Press, 1972), 49.
69. Gage, *Woman, Church, and State*, 467.
70. Ida Husted Harper, *The Life and Work of Susan B. Anthony* (Indianapolis: Bowen and Merrill, 1899), vol. 1: 77, www.gutenberg.org.
71. Stanton to Sara Underwood, March 31, 1889, Stanton Papers, Vassar College Library, in Kern, *Mrs. Stanton's Bible*, 91.
72. Kern, *Mrs. Stanton's Bible*, 91.
73. Frances Willard, *Woman in the Pulpit* (Boston: D. Lothrop, 1888), 23, 51.
74. Kern, *Mrs. Stanton's Bible*, 123
75. Stanton, *Woman's Bible*, 114.
76. 1 Cor 14:34–35; 11:4–6.
77. Kerr, *Lucy Stone*, 33.
78. Lucy Stone to brother William Bowman Stone, June 9, 1848, in *Lucy Stone*, ed. Kerr, 49.
79. Parker was quoting *The Sentinel* editorial "Reminiscences of Lucy Stone by Her Daughter Alice Stone Blackwell" in *Lucy Stone*, ed. Kerr, 53.
80. Kern, *Mrs. Stanton's Bible*, 214.
81. Matilda Joslyn Gage, *Woman, Church, and State* (1893; repr., New York: Arno Press, 1972), 58.
82. Gage, *Woman, Church, and State*, 54.
83. Grimké, *Sarah Grimké: Letters*, 95.
84. Quoted from editorial "Bigotry and the Woman's Bible," in *Free Thought Magazine* 16 (1898), 52, 433, cited in Kern, *Mrs. Stanton's Bible*, 209.

85. 1 Cor 11: 5; Phil 4:3; Rom 16:3–4.
86. Oddly, Willard's rendering of the verse adds the word "man" to "one," which does not reflect the Greek or the KJV.
87. Willard, *Woman in the Pulpit*, 27–32.
88. Stanton et al., *History of Woman Suffrage*, 4.132.
89. A few, like Garrison, considered the idea that the Bible might support slavery and if so, should be jettisoned, but there does not seem to be a thorough-going critique of the Bible by abolitionists. Given the proslavery argument that invokes biblical texts was already out there, such arguments would work against their aims.
90. Grimké learned with her brother Thomas as he prepared to enter Yale, Stanton won a prize for Greek in school as a teenager, and Stone resolved to learn languages to make sense of Gen 3:16, later attending Oberlin College. Stone and Antoinette Brown audited a rhetoric class and organized a women's debating society, in defiance of rules based on 1 Cor 14:34, which allegedly forbade women speaking in public. This last anecdote is from Henry Brown Blackwell, in Blackwell Family Collection, Library of Congress, reproduced in Amanda Moore Kerr, *Lucy Stone. Speaking Out for Equality* (New Brunswick: Rutgers University Press, 1992), 20.
91. Neither was overly reverential toward these methods, Stanton saying German scholarship was "too abstruse and inchoate for export," *Woman's Bible*, 56.

CHAPTER 3

1. Temperance was not a single group but a multiplicity of organizations over time. Jack Blocker recounts groups of farmers and immigrants, rural and urban folk, who identified with temperance, Jack Blocker, *American Temperance Movements* (Boston: Twayne Publishers, 1989), 106–11.
2. Ida B. Wells, "Temperance, and Race Progress," *AME Church Review* (1892), https://tinyurl.com/5n6fz7pb.
3. An understanding of drunkenness or alcoholism as a disease appears as early as 1811 in the writing of Benjamin Rush, a signatory of the Declaration of Independence, *An inquiry into the effects of ardent spirits upon the human body and mind* (New York: Cornelius Davis, 1811), https://tinyurl.com/5btnbbek.
4. Sinha follows a standard estimate of abolitionist members, *Slave's Cause*, 253. Information on WCTU membership is from Blocker,

American Temperance Movements, 84. Carol Mattingly gives numbers based on minutes of national meetings of NAWSA, *Well Tempered Women* (Carbondale, IL: Southern Illinois University, 2000), 188. The suffrage movement grew, garnering 404,000 signatures for a petition to Congress in 1910.

5. Blocker credits Willard with turning the movement progressive, *American Temperance Movements*, 84–85.

6. Prov 20:1; 23:31; Joel 1:5; Eph 5:18; Rom 13:13.

7. Psalm 104:15; Isa 62:8–9; Ecc 9:7.

8. Ex 29:40; Lev 23:12–13; Num 15:5; 28:14.

9. Isa 5:1–7; Joel 1:7; Mark 12;1–2; Matt 20:1–16.

10. Mark 14:22–25; Matt 26:26–30; Luke 22:14–20; 1 Cor 11:23–26; John 2:1–11.

11. Frances Willard, *Glimpses of Fifty Years. The Autobiography of an American Woman* (Chicago: Woman's Temperance Association Publication Association; H.J. Smith, 1889), 469.

12. See a picture from an action in Xenia, Ohio, in 1874: https://tinyurl.com/y6y7kdyt.

13. Anonymous, *Cincinnati Enquirer*, Feb. 3, 1874, in *"Give to the Winds thy Fears": the Women's Temperance Crusade, 1873–1874*, Jack Blocker, (Stuttgart: Holtzbrinck, 1985), 43.

14. Eliza D. "Mother" Stewart, *Memories of the Crusade. A Thrilling Account of the Great Uprising of the Women of Ohio in 1873 Against the Liquor Crime* (Chicago: H.J. Smith, 1890), 188, https://tinyurl.com/5b968uhe.

15. Stewart, *Memories of the Crusade*, 290.

16. Stewart, *Memories of the Crusade*, 188.

17. Stewart, *Memories of the Crusade*, 188.

18. Colleen McDannell, *Material Christianity* (New Haven: Yale, 1995), 68.

19. McDannell, *Material Christianity*, 73, 77, 79, 81, 83.

20. *The New York Times*, October 23, 1888, 2.

21. By 1879, the Ohio branch of the WCTU was using the Adair law to combat domestic violence. This law allowed wives to sue for damages from a saloonkeeper as well as the owner of the property if their sale of liquor to her husband caused suffering at home. Although the law had been on the books for twenty years, it was not until Ohio WCTU leaders like Eliza Stewart got behind it that it was enforced. See Erin M. Masson, "The Woman's Christian Temperance Union, 1874–1898:

Combating Domestic Violence," *William and Mary Journal of Women and the Law* 3 (1997), 163–88.

22. Willard courted white Southern support, suggesting the "great mass of southerners" act kindly toward Blacks, and that Blacks prone to drink are a threat, especially to women and children, "The Race Problem: Miss Willard on the Political Puzzle of the South," *The Voice*, October 23, 1890. Ida Wells castigated Willard in print for views that were sympathetic to lynching. Nativist sentiment is evident in the WCTU slogan, "For God, Home, and Native Land." Willard lamented in her 1889 presidential address that the country had become "the dumping ground of European cities," Tenth Presidential Address before the WCTU, November 8, 1889, Chicago, IL. In *Minutes of the National Women's Christian Temperance Union* (Chicago: Women's Temperance Publishing Association, 1889), 92–163; repr. in *Let Something Good Be Said. Speeches and Writings of Frances E. Willard*, eds. Carolyn De Swarte Gifford and Amy R. Slagell (University of Illinois Press: Urbana, 2007), 140. See also "Truth Telling: Frances Willard and Ida B. Wells," https://tinyurl.com/mvy2ck34.

23. Christopher H. Evans describes the public feud between Ida B. Wells and Willard, where Wells complained about Willard's lack of open support for her anti-lynching campaign and her affirming stereotypes of dangerous, over-sexed Black men as threats to white women. Willard defended herself but never retracted her early statements, *Do Everything: The Biography of Frances Willard* (New York: Oxford, 2022), 274–88. Evans notes the paradox of Willard's legacy as a proponent of the Christian home and a champion of equal rights for women and advocate for social justice. The former image has dominated memorializing of Willard until recently, 322.

24. See Katherine Gilbert Murdock, *Domesticating Drink: Women, Men, and Alcohol in America, 1870–1940* (Baltimore: Johns Hopkins University Press, 2002).

25. Frances Willard, *Do Everything: A Handbook for the World's White Ribboners* (Chicago: WCTU Publishing Association, 1895), 14, https://digital.lib.niu.edu/islandora/object/niu-gildedage%3A23717.

26. "Presidential Address," *Our Day: A Record and Review of Current Reform* 2.11 (1888), 482–4. https://tinyurl.com/y3dvp8n4.

27. Willard, "Presidential Address," 482.

28. Willard, "Presidential Address," 495.

29. *The Union Signal*, January 4, 1883, 13.

30. Num 6:2–3; Prov 28:7; Josh 24:24, *The Union Signal,* July 12, 1883, 7.
31. *The Union Signal,* July 12, 1883, 3.
32. *Do Everything: Handbook,* vii.
33. *Do Everything: Handbook,* 46.
34. *Do Everything: Handbook,* 36.
35. *Do Everything: Handbook,* 39.
36. For more information on these groups, Jack Blocker, *American Temperance Movements: Cycles of Reform* (Boston: Twayne, 1989), 95–106; https://westervillelibrary.org/antisaloon/; "Temperance and Prohibition," https://prohibition.osu.edu/.
37. Ernst Cherrington, ed., *The Standard Encyclopedia of the Alcohol Problem* (Westerville, OH: American Issue Publishing Company, 1924).
38. Moses Stuart, *Essay on the Prize Question, Whether the Use of Distilled Liquors is Compatible at This Time, with Making a Profession of Christianity* (New York: John F. Haven, 1830), https://tinyurl.com/2uddm6jw.
39. A summary of Maclean's work on biblical evidence for fermented wine appears in *An Examination of the Essays Bacchus and Anti-Bacchus published originally in the Princeton Review* (Princeton: John Bogart, 1841), http://resource.nlm.nih.gov/60620090R.
40. Reprinted as part 2 of his work, *The Bible Rule of Temperance* (Boston: National Temperance Society, 1868).
41. See discussion of the controversy in John L. Merrill, "The Bible and the American Temperance Movement: Text, Context, and Pretext," *Harvard Theological Review* 81.2 (1988), 145–70.
42. Zech 9:15; 10:7; Ps 78:65; Isa 5:11; Prov 23:29–30, George Duffield, *The Bible Rule of Temperance* (Boston: National Temperance Society, 1868), 152–55.
43. F. R. Lees and D. Burns, *The Temperance Bible Commentary* (London: S. W. Partridge, 1868). American edition (New York: Sheldon and Company, 1870).
44. Lee and Burns, *Temperance Bible Commentary,* Appendix, 397–411.
45. Amos 9:13, Lee and Burns, *Temperance Bible Commentary,* 406.
46. Matt 10:43, Lee and Burns, *Temperance Bible Commentary,* 408.
47. Marni Davis, *Jews and Booze* (New York: NYU Press, 2012), 46.
48. Wilbur and Sara Crafts, eds., *The World Book of Temperance,* 3rd ed. (Washington: International Reform Bureau, 1911), 221.
49. Jonathan Sarna, "Passover Raisin Wine, the American Temperance Movement, and Mordecai Noah," *Hebrew Union College Annual* 59

(1988), 271–76. An informal survey of my New York synagogue group revealed several people with memories of drinking raisin wine as children, provided by their grandparents, many of whom brought the recipes from Europe.

50. Crafts, *World Book of Temperance*, 3rd ed., 219–21.
51. Mark 8:15.
52. Davis, *Jews and Booze*, 46–56.
53. *The World Book of Temperance* was revised and enlarged by the Crafts three years later.
54. James Wallace, "Have We Bible Warrant for Wine Drinking?" leaflet reprinted in Crafts, *World Book of Temperance*, 3rd ed., 31.
55. Wallace, "Bible Warrant," 32.
56. Michael M. Homan, "Did the Ancient Israelites Drink Beer?" *BAR* 36.5 (Sept/Oct 2010), https://www.baslibrary.org/biblical-archaeology-review/36/5/4. Interestingly, some of the reactions to Homan's article online echo the discussion of different words for drink that took place in the nineteenth century.
57. Wallace, "Bible Warrant," 31. His language echoes Theodore Parker's well-known sermon, "A Discourse on the Transient and the Permanent in Christianity," delivered Roxbury, MA, 1841, and widely circulated in church newspapers.
58. Lee and Burns, *The Temperance Bible Commentary*, ix.
59. Tayler Lewis, Preface to First American edition, *The Temperance Bible Commentary* (New York: Sheldon and Company, 1870), xi.
60. Wallace, "Bible Warrant," 32.
61. Lev 14:14, Isa 57:14.
62. Wallace, "Bible Warrant," 32. Like others of his time, Wallace caricatures the Pharisees of the gospels, while current scholarship appreciates their movement as a legitimate expression of ancient Jewish devotion to God.
63. Merrill, "The Bible and the American Temperance Movement," 149–50.
64. Crafts, *World Book of Temperance*, 3rd ed., 26.
65. W. J. Beecher, "Drunkenness," in *A Dictionary of the Bible*, ed. James Hastings, 629–30.
66. *Elizabeth Cady Stanton*, eds. Stanton and Blatch, 2: 52–53.
67. Rosa Lindsay, "A Little Stimulant—A Temperance Tale," *Harper's* Dec 1850–May 1851, 361–64; Mrs. S. C. Hall, "The Drunkard's Bible," *Harper's* June–November, 1854, 385–90.

CHAPTER 4

1. See Kenyatta R. Gilbert, *A Pursued Justice: Black Preaching from the Great Migration to Civil rights* (Waco: Baylor University Press, 2016); David Swift, *Black Prophets of Justice: Activist Clergy Before the Civil War* (Baton Rouge: Louisiana State University Press, 1989). Sometimes neglected are the African American women preachers and activists such as Jarena Lee, Zilphia Elaw, Maria Stewart, Frances Harper, and others. See Bettye Collier-Thomas, *Daughters of Thunder: Black Women Preachers and their Sermons 1850–1979* (San Francisco: Jossey-Bass Publishers, 1997).

2. Richard T. Hughes, *Myths America Lives By: White Supremacy and the Stories That Give Us Meaning,* 2nd ed. (Champaign: University of Illinois, 2018). In his first edition, he delineated various founding myths including chosenness, innocence, and manifest destiny. In the second edition, he revised his material when he recognized the myths all rested on the fundamental myth of white supremacy.

3. Rom 8:37–39. Paul's term for the powerful forces both secular and cosmic. See also Eph 6:12; Col 1:16; 2:15; 1 Pet 3:22.

4. Part of a speech, "The Ballot or the Bullet," given at King Solomon Baptist Church, Detroit, in 1964.

5. James Cone offers Frederick Douglass and W. E. B. Dubois as representatives of the integrationist and nationalist views, respectively, *Martin and Malcolm and America: A Dream or A Nightmare?* (Ossining: Orbis Books, 1992).

6. See "What Can We Give Our Youth?" originally given in 1967, in *The Black Messiah* (Trenton, Africa World Press, 1989), 241–53.

7. "What Can We Give Our Youth?" in Cleage, *The Black Messiah,* 253.

8. Katherine Mellen Charron writes, "Baptist ministers predominated as leaders and grounded their leadership style in personal charisma. They roused the masses with their oratorical talents but very few had considered spreading leadership through a community, and they tended not to pay attention to the day-to-day upkeep of the movement that their words aimed to set in motion. They left such details to women," *Freedom's Teacher: The Life of Septima Clark* (Chapel Hill: University of North Carolina Press, 2009), 310.

9. Ann D. Gordon. with Bettye Collier-Thomas, *African American Women and the Vote 1837–1965* (Amherst: University of Massachusetts Press, 1997); Rosalyn Terborg-Penn, *African American Women in the Struggle for the Vote, 1850–1920* (Bloomington: Indiana University Press, 1998).

10. Charron, *Freedom's Teacher*, 310.

11. Because women's contributions were less celebrated, they cast a much smaller shadow in the classic scholarship on the movement. Taylor Branch does not hide the conscious sidelining of women like Ella Baker and Septima Clark, dedicating his work to Clark, *Parting the Waters: America in the King Years, 1954–1963* (New York: Simon and Schuster, 1988), 231–33, 247, 880. David Garrow notes Clark's complaint that her CEP work was not sufficiently dramatic to be appreciated, *Bearing the Cross: Martin Luther King and the Southern Christian Leadership Conference* (New York: Harper Collins, 1986), 309. David Chappell's more recent work mentions Fannie Lou Hamer throughout but not in depth, *A Stone of Hope: Prophetic Religion and the Death of Jim Crow* (Chapel Hill: University of North Carolina, 2004), 71–75 and passim. Works addressing the role of women in the movement directly include Lynne Olson, *Freedom's Daughters: The Unsung Heroines of the Civil Rights Movement from 1830 to 1970* (New York: Scribners, 2001); Vicki Crawford, Jacqueline Anne Rouse, and Barbara Woods, *Women in the Civil Rights Movement: Trailblazers and Torchbearers 1941–1968* (Bloomington: Indiana University Press, 1993). Crawford's work includes two articles on Clark and the CEP. See "Women in the Civil Rights Movement," part of the Library of Congress Civil Rights History Project, https://tinyurl.com/3e83sufy.

12. Septima Clark, interview by Peter H. Wood, Charleston, SC, February 3, 1981, Southern Oral History Project, Wilson Library, UNC, in *Freedom's Teacher*, Charron, 48. Septima Clark papers, Avery Research Center for African American History and Culture, College of Charleston, Charleston, SC.

13. Septima Clark, *Ready from Within*, ed. with an introduction by Cynthia Stokes Brown, *Ready from Within* (Trenton, NJ: Wild Trees Press, 1990), 83.

14. Charron, *Freedom's Teacher*, 70–77.

15. Mary Church Terrell, Ida Well-Barnett, and others founded the National Association for Colored Women, its motto, "Lifting As We Climb."

16. Clark, *Ready from Within*, 34.

17. Clark, *Ready from Within*, 49. Charron cites the role of the beauty shop as a safe woman-centered space in the deep South, where women could talk freely about their lives. Black beauticians recruited for the NAACP and raised funds for community aid in their shops, *Freedom's Teacher*, 279–81.

18. Isa 61:1.

19. Septima Clark, "Citizenship and Gospel," *Journal of Black Studies* 10.4 (1980), 463.

20. Clark, "Citizenship and Gospel," 464.

21. Septima Clark, "The Bible and the Ballot," Septima Clark papers, box 3, folder 36, *Low Country Digital Library,* lcdl.library.cofc.edu.

22. Clark, *Echo in My Soul*, 132.

23. Septima Clark letter to the Warings, June 30, 1955, box 9, folder 227, J. W. Warings papers, in Charron, 231.

24. Anne Moody, *Coming of Age in Mississippi* (New York: Random House, 1968), 275–76.

25. Fannie Lou Hamer, "We're on Our Way," in Maegan Parker Brooks and Davis W. Houck, *To Tell It like It Is: The Speeches of Fannie Lou Hamer* (Jackson: University Press of Mississippi, 2011), 55.

26. Clark, *Echo in My Soul*, 118.

27. Septima Clark, "God kept me that night, so I'll put my body in his care each night thereafter and I did," Septima Clark to Josephine Carson, August 31, 1966, box 4, folder 18, Septima Clark papers, Avery Research Center for the Study of African American History and Culture, College of Charleston, Charleston, SC. In Charron, *Freedom's Teacher*, 322, 420, n. 44.

28. Septima Clark, "Why I Believe There Is a God," Septima Clark papers, Low Country Digital Library, lcdl.library.cofc.edu.

29. Fannie Lou Hamer describing her beating at a jail in Winona, MS, excerpt from a mass meeting in Greenwood, Mississippi, 1963, reprinted in Claudia Setzer and David A. Shefferman, *The Bible and American Culture* (London and New York: Routledge Press, 2011), 191.

30. Interview with Fannie Lou Hamer by Robert Wright, August 9, 1968, Oral History Collection, Civil Rights Documentation Project, Moorland-Springarn Research Center, Howard University, cited in Meagan Parker Brooks, *A Voice That Could Stir an Army: Fannie Lou Hamer and the Rhetoric of the Black Freedom Movement* (Jackson: University Press of Mississippi, 2014), 37.

31. Brooks, *Voice,* 54–56; Charron, *Freedom's Teacher,* 321.

32. One sharecropper took it upon herself to carefully track her family's loan share of land, expenses, and the price of cotton in the area, calculating that they should have been paid $4000 for a year's work, but the plantation owner paid them $200. J. Todd Moye, *Let The People Decide,* in Brooks, *Voice,* 14–15.

33. Setzer and Shefferman, *Bible and American Culture*, 190–91.

34. All references are from the speech in Greenwood, MS, in Setzer and Shefferman, *Bible and American Culture*, 190–91.

35. This term was coined by James C. Scott, *Domination and the Arts of Resistance* (New Haven: Yale University Press, 1992).

36. A recent work gathers scholarship from all over the world examining the Bible's role in both colonization and resistance to it. See Jione Havea, *Scripture and Resistance* (Lanham, MD: Lexington Books/Fortress Academic Press, 2019). Countless earlier scholars have turned our attention to the politically subversive aspects of scripture, including Richard A. Horsley, Warren E. Carter, Elisabeth Schüssler Fiorenza, and Vincent Wimbush.

37. 1 Cor 15:23–25. See Paul Duff, "Processions," *Anchor Bible Dictionary*, vol. 5, ed. David Noel Freedman (New York: Doubleday, 1992), 469–473. For Paul's anti-imperial strategy, see the collection of essays, *Paul and Empire*, ed. Richard Horsley (Harrisburg, PA, 1997) and Neil Elliott, *The Arrogance of Nations* (Minneapolis: Fortress, 2010).

38. Gal 6:7; Proverbs 26:27.

39. Matt 5:18.

40. Acts 17:26.

41. Setzer and Shefferman, *Bible and American Culture*, 190–91.

42. Matt 5:15–16. Setzer and Shefferman, *Bible and American Culture*, 190–91. Also in Brooks and Houck, *Speeches of Fannie Lou Hamer*, 3–6. The song was originally a children's song and a spiritual but became an anthem in the movement.

43. Dawn Coleman, "The Bible and the Sermonic Tradition," in *Oxford Handbook of the Bible in America*, ed. Paul Gutjahr (New York: Oxford University Press, 2017), 251.

44. David Howard-Pitney, *The African American Jeremiad: Appeals for Justice in America* (Philadelphia: Temple University, 2005).

45. Fannie Lou Hamer, "We're On Our Way," speech delivered at a Mass Meeting in Indianola, MS, September, 1964, in Brooks and Hauck, *Speeches of Fannie Lou Hamer*, 48.

46. Fannie Lou Hamer, "We're on Our Way," in Brooks and Hauck, *Speeches of Fannie Lou Hamer*, 55–56.

47. Fannie Lou Hamer, "The Only Thing We Can Do Is Work Together," Brooks and Hauck, *Speeches of Fannie Lou Hamer*, 70–73.

48. Fannie Lou Hamer, "The Only Thing We Can Do Is Work Together," Brooks and Hauck, *Speeches of Fannie Lou Hamer*, 70–73.

49. Fannie Lou Hamer, Brooks and Hauck, "What Have We to Hail?" *Speeches of Fannie Lou Hamer*, 82.

50. Martin Luther King, Jr., "The Drum Major Instinct," in *A Testament of Hope. The Essential Writings of Martin Luther King, Jr.*, ed. James M. Washington (New York: Harper and Row, 1986), 264.

51. Harry Emerson Fosdick, "Handling Life's Second Bests," in *Answers to Real Problems: Harry Emerson Fosdick Speaks to Our Time*, ed. Mark E. Yurs (Eugene, OR: Wipf and Stock, 2008), 25.

52. Gary G. Porton, for example, sees the parables in the Hebrew Bible as the earliest examples in the Near East where the actors are human beings rather than talking animals and plants, "The Parable in the Hebrew Bible and Rabbinic Literature," in *The Historical Jesus in Context*, eds. Amy-Jill Levine, Dale C. Allison, and John Dominic Crossan (Princeton: Princeton University Press, 2007), 206–21. Significant literature around parables since the writing of Adolph Jülicher. A recent treatment underlines the provocative quality of Jesus's parables, as well as the anti-Jewish tendencies of later interpreters. See Amy-Jill Levine, *Short Stories by Jesus* (San Francisco: Harper Collins, 2014).

53. David Stern notes a "family resemblance" in format between early Jewish and Christian interpretations, "Midrash and Parables," *Jewish Annotated New Testament*, 2nd ed., 707–10.

54. Levine, *Short Stories*, 4.

55. Mark 10:43–44.

56. King, "Drum Major Instinct," 265, 267.

57. Isa 11:6; *Hamlet*, Act 5, scene 2. Martin Luther King, Jr., "Eulogy for the Martyred Children," in *Testament of Hope*, ed. James M. Washington (New York: Harper and Row, 1986), 221–23.

58. Job 38:7. King, "Facing the Challenge of a New Age," in *Testament of Hope*, 135–44.

59. King, "Letter from Birmingham Jail," in *Testament of Hope*, 289–302.

60. He repeats this phrase throughout his speaking career, in "The Power of Non-Violence" (1957), "The Current Crisis in Race Relations" (1958), and "The American Dream" (1968), in *Testament of Hope*, 15, 89, 216, respectively.

61. David Burns, *The Life and Death of the Radical Historical Jesus* (New York: Oxford University Press, 2013).

62. Thurman, *Jesus and the Disinherited*, 11.

63. Abraham Smith, "'Low in the Well': A Mystic's Creative Message of Hope," *Journal for the Study of the Historical Jesus* 17 (2019), 185–200.

64. Howard Thurman, "Good News for the Underprivileged," *Religion and Life* 4 (1935), 409.

65. Contemporary scholars are exploring the historical Paul and under-scoring his embeddedness in Judaism. Fundamental to the sea change in understanding Paul was Krister Stendahl's "The Apostle Paul and the Introspective Conscience of the West," who showed the filtering of Paul through Augustine and Luther transformed an issue about Jewish and Gentile inclusion into the individual's existential struggle with sin. *Harvard Theological Review* 56 (1963), 199–215. See also Paula Fredriksen, "What Does It Mean to See Paul within Judaism?" *JBL* 141 (2022), 359–380, Mark Nanos, ed., *Paul within Judaism* (Minneapolis: Fortress, 2015), and Pamela Eisenbaum, *Paul Was Not a Christian* (San Francisco: Harper One, 2010), to name only a few of the scholars working on this question.

66. Bowens, *African American Readings of Paul*, 246–53.

67. Bowens, *African American Readings of Paul*, 241–46.

68. Amos 5:21–22.

69. Howard-Pitney, *The African American Jeremiad*, 13.

70. One of several examples is King, "The Case against Tokenism," in *Testament of Hope*, 107–8.

71. King, "Showdown for Nonviolence," in *Testament of Hope*, 65.

72. King, "Drum Major Instinct," 265, 267.

73. King, "Showdown for Non-violence," 71–72.

74. King, "Showdown for Non-violence," 64–72.

75. King, "Where Do We Go From Here?", 251.

76. 1 John 4:16. Washington, *Testament of Hope*, 250.

77. John 3:1–10.

78. Micah 6:8.

79. Amos 5:24; Isa 11:6, commonly misquoted; Micah 4:4; Acts 17:26.

80. David Stern, "Vayikra Rabbah and My Life in Midrash," *Prooftexts* 21 (2001), 37. Stern suggests some works, like *Vayikra Rabbah*, may contain midrash and word play used in actual sermons by the ancient rabbis.

81. Gilbert, in *A Pursued Justice*, examines the prophetic preaching of three northern preachers from the early twentieth century during failed Reconstruction, the rise of Jim Crow, and the Great Migration in the interwar years.

82. Richard Lischer, *The Preacher King* (New York: Oxford, 1995), 43

83. Tinsley Yarbrough, *A Passion for Justice: J. Waties Waring and Civil Rights* (New York: Oxford, 1987), 229.

84. Powery and Sadler, *Genesis of Liberation*, 169.

85. Mitzi J. Smith, *Insights from African American Interpretation* (Minneapolis: Fortress, 2017), 66.

86. Prov 26:27.

87. For a helpful summary of the form and literature, see Carol Bakhos, "Midrash," in *Oxford Research Encyclopedia of Literature*, ed. Paula Rabinowitz (Oxford University Press, 2015), https://tinyurl.com/m6xf66vv.

88. Brennan Breed, *Nomadic Text: A Theory of Biblical Reception History* (Bloomington: Indiana University Press, 2014).

89. See Bowens, *African American Readings of Paul*, 301–2; Nyasha Junior and Jeremy Schipper, *Black Samson* (New York: Oxford, 2020).

90. See, for example, articles in Havea, *Scripture and Resistance* and in R. Sugirtharajah, ed., *The Postcolonial Biblical Reader* (Malden, MA: Blackwell Publishing, 2006).

CHAPTER 5

1. Hillary Clinton, United Nations Fourth World Conference on Women, Beijing, China, Sept. 5, 1995.

2. Tarana Burke, *Unbound. My Story of Liberation and the Birth of the Me Too Movement* (New York: Flatiron Books, 2021), 29–30.

3. Burke, *Unbound*, 33.

4. Burke, *Unbound*, 223–24.

5. Burke, *Unbound*, 227.

6. Olga M. Segura, "#MeToo Founder Tarana Burke: 'Jesus Was the First Activist That I Knew,'" *Sojourners*, Sept. 24, 2018, https://tinyurl.com/mrwu7u3v.

7. Tarana Burke interview with Erinn Haines, Oct. 14, 2022, https://tinyurl.com/3ejfcjab.

8. Johanna Stiebert, *Rape Myths, the Bible, and #MeToo* (London: Routledge, 2020), 49.

9. Gen 34:1–4 2; Sam 13:1–14; Judg 19:22–26.

10. Stiebert, *Rape Myths*, 24.

11. Stiebert, *Rape Myths*, 50–60.

12. Amy Kalmanofsky expresses her shock when she discovered the extent to which sacred texts often were not safe places for women. She argues that feminist scholarship can aid those who suffer sexual abuse by helping to name and interpret events, "How Feminist Biblical Scholarship Can Heal Victims of Sexual Violence," in *Sexual Violence and Sacred Texts*, ed. Amy Kalmanofsky (2017; repr., Eugene, OR: Wipf and Stock, 2020), 14–15.

13. Kalmanofsky argues that feminist interpretation can be a factor in healing, "Interpretation is an empowering activity. It helps violated individuals name, condemn, and resist the violence in their own lives, and more importantly, it helps them assume an agency that moves them from being victims to being survivors of sexual violation," "How Feminist Biblical Scholarship Can Heal," 15.

14. Ruth Everhart, *The #MeToo Reckoning: Facing the Church's Complicity in Sexual Abuse and Misogyny* (Downers Grove, IL: Intervarsity Press, 2020), 54.

15. Mark 5:25–34; Mark 5:21–24, 35–43.

16. Everhart, *#MeToo Reckoning*, 113–28.

17. 2 Sam 11–12.

18. Everhart, *#MeToo Reckoning*, 128.

19. When I taught this story to earlier generations of undergraduates, there was often one male student who offered, "she was asking for it." Fortunately, such remarks have long since disappeared.

20. Everhart, *#MeToo Reckoning*, 147.

21. Everhart, *#MeToo Reckoning*, 146–53.

22. Deut 16:20.

23. Julian E. Zelizer, *Abraham Joshua Heschel: A Life of Radical Amazement* (New Haven: Yale University Press, 2021), 151

24. Abraham Joshua Heschel, "Reasons for my involvement in peace movement," 1973, in *Moral Grandeur and Spiritual Audacity*, ed. Susannah Heschel (New York, Farrar, Straus, Giroux, 1997), 224.

25. Jill Jacobs, *There Shall Be No Needy. Pursuing Social Justice Through Jewish Law and Tradition* (Woodstock, VT: Jewish Lights Publishing, 2009), 16.

26. In rabbinic times, Hillel modified this command with the *prozbul*, which allowed the temporary transfer of a debt to a court, which meant it could be repaid. In an imperfect world, maintaining the system of lending and borrowing was desirable.

27. Jacobs, *There Shall Be No Needy*, 22.

28. Abraham Unger, *A Jewish Public Theology. God and the Global City* (Lanham, MD: Lexington Books, 2019), 70.

29. https://dayenu.org/.

30. Abraham Joshua Heschel, *Moral Grandeur and Spiritual Audacity*, ed. Susannah Heschel (New York: Farrar, Starus, Giroux, 1997).

31. Jennie Rosenn, "Speak Torah to Power," https://www.youtube.com/watch?v=Ld4hSu_acnY.

32. https://dayenu.org/climateinvest/.

33. https://www.breachrepairers.org/about-us.

34. https://www.breachrepairers.org/moral-agenda.

35. William Barber, "A National Call for Moral Revival," in "Pain and Poverty in America. The Poor People's Campaign," https://www.youtube.com/watch?v=zj5aVF54p-0&t=253s.

36. Deut 10:19; Ex 23:9; Gen 2:1–3; Ex 20:8–11; Deut 5:12–15.

37. Gen 1:26–27. Rick Lowery, "The Prophetic Word Is Political," in *Revive Us Again. Vision and Action in Moral Organizing*, eds. William J. Barber II, Liz Theoharis, and Rick Lowery (Boston: Beacon, 2018), 9.

38. Liz Theoharis, *We Cry Justice: Reading the Bible with Poor People* (Minneapolis: Broadleaf Books, 2021), 9–10.

39. Solita Alexander Riley, "What We Wish For," in *We Cry Justice*, Theoharis, 13–15.

40. Claire, "Pain and Poverty in America: The Poor People's Campaign," https://www.youtube.com/watch?v=zj5aVF54p-0&t=253s.

41. William J. Barber II, *We Are Called to Be a Movement* (New York: Workman Publishing Co, 2020), 18.

42. Luke 4:16–19; Isa 61:1–2.

43. Matt 6:25–34.

44. Theoharis, "Blessed Are the Rejected, for They Shall Lead the Revival," in *Revive Us Again*, eds. Barber, Theoharis, and Lowery, 12–13.

45. Paul Duff argues that "the poor," which some have argued is an honorific title for the Jerusalem church, probably also represents the literal truth of the economic situation of the Jerusalem church, "Paul's Collection for the Poor in Jerusalem," https://global.oup.com/obso/focus/focus_on_paul_collection/.

46. Mark 10:17–21; Luke 6:24; 16:19–31.

47. James Baldwin is cited in Stephen Pavey, "You Must Let Us Wail," in *We Cry Justice*, 54–55.

48. Stephen Pavey, "You Must Let Us Wail," in *We Cry Justice*, 55–57.

49. Jer 31:15.

50. Martin Luther King, "Where Do We Go From Here?"

51. Charon Hribar, "Woe to You Who Pass Unjust Laws," in *We Cry Justice*, 176–79.

52. Aaron Scott, "Same Sin, Different Day," in Theoharis, *We Cry Justice*, 219–221.

53. Ex 12:38; 6:6. Daniel Jones, "A Mixed Multitude," *We Cry Justice*, 110.

54. Ex 16:15–25. Daniel Jones, "God Created Enough," *We Cry Justice*, 21–23.

55. Interview with Paul Neuhauser, "The ICCR Story," *The Arc of Change* podcast July 16, 2009, https://tinyurl.com/bdfd8cfz.
56. Interview with Paul Neuhauser, "The ICCR Story," *The Arc of Change*.
57. *PAB 40th Anniversary Commemorative Brochure*, 4, adriandominicans.org.
58. Interview with Annette Sinagra, "Ending Modern-Day Slavery: Annette Sinagra Talks about fighting Human Trafficking," *The Arc of Change*, podcast Feb. 19, 2010, https://tinyurl.com/6hj46xke.
59. Dashka Slater, "Resolved: Public Corporations Shall Take Us Seriously," *New York Times*, Aug. 12, 2007, n.p.
60. "Women of Faith in Finance," iasj.org/sr-pat-daly-women-of-faith-in-finance/.
61. Catholic Social Teaching rests on seven principles, which it roots in scripture: the Life and Dignity of the Human Person, a Call to Family and Community, Rights and Responsibilities to support Human dignity, an Option (or preferential treatment) of the Poor and Vulnerable, the Dignity of Work and the Rights of Workers, Solidarity with all other members of the Human Family, and Care for God's Creation. See https://tinyurl.com/2r4293yu.
62. Seamus Finn, "Faith and Finance: A Catholic Consideration," in *Building Bridges Across Financial Communities: The Global Financial Crisis, Social Responsibility, and Faith-Based Finance*, ed. Nazim Ali (Cambridge: Harvard Law School, ILSP, Islamic Finance Project, 2012), 263–79. See also US Council of Catholic Bishops, "Economic Justice for All: Pastoral Letter on Catholic Social Teaching and the U.S. Economy," https://www.usccb.org/resources/economic-justice-all-pastoral-letter-catholic-social-teaching-and-us-economy, 8–14.
63. Gen 1:31; 14:19–22; Isa 40:28; 45:18; Gen 2:15; 1:28; Wis 9:2–3.
64. Ex 23:10–11; Lev 25:1–17; Deut 15:1–11; Lev 25:8–17.
65. Matt 25:31–46.

CONCLUSION

1. Our dual heritage as Americans comes from an intertwined legacy of early religious settlers who were founding a theocracy and the later statesmen who penned a constitution that rejected state religion. Frank Lambert joins the term "Planting Fathers" to "Founding Fathers" to express the mixed religious and republican heritage of America, *The*

Founding Fathers and the Place of Religion in America (Princeton: Princeton University Press, 2003).

2. https://tinyurl.com/2rcjf6z8.

3. Philip Goff, Arthur Farnsley II, and Peter Thuesen considered two national surveys from 2012. The number of Americans who read the Bible in the previous year, a very low bar, was only 50.2 percent. Yet roughly two thirds of those who did not read the Bible still regarded it at the inerrant word of God or divinely inspired, *The Bible in American Life* (New York: Oxford University Press, 2017), 6–7.

4. Thanks to my assistant Kyle Hahn, who uncovered many examples, from the Simpsons network show to the video game on the Binding of Isaac, as well as material on the gaming platforms Fortnite and Minecraft.

SELECT BIBLIOGRAPHY

PRIMARY LITERATURE

African Servitude. New York: Davies and Kent, 1860. https://tinyurl. com/59rwfm5r.

Banneker, Benjamin. "Benjamin Banneker's Letter to Thomas Jefferson." Philadelphia, 1791. https://tinyurl.com/2w528nd4.

Barber, William J., with Liz Theoharis and Rick Lowery, eds. *Revive Us Again. Vision and Action in Moral Organizing.* Boston: Beacon, 2018.

Barber, William J. *We Are Called to Be a Movement.* New York: Workman Publishing Co, 2020.

Barnes, Albert. *An Inquiry into the Scriptural Views of Slavery.* Philadelphia: Perkins and Purves, 1846. Boston Public Library. https://tinyurl. com/8c6f4awh.

———. *The Church and Slavery.* Philadelphia: Parry and McMillan, 1857. Repr. Ann Arbor: University of Michigan, 2005. http://name.umdl. umich.edu/ABT8113.0001.001.

Bibb, Henry. *Narrative of the Life and Adventures of Henry Bibb, an American Slave, Written by Himself,* with introduction by Lucius C. Whitlock (1849). Reprinted in *Slave Narratives.* Edited by William L. Andrews and Henry Louis Gates, Jr. New York: The Library of America, 2000.

Birney, James Gillespie. *The Sinfulness of Slaveholding in All Circumstances Tested by Reason and Scripture.* Detroit: Charles Willcox, 1846. https:// tinyurl.com/43x4pr4f.

Bourne, George. *The Book and Slavery Irreconcilable* (1816). Reprinted in *George Bourne and the Book and Slavery Irreconcilable.* Edited by John W. Christie and Dwight L. Dumond. Wilmington: Historical Society of Delaware, 1969.

Brown, William Wells. *Narrative of William W. Brown, A Fugitive Slave, Written by Himself* (1847). Reprinted in *Slave Narratives.* Edited by William L. Andrews and Henry Louis Gates, Jr., 369–423. New York: The Library of America, 2000.

Burke, Tarana. *Unbound: My Story of Liberation and the Birth of the Me Too Movement*. New York: Flatiron Books, 2021.

Cherrington, Ernst, ed. *The Standard Encyclopedia of the Alcohol Problem*. Westerville, OH: American Issue Publishing Company, 1924.

Clark, Septima. "The Bible and the Ballot." Septima Clark papers, box 3, folder 36, Low Country Digital Library, lcdl.library.cofc.edu.

———. "Citizenship and Gospel." *Journal of Black Studies* 10 (1980): 461–66.

———. *Echo in My Soul*. New York: E. P. Dutton, 1963.

———. *Ready from Within*. Edited, with an introduction by Cynthia Stokes Brown. Trenton, NJ: Wild Trees Press, 1990.

———. Septima Clark Papers. Low Country Digital Library, lcdl.library.cofc. edu.

Crafts, Wilbur and Sara Crafts, eds. *The World Book of Temperance*, 3rd ed. Washington: International Reform Bureau, 1911.

Do Everything: A Handbook for the World's White Ribboners. Chicago: WCTU Publishing Association, 1895. https://tinyurl.com/yc5sreee.

Douglass, Frederick. "Address . . . January 9th, 1894, on the Lessons of the Hour—Folder 1 of 8," 9 January, 1894. Courtesy of Library of Congress. https://tinyurl.com/yck2msfy.

———. *My Bondage and My Freedom* [1855]. In *Frederick Douglass: Autobiographies*. Edited by Henry Louis Gates, Jr., 103–124. LOA 68. New York: The Library of America, 1994.

———. *Narrative of the Life of Frederick Douglass, an American Slave, Written by Himself* [1845]. In *Frederick Douglass: Autobiographies*. Edited by Henry Louis Gates, Jr., 1–102. LOA 68. New York: The Library of America, 1994.

———. *The Frederick Douglass Papers,* ser. 1, vol. 2. Edited by John Blassingame, John McKivigan, Richard Carlson, Clarence Mohr. New Haven: Yale University Press, 1982.

———. *The Frederick Douglass Papers*, ser. 1, vol. 4. Edited by John Blassingame, John McKivigan. New Haven: Yale University Press, 1991.

———. *The Frederick Douglass Papers*, ser. 1, vol. 5. Edited by John Blassingame, John McKivigan. New Haven: Yale University Press, 1992.

Duffield, George. *The Bible Rule of Temperance*. Boston: National Temperance Society, 1868.

Everhart, Ruth. *The #MeToo Reckoning: Facing the Church's Complicity in Sexual Abuse and Misogyny*. Downers Grove, IL: Intervarsity Press, 2020.

Finn, Seamus. "Faith and Finance: A Catholic Consideration." In *Building Bridges Across Financial Communities: The Global Financial Crisis, Social*

Responsibility, and Faith-Based Finance. Edited by S. Nazim Ali, 263–79. Cambridge: Harvard Law School, ILSP, Islamic Finance Project, 2012.

Foner, Philip S., ed. *Frederick Douglass: Selected Speeches and Writings.* Chicago: Lawrence Hill Books, 1999.

Foster, Frances Smith, ed. *A Brighter Coming Day: A Frances Ellen Watkins Harper Reader.* New York: The Feminist Press at City College of New York, 1990.

Gage, Matilda Joslyn. *Woman, Church, and State.* 1893. Reprint, New York: Arno Press, 1972.

Garnet, Henry Highland Garnet. "An Address to the Enslaved people of the United States of America." https://tinyurl.com/yt5yun95.

Garrison, William Lloyd. *No Compromise with the Evil of Slavery.* New York: American Anti-Slavery Society, 1854.

———. *An Address Delivered in Marlboro Chapel, Boston, July 4, 1838.* Boston: Isaac Knapp, 1838. https://tinyurl.com/bdyfsyks.

Grimké, Angelina. *An Appeal to the Christian Women of the South.* https://tinyurl.com/57f3tef3.

———. "Speech at Pennsylvania Hall." https://tinyurl.com/yvs73h86.

———. Sarah Moore Grimké and Theodore Dwight Weld. *American Slavery As It Is.* New York: Anti-Slavery Society, 1839. https://tinyurl.com/yc3yfa5u.

Grimké, Sarah. *Sarah Grimké: Letters on the Equality of the Sexes and Other Essays.* Edited by Elizabeth Ann Bartlett. New Haven: Yale University Press, 1988.

Harper, Ida Husted. *The Life and Work of Susan B. Anthony.* Vol. 1. Indianapolis: Bowen and Merrill, 1899. www.gutenberg.org.

Jacobs, Harriet. *Incidents in the Life of a Slave Girl, Written by Herself.* 1861. Reprinted in *Slave Narratives* Edited by William L. Andrews and Henry Louis Gates, Jr., 743–948. LOA 114. New York: The Library of America, 2000.

Jacobs, Jill. *There Shall Be No Needy: Pursuing Social Justice Through Jewish Law and Tradition.* Woodstock, VT: Jewish Lights Publishing, 2009.

King, Martin Luther, Jr. *A Testament of Hope: The Essential Writings of Martin Luther King, Jr.* Edited by James M. Washington. New York: Harper and Row, 1986.

Lerner, Gerda. *The Grimké Sisters from South Carolina.* Chapel Hill: University of North Carolina, 2004.

Maclean, John. *An Examination of the Essays Bacchus and Anti-Bacchus published originally in the Princeton Review.* Princeton: John Bogart, 1841. http://resource.nlm.nih.gov/60620090R.

Moody, Anne. *Coming of Age in Mississippi*. New York: Random House, 1968.

Neuhauser, Paul, "The ICCR Story," podcast *The Arc of Change*, July 16, 2009. https://tinyurl.com/bdfd8cfz. Parker, Theodore. *A Sermon of Slavery*. Boston: Thurston and Torry, 1843. https://tinyurl.com/msmur4ny.

Richardson, Marilyn. *Maria W. Stewart. America's First Black Woman Political Writer*. Bloomington: Indiana University Press, 1987.

Ripley, C. Peter et al., eds. *Black Abolitionist Papers*. Vols. 1–5. Chapel Hill: University of North Carolina, 1985–2015.

Rosenn, Jennie. "Speak Torah to Power," https://www.youtube.com/watch?v=Ld4hSu_acnY.

Setzer, Claudia, and David A. Shefferman. *The Bible and American Culture. A Sourcebook*. London: Routledge Press, 2011.

Sinagra, Annette. "Ending Modern-Day Slavery: Annette Sinagra Talks about fighting Human Trafficking," podcast *The Arc of Change*. February 19, 2010. https://soundcloud.com/iccronline/the-arc-of-change-february-19.

Stanton, Elizabeth Cady. *Eighty Years and More*. 1898. Reprint, Charleston, SC: BiblioBazaar, 2006.

———. "Temperance and Women's Rights." Temperance and Women's Rights. https://tinyurl.com/mrtsupe5.

———. *The Woman's Bible*. 1895–98. Reprint, Mineola, NY: Dover Publications, 2002.

Stanton, Elizabeth Cady, Susan B. Anthony, Matilda Joslyn Gage, and Ida Husted Harper, eds. *History of Woman Suffrage*. Rochester: Charles Mann Press, 1881–1922.

Stanton, Theodore, and Harriett Stanton Blatch, eds. *Elizabeth Cady Stanton*. New York: Arno Press and the New York Times, 1969.

Stewart, Eliza D. *Memories of the Crusade. A Thrilling Account of the Great Uprising of the Women of Ohio in 1873 Against the Liquor Crime*. Chicago: H.J. Smith, 1890. https://tinyurl.com/yckavzdh.

Stone, Lucy. Letters between Lucy Stone and Antoinette Brown Blackwell. https://tinyurl.com/3n9p8zux.

Stringfellow, Thornton. *Scriptural and Statistical Views in Favor of Slavery*. 1856. *Documenting the American South*. University Library, University of North Carolina at Chapel Hill, 2000. https://docsouth.unc.edu/church/string/string.html.

Stuart, Moses. *Essay on the Prize Question: Whether the Use of Distilled Liquors is Compatible at this Time, with Making a Profession of Christianity*. New York: John F. Haven, 1830. https://tinyurl.com/5x9apy26.

Taylor, Marion Ann, and Christiana De Groot, eds. *Women of War, Women of Woe: Joshua and Judges through the Eyes of Nineteenth-Century Female Biblical Interpreters.* Grand Rapids: Eerdmans, 2016.

Taylor, Marion Ann and Heather E. Weir, eds. *Women in the Story of Jesus: The Gospels through the Eyes of Nineteenth-Century Female Biblical Interpreters.* Grand Rapids: Eerdmans, 2016.

Theoharis, Liz. *We Cry Justice: Reading the Bible with Poor People.* Minneapolis: Broadleaf Books, 2021.

Truth, Sojourner. *Narrative of Sojourner Truth, A Northern Slave.* 1850. Reprinted in *Slave Narratives.* Edited by William L. Andrews and Henry Louis Gates, Jr., 567–676. New York: The Library of America, 2000.

Unger, Abraham. *A Jewish Public Theology. God and the Global City.* Lanham, MD: Lexington Books, 2019.

Walker, David. *Walker's Appeal in Four Articles; together with a preamble, to the Coloured Citizens of the World.* 1829. https://docsouth.unc.edu/nc/walker/walker.html.

Watson, Henry. *Narrative of Henry Watson: A Fugitive Slave.* Boston: Bela Marsh, 1848.

Weld, Theodore Dwight. *The Bible Against Slavery, or, An Inquiry into the genius of the Mosaic system, and the teachings of the Old Testament on the subject of human rights.* 1864. Reprint, Detroit: Negro History Press, 1970.

Wells, Ida B. "Ida B. Wells on Temperance." *AME Church Review* (1892). https://tinyurl.com/5cfczh88.

Willard, Frances. *Glimpses of Fifty Years. The Autobiography of an American Woman.* Chicago: Woman's Temperance Association Publication Association; H.J. Smith, 1889.

———. "Presidential Address." *Our Day. A Record and Review of Current Reform* 2.11 (1888), 482–4. https://tinyurl.com/sw72d2s7.

———. *Woman in the Pulpit.* 1888. Reprinted in *The Defense of Women's Rights to Ordination in the Methodist Episcopal Church,* ed. Carolyn DeSwarte Gifford. New York: Garland, 1987.

"Women in the Civil Rights Movement." Library of Congress Civil Rights History Project. https://tinyurl.com/3e83sufy.

SECONDARY LITERATURE

Bacon, Jacqueline. *"The Humblest May Stand Forth": Rhetoric, Empowerment, and Abolition.* Columbia: University of South Carolina, 2002.

Bercovitch, Sacvan. *The American Jeremiad.* Madison: University of Wisconsin, 1978.

Blackwell, Alice Stone. *Lucy Stone: Pioneer of Woman's Rights*. 1930. Reprint, Charlottesville: University of Virginia, 2001. Blight, David. *Frederick Douglass: Prophet of Freedom*. New York: Simon and Schuster, 2018.

Blocker, Jack. *American Temperance Movements*. Boston: Twayne Publishers, 1989.

———. *"Give to the Winds Thy Fears": The Women's Temperance Crusade, 1873–1874*. Stuttgart: Holtzbrinck, 1985.

Bowens, Lisa. *African American Readings of Paul*. Grand Rapids: Eerdmans, 2020.

Brekus, Catherine. *Strangers and Pilgrims: Female Preaching in America 1740–1845*. Chapel Hill: University of North Carolina Press, 1998.

Brooks, Meagan Parker. *A Voice That Could Stir an Army: Fannie Lou Hamer and the Rhetoric of the Black Freedom Movement*. Jackson: University Press of Mississippi, 2014.

———, and Davis. W. Houck. *To Tell It like It Is: The Speeches of Fannie Lou Hamer*. Jackson: University Press of Mississippi, 2011.

Burns, David. *The Life and Death of the Radical Historical Jesus*. New York: Oxford University Press, 2013.

Callahan, Allen Dwight. *The Talking Book*. New Haven: Yale University Press, 2006.

Charron, Katherine Mellen. *Freedom's Teacher: The Life of Septima Clark*. Chapel Hill: University of North Carolina Press, 2009.

Cleaver, Kenneth. "An Examination of Albert Barnes' Handling of the Bible in the Debate of Slavery in the Mid-Nineteenth Century." PhD diss., Trinity Evangelical Divinity School, 2002. https://digitalcommons.liberty.edu/fac_dis/25/.

Collier-Thomas, Bettye. *Daughters of Thunder: Black Women Preachers and their Sermons 1850–1979*. San Francisco: Jossey-Bass Publishers, 1997.

Cooper, Valerie. *Word, Like Fire: Maria Stewart, The Bible, and the Rights of African Americans*. Charlottesville: University of Virginia Press, 2011.

Crawford, Vicki, Jacqueline Anne Rouse, and Barbara Woods. *Women in the Civil Rights Movement: Trailblazers and Torchbearers 1941–1968*. Bloomington: Indiana University Press, 1993.

Dudden, Faye. *Fighting Chance: The Struggle Over Woman Suffrage and Black Suffrage in Reconstruction America*. New York: Oxford University Press, 2011.

Evans, Christopher H. *Do Everything: The Biography of Frances Willard*. New York: Oxford, 2022.

Free, Laura. *Suffrage Reconstructed*. Ithaca: Cornell University Press, 2015.

Frost, Elizabeth, and Kathryn Cullen-Dupont. *Women's Suffrage in America*. New York: Facts on File, 1992.

Garroway, Joshua. "Pharisees," https://tinyurl.com/5n6zupmf. Gordon, Ann D., and Bettye Collier-Thomas. *African American Women and the Vote 1837–1965*. Amherst: University of Massachusetts Press, 1997.

Gifford, Carolyn De Swarte and Amy R. Slagell, eds. *Let Something Good Be Said. Speeches and Writings of Frances E. Willard*. Urbana: University of Illinois Press, 2007.

Green, Emma. "A Pastor's Case for the Morality of Abortion." *The Atlantic*, May 26, 2019. https://tinyurl.com/wvfzty8x.

Greenidge, Kerri. *The Grimkés: The Legacy of Slavery in an American Family*. New York: Liveright, 2023.

Harrill, J. Albert. "The Use of the New Testament in the American Slave Controversy." *Religion and American Culture* 10 (2000): 149–86.

———. *Enslaved people in the New Testament. Literary, Social, and Moral Dimensions*. Minneapolis: Fortress, 2005.

Howard-Pitney, David. *The African American Jeremiad*. 1990. Reprint, Philadelphia: Temple University Press, 2005.

Hughes, Richard T. *Myths America Lives By: White Supremacy and the Stories that Give Us Meaning*. 2nd ed. Champaign: University of Illinois, 2018.

Jones, Martha S. *All Bound Up Together: The Woman Question in African American Public Culture*. Chapel Hill: University of North Carolina, 2007.

Kalmanofsky, Amy, ed. *Sexual Violence and Sacred Texts*. Eugene, OR: Wipf and Stock, 2020.

Keel, Terence. *Divine Variations: How Christian Thought Became Racial Science*. Stanford: Stanford University Press, 2018.

Kern, Kathi. *Mrs. Stanton's Bible*. Ithaca: Cornell University Press, 2001.

Kerr, Amanda. *Lucy Stone: Speaking Out for Equality*. New Brunswick: Rutgers University Press, 1992.

Lees, F. R., and D. Burns, *The Temperance Bible Commentary*. London: S. W. Partridge, 1868. American edition New York: Sheldon and Company, 1870.

Lischer, Richard. *The Preacher King*. New York: Oxford, 1995.

Marbury, Herbert Robinson. *Pillars of Cloud and Fire: The Politics of Exodus in African American Biblical Interpretation*. New York: New York University Press, 2015.

McDannell, Colleen. *Material Christianity*. New Haven: Yale, 1995.

McKelvey, Tara. "What does it mean to be a progressive in the US?" February 5, 2016. https://www.bbc.com/news/world-us-canada-35467470.

Merrill, John L. "The Bible and the American Temperance Movement: Text, Context, and Pretext." *Harvard Theological Review* 81 (1988), 145–70.

Mullen, Lincoln A. "Bible filled Pages: Newspaper pages that were primarily Bible quotations." *America's Public Bible: A Commentary.* Stanford University Press, 2023. https://americaspublicbible.supdigital.org/essay/super-pages/.

Murdock, Katherine Gilbert. *Domesticating Drink: Women, Men, and Alcohol in America, 1870–1940.* Baltimore: Johns Hopkins University Press, 2002.

Newton, Richard. "The African American Bible: Bound in a Christian Nation." *Journal of Biblical Literature* 136 (2017), 221–28.

Noll, Mark. *The Civil War as a Theological Crisis.* Chapel Hill: University of North Carolina, 2006.

———. *America's God: From Jonathan Edwards to Abraham Lincoln.* New York: Oxford University Press, 2005.

O'Brien, C. C. "'The White Women All Go For Sex,': Frances Harper on Suffrage, Citizenship, and the Reconstruction South." *African American Review* 43 (2009), 605–20.

Olson, Lynne. *Freedom's Daughters: The Unsung Heroines of the Civil Rights Movement from 1830 to 1970.* New York: Scribners, 2001.

Park, Wongi. "The Blessing of Whiteness: Reading Gen 9:18–29 in the Antebellum South." *Religions* 12 (2021) 928; https://doi.org/10.3390/rel12110928.

Powery, Emerson, and Rodney Sadler, Jr. *The Genesis of Liberation.* Louisville: Westminster John Knox, 2016.

Scanlon, Leslie Ann. "A Q and A with minister and professor Rebecca Todd Peters." *The Presbyterian Outlook*, December 3, 2021, updated February 13,2022. https://tinyurl.com/3txjvy8w.

Segura, Olga. "#MeToo Founder Tarana Burke: 'Jesus Was the First Activist That I Knew,'" *Sojourners*, September 24, 2018. https://tinyurl.com/mrwu7u3vSinha, Manisha. *The Slave's Cause.* New Haven: Yale University Press, 2016.

Sklar, Kathryn Kish. *Women's Rights Emerges Within the Antislavery Movement, 1830–1870.* 2nd ed. Boston: Bedford/St. Martins, 2019.

Smith, Abraham. "'Low in the Well': A Mystic's Creative Message of Hope." *Journal for the Study of the Historical Jesus* 17 (2019), 185–200.

———. "Paul and African American Biblical Interpretation." Pages 31–42 in *True to Our Native Land: An African American New Testament Commentary.* Edited by Brian Blount, Cain Hope Felder, Clarice J. Martin, and Emerson B. Powery, 31–42. Minneapolis: Fortress Press, 2007.

Stiebert, Johanna. *Rape Myths, the Bible, and #MeToo*. London: Routledge, 2020.

Terborg-Penn, Rosalyn. *African American Women in the Struggle for the Vote, 1850–1920*. Bloomington: Indiana University Press, 1998.

Thurman, Howard. *Jesus and the Disinherited*. 1949. Reprint, Boston: Beacon, 1976.

Vetter, Lisa. *The Political Thought of America's Founding Feminists*. New York: New York University Press, 2017.

Waters, Kristin. "Crying Out for Liberty: Maria W. Stewart and David Walker's Black Revolutionary Liberalism." *Philosophia Africana* 15 (2013), 35–60.

Zelizer, Julian E. *Abraham Joshua Heschel: A Life of Radical Amazement*. New Haven: Yale University Press, 2021.

INDEX